Professional UML with Visual Studio® .NET
Unmasking Visio® for Enterprise Architects

D0506724

Andrew Filev
Tony Loton
Kevin McNeish
Ben Schoellmann
John Slater
Chaur G. Wu

wrox
Programmer to Programmer

Professional UML with Visual Studio® .NET:
Unmasking Visio® for Enterprise Architects

Published by
Wiley Publishing, Inc.
10475 Crosspoint Boulevard
Indianapolis, IN 46256
www.wiley.com

Copyright © 2003 by Wiley Publishing, Inc., Indianapolis, Indiana

Published simultaneously in Canada

Library of Congress Card Number: 2003107079

ISBN: 0-7645-4376-8

Manufactured in the United States of America

10 9 8 7 6 5 4 3 2 1

1B/QU/QW/QT/IN

Trademark Acknowledgments

Credits

Authors
Andrew Filev
Tony Loton
Kevin McNeish
Ben Schoellmann
John Slater
Chaur G. Wu

Technical Reviewers
Kourosh Ardestani
Paul Churchill
Mitch Denny
Mark Horner
Andrew Krowczyk
Christian Nagel
Ben Schoellmann
David Schultz
Bill Sempf
Erick Sqarbi
Helmut Watson

Managing Editor
Louay Fatoohi

Commissioning Editors
Douglas Paterson
Gerard Maguire

Technical Editors
Gerard Maguire
Douglas Paterson

Project Manager
Charlotte Smith

Production Coordinator
Sarah Hall

Cover
Natalie O'Donnell

Indexer
Andrew Criddle

Proofreader
Chris Smith

About the Authors

Andrew Filev

Andrew Filev is President of dotSITE Software. This company specializes in cost-effective development on the .NET platform. Andrew's team has been developing commercial solutions using .NET since the first public announcement of this new Microsoft strategy. Andrew set up one of the first .NET portals, and has held a number of seminars and lectures dedicated to .NET in state and private companies.

Andrew has implemented numerous solutions in various high-tech fields – Web Services, ERP applications, medical systems, development frameworks, among others. He can be reached at andrew@dotsitesoftware.com or www.dotsitesoftware.com.

Special thanks for my friend Igor for his help with the book, also for Doug, Charlotte, and Gerard for their great editorial work. Thanks for dotSITE team without whom I would never take a part in working on the architecture of such interesting projects.

Tony Loton

Tony Loton works through his company LOTONtech Limited (http://www.lotontech.com) as an independent consultant, course instructor, and technical writer. The current area of interest at LOTONtech is the enhancement of UML visual modeling tools – specifically Rational Rose and Visio for Enterprise Architects – to facilitate .NET application design. Further details can be found at http://www.lotontech.com/visualmodeling.

Tony graduated in 1991 with a BSc. Hons. degree in Computer Science and Management and he currently holds an appointment as associate lecturer with the Open University in the UK.

My contribution is dedicated to my wife and children, for respecting my need to "get on with it".

Kevin McNeish

Kevin is President of Oak Leaf Enterprises, a company that specializes in object-oriented developer tools, training, and software. He started his programming career twenty years ago working with Assembly Language, then moved to C, Visual FoxPro, and currently uses C# as his primary .NET development tool. He authored the book *.NET for Visual FoxPro Developers* and teaches both .NET and UML training classes in North America and Europe.

He has also written UML articles for *CoDe*, *FoxPro Advisor,* and *FoxTalk* magazines. Kevin, a Microsoft MVP, is the creator of a .NET business application framework called "The Mere Mortals Framework for .NET". He also mentors software companies in a variety of vertical markets to design and build component-based applications that scale from the desktop to the Internet. He can be reached at oakleaf@oakleafsd.com or www.oakleafsd.com.

As always, thanks to my wife Nicole and my sons Jordan, Timothy, and Alexander for their love and support while writing this book!

Ben Schoellmann

Benjamin Schoellmann credits his move to sunny Houston, Texas, with providing the inspiration necessary to pursue a development and writing career. Currently he is involved with evangelizing .NET technologies among his coworkers at Synhrgy HR Technologies. Among his favored activities are golfing, tinkering with his network, talking incessantly, and integrating hardware and software solutions, primarily home automation, to enhance his leisurely pursuit of Slack. He maintains several content-free WEB domains, including Benjammin.com. He is obsessive about keeping pace with emerging technologies, and is very quick to credit his developer friends with all his success in the IT field.

And while he's quick to blame the dog for just about everything, his friends know better.

> *I'd like to thank all my friends and family for putting up with me during this process... and the rest of the time as well.*

John Slater

John Slater is a project manager at Management Reports International in Cleveland, OH. At MRI he is currently developing applications for the property management industry. Right now, he is working on several projects using .NET development tools and .NET Enterprise servers.

In his free time John enjoys outdoor activities and playing with his children Rachel and Nathan. He can be reached at jr_slater@hotmail.com.

Chaur G. Wu

Chaur Wu currently works for Trend Micro Inc. as a senior software engineer. He started software programming before was old enough to qualify for a driving license. The first program he wrote was a bingo game – in assembly code on a 8051 single chip. To capitalize on the program, he ran a small casino in the lab – he developed primitive game boxes that connected his pals and allowed them to place bets.

He's also been involved in much larger projects. For example, he developed a program in C++ to simulate the movement and geographical coverage of GPS satellites. As a research assistant in his graduate study, he implemented a wavelet-based video compression algorithm for a traffic surveillance system sponsored by Boston City Department of Transportation. He also helped solve a blurred image problem using inverse filters and other image processing algorithms for a client who designs fiber optics components in San Jose, CA.

His technical interests include distributed software systems in Java, COM, and .NET, generative programming, software design, and neural networks. Outside of work, his favorite vacation combines a one-night gambling trip to Reno followed by a day of skiing at some resort near Lake Tahoe.

You can e-mail Chaur at cha_urwu@hotmail.com.

> *I would like to dedicate my efforts in this book to my two-year-old daughter, Sarah.– CGW*

Table of Contents

Table of Contents

Table of Contents

Table of Contents

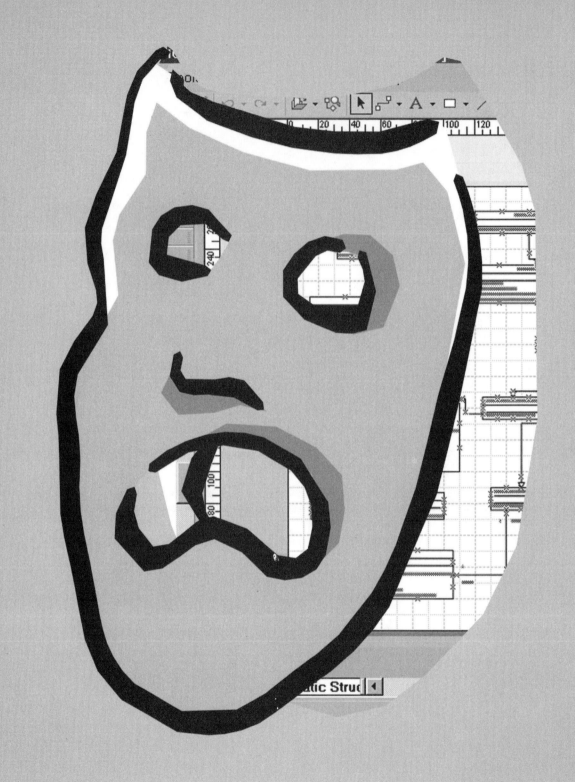

Introduction

To many, Visio for Enterprise Architects appears to be a mysterious diagramming tool. In conjunction with Visual Studio .NET Enterprise Architect it potential seems clear – going from design to code, and back from code to design offers the developer tremendous benefits for rapidly developing applications. Why do we say 'mysterious'? This is because Visio's range of features can daunt the user, but most importantly, many aspects of its use directly relevant to software developers are frustratingly lacking in explanation.

This book aims to address this problem – here we focus exclusively on Visio's features for developing .NET applications, encompassing:

- ❏ UML diagrams
- ❏ Generating code from UML diagrams
- ❏ Reverse engineering source code into UML diagrams
- ❏ Database modeling

Along the way, we'll see some more general applications of Visio to the software development lifecycle, and also learn about Visio's idiosyncrasies, which almost every user of Visio will have encountered, and wondered "Is it just me?"

In other words, this book will allow you to finally unmask Visio for Enterprise Architects.

What Does This Book Cover?

Chapter 1 starts us off by reviewing the key UML concepts, the main diagram types, and the role of those diagrams within the software development process. If you're quite new to UML this will serve as a practical introduction that will help you make sense of the rest of the book.

In Chapter 2 we have our first dip into Visio, and have a look around the general Visio environment. Before we hit the main feature of the book, the UML diagrams, we look at other aspects of Visio that aid software development, and make an attempt to familiarize ourselves with Visio, its pages, shapes, and connectors.

In Chapter 3 we cover using Visio for object modeling – defining data access base classes for your .NET applications, defining a business object base class, deriving business classes from use cases, working with abstract and concrete classes, and using sequence diagrams to model the flow of messages between objects. Along the way we'll meet many of Visio's UML diagramming features, setting us up for the next chapter.

Visio for Enterprise Architects can generate skeleton source code from an existing UML diagram in C#, Visual Basic .NET, or C++. Moreover, Visio provides further options that give the developer greater control over the implementation of this source code. In Chapter 4 we look at how to generate code from a UML model in Visio, the various options available for generating code, including the use of code templates to specify the structure of the source code generated by Visio. We look at a variety of UML to code mappings, typical of the situations you will encounter in more complex models.

The Visual Studio .NET Enterprise Architect and Visio for Enterprise Architects combination provides a facility for reverse engineering existing C#, VB.NET, or C++.NET source code into a Visio UML static structure model. In Chapter 5 we'll look at this reverse engineering feature and cover why reverse engineering is useful how to reverse engineer .NET source code from within the Visual Studio .NET IDE, explore the structure of a typical reverse-engineered Visio UML model, and look at the code to UML mappings for important constructs such as generalization (inheritance) and association. We finish the chapter by using reflection to reverse engineer .NET assemblies to provide .NET Framework base class models for our UML diagrams.

In Chapter 6, we take a step back from the world of diagramming, generating code, and generating more diagrams from code, and look at the role of Visio and UML in the entire software development lifecycle. In effect, we'll be discussing how we document our work at different stages of a typical development project using Visio and UML – at the end of this chapter you'll take away some deeper insight into using Visio and UML in the course of working on your own projects.

Chapter 7 sees us move on to another area of using Visio to assist with general design issues. Designing a distributed system is an iterative process from **requirements analysis** to **modular breakdown** and to **packaging** and **deployment strategies**. However, designing a distributed system is different from designing a non-distributed one. In this chapter we look at a .NET Remoting example, a Bank application. We begin with an overview of .NET Remoting, and we see how to decide which classes in our application should be .NET Remoting types, how to decide the activation mode of each .NET remoting type, and how this can be diagrammed in Visio, what code elements should be grouped in a component, how to prepare a component diagram, and how to prepare a deployment diagram.

Chapter 8 moves us on to yet another aspect of Visio directly relevant to the enterprise developer – data modeling. We take a detailed walk through database modeling and Object Role Modeling (ORM), looking at Visio's ORM Source Diagrams and Entity Relationship Source Diagrams. We then see how to generate a database schema from these models, and further tweak the design with reverse engineering of the database into ORM and ER models, and updating the database with our modifications to yield round-trip database engineering.

Who Is This Book For?

This book is for the .NET developer who:

❑ Is comfortable with the basic concepts of UML

❑ Wants to learn how to use Visio for Enterprise Architects effectively

❑ Wants to see how UML and Visio can benefit their projects in general

What You Need to Use This Book

This book is based around the following combination:

❑ Visual Studio .NET Enterprise Architect Edition

❑ Visio for Enterprise Architects

Thus, having access to each is a prerequisite for using this book.

Conventions

We've used a number of different styles of text and layout in this book to help differentiate between different kinds of information. Here are examples of the styles we used and an explanation of what they mean.

Code has several fonts. If it's a word that we're talking about in the text – for example, when discussing a `for (...)` loop, it's in this font. If it's a block of code that can be typed as a program and run, then it's also in a gray box:

```
public Employee this[int index]
```

Sometimes we'll see code in a mixture of styles, like this:

```
public Employee this[int index]
{
    get
    {
        foreach (Employee em in employees)
        {
            if (em.ID == index)
```

```
                    return em;
          }
      return null;
      }
   }
```

In cases like this, the code with a white background is code we are already familiar with; the line highlighted in gray is a new addition to the code since we last looked at it.

Advice, hints, and background information come in this type of font.

Important pieces of information come in boxes like this.

Bullets appear indented, with each new bullet marked as follows:

❑ **Important Words** are in a bold type font.

❑ Words that appear on the screen, or in menus like the Open or Close, are in a similar font to the one you would see on a Windows desktop.

❑ Keys that you press on the keyboard, like *Ctrl* and *Enter*, are in italics.

Customer Support

We always value hearing from our readers, and we want to know what you think about this book: what you liked, what you didn't like, and what you think we can do better next time. You can send us your comments, either by returning the reply card in the back of the book, or by e-mail to feedback@wrox.com. Please be sure to mention the book title in your message.

How to Download the Sample Code for the Book

When you visit the Wrox web site, www.wrox.com, locate the title through our Find a Book facility or by using one of the title lists. Click Download Code on the book's detail page, or on the Download item in the Code column for title lists.

The files that are available for download from our site have been archived using WinZip. When you've saved the archive to a folder on your hard drive, you need to extract the files using a decompression program such as WinZip or PKUnzip. When you extract the files, the code will be extracted into separate folders for each chapter of this book, so ensure your extraction utility is set to use folder names.

Errata

We've made every effort to make sure that there are no errors in the text or in the code. However, no one is perfect and mistakes do occur. If you find an error in one of our books, such as a spelling mistake or a faulty piece of code, we would be very grateful to hear about it. By sending in errata you may save another reader hours of frustration, and, of course, you will be helping us to provide even higher quality information. Simply e-mail the information to support@wrox.com – your information will be checked and, if correct, posted to the errata page for that title, and used in reprints of the book.

To find errata on the web site, go to www.wrox.com, and simply locate the title through our **Advanced Search** or title list. Click the **Book Errata** link below the cover graphic on the book's detail page.

E-Mail Support

If you wish to query a problem in the book with an expert who knows the book in detail, then e-mail support@wrox.com with the title of the book and the last four numbers of the ISBN in the subject field of the e-mail. A typical e-mail should include the following things:

- ❑ The **title of the book**, the **last four digits of the ISBN** (7957), and the **page number** of the problem.

- ❑ Your **name**, **contact information**, and the **problem** in the body of the message.

We need the above details to save your time and ours – we *never* send unsolicited junk mail. When you send an e-mail message, it will go through the following chain of support:

- ❑ Customer Support – Your message is delivered to our customer support staff, who are the first people to read it. They have files on most frequently asked questions and will answer anything general about the book or the web site immediately.

- ❑ Editorial – Deeper queries are forwarded to the technical editor responsible for that book. They have experience with the programming language or particular product, and are able to answer detailed technical questions on the subject.

- ❑ The Authors – Finally, in the unlikely event that the editor cannot answer your problem, they will forward the request to the author. Wrox authors are glad to help support their books. They will e-mail the customer and the editor with their response, and again all readers should benefit.

The Wrox support process can only offer support for issues that are directly pertinent to the content of our published title. Support for questions that fall outside the scope of normal book support is provided via the community lists of our http://p2p.wrox.com/ forum.

p2p.wrox.com

For author and peer discussion, join the P2P mailing lists. Our unique system provides **programmer to programmer**™ contact on mailing lists, forums, and newsgroups, all in addition to our one-to-one e-mail support system. If you post a query to P2P, you can be confident that the many Wrox authors and other industry experts who are present on our mailing lists are examining it. At p2p.wrox.com, you will find a number of different lists that will help you not only while you read this book, but also as you develop your own applications. Particularly appropriate to this book are the **vs_dotnet** and **uml** lists.

To subscribe to a mailing list, just follow these steps:

1. Go to http://p2p.wrox.com/.

2. Choose the appropriate category from the left menu bar.

3. Click on the mailing list you wish to join.

4. Follow the instructions to subscribe, and fill in your e-mail address and password.

5. Reply to the confirmation e-mail you receive.

6. Use the subscription manager to join more lists and set your e-mail preferences.

Why This System Offers the Best Support

You can choose to join the mailing lists, or you can receive them as a weekly digest. If you don't have the time (or the facility) to receive the mailing lists, then you can search our online archives. Junk and spam mails are deleted, and your own e-mail address is protected by the Lyris system. Queries about joining or leaving lists, and any other general queries about lists, should be sent to listsupport@p2p.wrox.com.

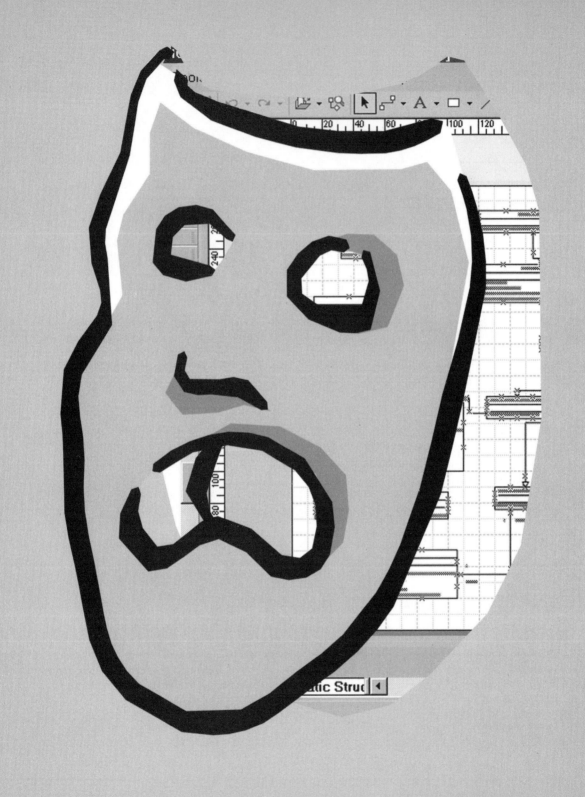

Review of UML

The purpose of this chapter is to set the scene by reviewing the key UML concepts, the main diagram types, and the role of those diagrams within the software development process. If you're quite new to UML this will serve as a practical introduction that will help you make sense of the rest of the book, before you move on to further reading. If you're experienced with UML the chapter will serve as handy revision and you might just find some nuggets of information that have so far eluded you.

Either way we'll all be moving on from roughly the same starting point: with the same appreciation of UML notation, with an understanding of relevant software development processes, and with a common bias towards .NET and the Visio for Enterprise Architects tool.

The final point is quite important, and the raison d'être for this book. In recent years the body of UML literature has focused mainly on Java development and the use of modeling tools such as Rational Rose. In this book we're applying a .NET development perspective at the same time as demonstrating the so far under-documented Visio modeling tool that comes bundled with the Visual Studio .NET Enterprise Architect.

With all this in mind we can now press on with the introduction to – or revision of, depending on your background – the Unified Modeling Language.

What is the Unified Modeling Language?

When discussing UML, we need to establish one important point right up front.

> The **Unified Modeling Language** is a **notation**; that is a set of diagrams and diagram elements that may be arranged to describe the design of a software system. UML is not a **process**, nor is it a **method** comprising a notation and a process.

In theory you can apply aspects of the notation according to the steps prescribed by any process that you care to choose – traditional **waterfall, extreme programming, RAD** – but there are processes that have been developed specifically to complement the UML notation. You'll read more about the complementary process(es) later in this chapter.

Why use UML?

Hidden inside that specific question there's a more generic question, which is **"Why use a formal analysis and design notation, UML or otherwise?"** Let's start to answer that question by drawing an analogy.

Suppose you wanted to make a bridge across a small stream. You could just place a plank of wood across from one side to the other, and you could do so on your own. Even if it failed to hold your weight, the only downside would be wet feet.

Now suppose you wanted to make a bridge across a narrow river. You'd need to do some forward planning to estimate what materials you'd need – wood, brick, or metal – and how much of each. You'd need some help, and your helpers would want to know what kind of bridge you're building.

Finally, suppose you wanted to build a bridge across a very wide river. You'd need to do the same kind of forward planning as well a communicating your ideas to a much bigger team. This would be a commercial proposition with payback from fare-paying passengers, so you'd need to liaise with the relevant authorities and comply with health-and-safety requirements. You'd also be required to leave behind sufficient documentation to allow future generations to maintain the structure long into the future.

In a software context, this means that formal design becomes increasingly important as a function of the size and complexity of the project; in particular, as a function of the number of people involved. Based on that analogy, and wider project experience, we could conclude that a formal design notation is important in:

- ❑ Establishing a blueprint from the application
- ❑ Estimating and planning the time and materials
- ❑ Communicating between teams, and within a team
- ❑ Documenting the project

Of course, we've probably all encountered projects in which little or no formal design has been done up-front (corresponding with the first three bullet points in that list); in fact more projects than we care to mention! Even in those situations, UML notation has been found to be invaluable in documenting the end result (the last bullet point in that list). Though not recommended, if that's the extent of your commitment to UML you'll be most interested in the Reverse Engineering discussion in Chapter 5.

Now that we've answered the generic question, let's return to the specific question of **why use UML?**

Well it's become something of an **industry standard**, which means that there's a good chance of finding other people who understand it. That's very important in terms of the **communication** and **documentation** bullet points in our list. Also if you or anyone else in the team does not understand it, there's a good chance of finding relevant training courses, or books like this one.

That's very pragmatic reasoning and perhaps more convincing than a more academic (or even commercial) argument such as:

"The application of UML has a proven track record in improving the quality of software systems."

A Brief History of UML

Taking the phrase **Unified Modeling Language** as our starting point, we've discussed in the previous section the "language" (namely, notation) aspect. In the next section, we'll investigate the "modeling" aspect, which leaves us here with the word "unified". What, or who, preceded the UML and how did it all become **unified**? This will become clear as we step through a brief history of UML.

In the beginning although there was a plethora of object-oriented "methods", there were three principal methods:

❑   The **Booch** method devised by Grady Booch

❑   **Object Modeling Technique** (OMT) devised by Jim Rumbaugh

❑   **Object Oriented Software Engineering** (also known as Objectory) devised by Ivar Jacobson

These three methods have many ideas in common, yet different notation for expressing those ideas. Some of you may remember that in an OMT class diagram the classes were represented as rectangular boxes whereas in the Booch method they were represented as stylized cloud shapes. Also, each method placed emphasis on different aspects of object-oriented software development. For example Jacobson introduced the idea of use cases, not addressed by the other methods.

> In simple terms, a use case is a unit of functionality provided by the system to an actor (such as a user). For example, in a word-processing application one of the use cases might be "Run spell checker".

The unification of these three methods combined the best bits of each method with a common notation (UML) for the common concepts – the end result being an industry-standard notation for analysis and design. If you speak with anyone who claims to be doing **object modeling**, chances are they'll be using UML.

So how did this unification play out in time? The key dates are:

❑   OOPSLA '94 – Jim Rumbaugh leaves General Electric to join Grady Booch at Rational Software, so as to merge their methods and achieve standardization across the industry.

❑   OOPSLA '95 – Booch and Rumbaugh publish version 0.8 of the **Unified Method**. Rational Software buys Objectory and Ivar Jacobson joins the company.

❑   January 1997 – Booch, Rumbaugh, and Jacobson (**the three amigos**) release – through Rational – a proposal for the UML version 1.0.

❑   September 1997 – UML version 1.1 is adopted by the Object Management Group (OMG).

The Object Management Group, previously best known for the CORBA standard, is a non-profit organization – comprising many member companies – that encourages, standardizes, and supports the adoption of object technologies across the industry. You can find out more about the OMG at http://www.omg.org.

If we've given the impression that the Unified Modeling Language is the exclusive work of only three contributors, the three amigos, then let's set the record straight. Some of the concepts are based in the early work of other individuals – for example, David Harel's work on Statechart diagrams – and some further enhancements have come from other member organizations of the OMG; for example, the Object Constraint Language (OCL) devised by IBM.

> *OCL was devised so that additional rules could be added to a UML model in a language that less ambiguous than English. For example, the statement "Person.Employer=Person.Manager.Employer" may be less ambiguous than "a person and their manager must both work for the same company."*

More information on OCL can be found at http://www-3.ibm.com/software/ad/library/standards/ocl.html.

At the time of writing, the UML specification is at version 1.4 and in mid-2001 the OMG members started work on a major upgrade to UML 2.0. Modeling tools – including Visio for Enterprise Architects – will always be one or two steps behind in their support for the specification, but that's not usually a big problem because the core concepts discussed in the next section are now quite mature and stable.

At the time of writing, the version of Visio for Enterprise Architects used in the construction of this chapter provides support for UML at least up to version 1.2 – this can be determined from the *About error checking in the UML model* section of the Microsoft Visio Help:

> *"Semantic error checking occurs automatically, noting errors in the design of UML model elements, based on the well-formedness rules in the UML 1.2 specification."*

End-to-End UML Modeling

Having looked at why UML is useful, and where it came from, we'll now look at the notation itself. To cover the complete notation in a single chapter would be impossible, so for a deeper coverage I'll refer you to some other works.

- ❑ **Instant UML** by Pierre-Alain Muller (Wrox Press, ISBN 1-86100-087-1).

- ❑ **The Unified Modeling Language User Guide** by Grady Booch, James Rumbaugh, and Ivar Jacobson (Addison Wesley, ISBN 0-201-57168-4).

- ❑ **UML Distilled** by Martin Fowler with Kendall Scott (Addison Wesley, ISBN 0-201-65783-X).

What we'll do here is cover the essential notation and core concepts that will allow us to progress through the rest of the book with a common understanding.

We'll also aim to address one of the problems of many UML courses and books. The problem being, that all too often the various diagrams are presented in isolation without a clear indication of how they relate to one another. To make matters worse, different examples are often used to demonstrate the different diagrams, not one of those examples being for a system that you might actually want to build. Think here of a **statechart diagram** that describes a motor car gearbox, or a **sequence diagram** that describes the operation of a hotel elevator.

So in the following section we'll have a single example, an Order Processing system, which you should be able to relate to even if you don't intend to build such a thing, and at the end, we'll pull it all together.

UML Essential Notation and Core Concepts

Now we'll step through the UML diagrams in turn, all the way from an **activity diagram** through to a **deployment diagram** in this order:

- ❏ Activity Diagram
- ❏ Use Case Diagram
- ❏ Sequence and Collaboration Diagram
- ❏ Statechart Diagram
- ❏ Static Structure Diagram
- ❏ Component Diagram
- ❏ Deployment Diagram

Each diagram is labeled in light gray with some of the names given to the UML elements that are shown, which – for the record – reflects the **UML metamodel**.

> The UML Metamodel is itself a UML model, which defines the rules for constructing other UML models. Whereas in one of your own models you might state "Bank is associated with one or more Accounts", the metamodel would state a more generic relationship of "a Class may be associated with any Other Class".

On the whole, the model elements have been labeled using Visio EA terminology so as to reduce the potential for confusion when you come to use the tool. Historically – and in other modeling tools – you may have encountered alternative UML terminology. The alternative terms have been tabulated towards the end of this chapter.

As you'll see later in this chapter, the software development process that you follow might well be described as **use-case driven**, which implies the **use case diagram** as an obvious starting point. But those use cases will doubtless fit into some kind of overall **business process**, perhaps modeled up-front by a business analyst. So we'll take a business process as our starting point and use this as a vehicle for demonstrating the most suitable diagram for that purpose; the **activity diagram**.

Activity Diagram

The activity diagram is the closest you'll get in UML to a **flow chart**, and the closest you'll get to a **business process diagram**. Here is a sample activity diagram with the important UML elements labeled, followed by a description of those elements.

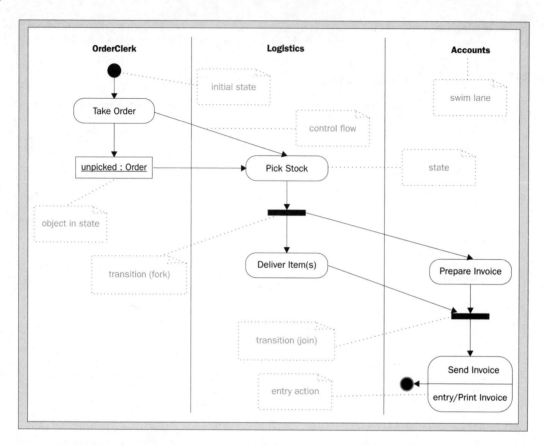

❑ **Initial state** is where the diagram begins.

❑ **Control flow** shows a transfer of control from one activity to another.

❑ **State** represents a period of time during which a piece of work is carried out by person or team.

❑ **Transition (fork)** shows the point as which two or more parallel activities will commence.

❑ **Transition (join)** shows the point as which two or more parallel activities must synchronize and converge.

❑ **Swim lane** allows all of the activities carried out by a particular person or team arranged into a column.

❑ **Entry action** shows what must happen when the activity begins.

❑ **Object in state** shows an object that is produced or consumed in the course of an activity, with the production or consumption (object flow) being represented by the dashed line.

What the diagram shows

The Order Processing business process begins when an Order Clerk performs the Take Order activity. This activity results in an Order object being created in unpicked state. Next, the Pick Stock activity is performed (for the Order) by the Logistics team.

At this point some parallel behavior occurs – the Logistics team Deliver Item(s) around the same time that the Accounts department Prepare Invoice. Only when the items have been delivered and the invoice has been prepared can the Accounts department then Send Invoice. Immediately prior to sending the invoice they must Print Invoice.

Those are the essential points of an activity diagram, but not a complete coverage. In particular you will see some additional syntax in the description of a Statechart diagram.

Use Case Diagram

Here is a sample use case diagram with the important UML elements labeled, followed by a description of those elements.

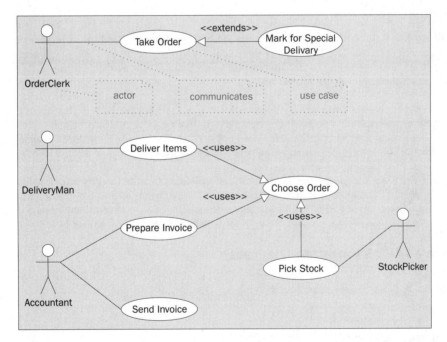

❑ **Actor** represents a person or external system that initiates a use case in order to get some value from the application.

❑ **Use case** is a well-defined unit of functionality that the system provides to one or more actors.

❑ **Communicates** shows that a particular actor makes use of a particular use case.

❑ A <<uses>> relationship shows where a piece of potentially-reusable functionality has been factored out into a separate use case.

15

❑   An <<extends>> relationship shows where some additional functionality may be provided in support of a use case, that extended functionality having been factored out into a separate use case.

A Note about Stereotypes

You might wonder why the words <<uses>> and <<extends>> are enclosed within angled brackets << like this >>. It's because they are **stereotypes**; these allow a single UML element (in this case a generalization line with a triangular head) to represent slightly different concepts.

> **Any UML element may be stereotyped and later you will see components stereotyped as <<executable>> or <<library>> in a component diagram.**

What the Diagram Shows

Taking the original activity diagram as a starting point, each of the activities – Take Order, Pick Stock, Deliver Items, Prepare Invoice, and Send Invoice – has been represented as a use case. A one-to-one correspondence between activities and use cases is not mandatory, but here it shows the potential for traceability between the diagrams.

You will also see a correspondence between the actors in this diagram and the swim lanes from the original activity diagram. The Order Clerk swim lane is represented as an Order Clerk actor, the Logistics swim lane is represented by DeliveryMan and StockPicker actors, and the Accounts swim lane is represented as an Accountant actor.

Choose Order represents functionality that is common to (used by) the Deliver Items, Prepare Invoice, and Pick Stock use cases. To deliver items, prepare an invoice, or pick stock the actor must first choose an order, but to take a new order the actor does not need to first choose an order (obviously) and to send an invoice the actor need not chose an order (because they will choose an invoice).

In the course of taking an order, the Take Order use case may be extended by functionality to Mark for Special Delivery. This has been modeled separately as an extension so that the extended behavior may be changed with no impact on the main use case; for example, this extension may bypass the standard procedure and instead send an instant message to the Stock Picker and Delivery Man.

Sequence and Collaboration Diagram

Use cases are realized (that is, described in terms of interactions between collaborating objects) using interaction diagrams, of which there are two types:

❑   Sequence diagrams

❑   Collaboration diagrams

Here is a sample sequence diagram with the important UML elements labeled, followed by a description of those elements.

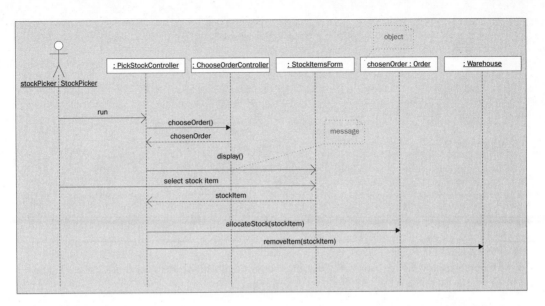

- **Object** refers to an object instance that sends messages to, or receives messages from, other object instances. The objects are labeled as instanceName : ClassName where the instance name is commonly omitted to show no particular instance of the class in question.

- **Message** shows an interaction between two objects, which may be labeled using descriptive text (such as select stock item above) or may be labeled with the name of an operation on the receiving class, such as allocateStock above. A return message may be shown as a dotted line.

Here is an equivalent **collaboration diagram** showing the same set of interactions. Whereas a sequence diagram has a top-to-bottom time line to show the order of events, a collaboration diagram uses a numbering scheme. Apart from the visualization style, sequence diagrams and collaboration diagrams may be thought of as equivalent to the extent that some modeling tools, such as Rational Rose, allow automatic switching between the visualization styles.

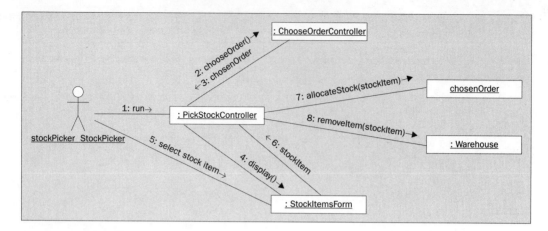

What these Diagrams Show

Both diagrams show the sequence of object interactions that support the PickStock use case. The sequence is:

1. The StockPicker actor runs the PickStockController (which in this design is a control class responsible for the use case).

2. The PickStockController calls the chooseOrder() operation on the ChooseOrderController which results in...

3. a chosenOrder being returned. This interaction represents the fact that the Pick Stock use case <<uses>> the Choose Order use case.

4. The PickStockController calls the display() operation of a StockItemsForm.

5. The StockPicker actor selects a stock item on the StockItemsForm.

6. The selected stockItem is returned to the controller.

7. To allocate the stock to the order, the PickStockController calls the allocateStock() operation of the Order – specifically the chosenOrder that was retrieved in Step 3. The stockItem from Step 6 is passed as a parameter.

8. To remove the item from stock, the PickStockController calls the removeItem() operation of the Warehouse passing stockItem as a parameter.

Statechart Diagram

The inclusion of Order as an object in state in the original activity diagram hints at the fact that this will be a state-full class. We could have included the object multiple times on that diagram to show the state changes of an Order that result from the various activities, but for clarity we didn't.

To show the complete set of states for an **Order**, and – most importantly – to show the circumstances in which an **Order** will transition from one state to another, we draw a **Statechart** diagram.

Here is a sample Statechart diagram with the important UML elements labeled, followed by a description of those elements.

- ❑ **State** represents the status of an object (a function of its attributes and links) over a period of time between transitions.
- ❑ **Transition** is a movement of the object from one state to another, triggered by the object receiving an event.
- ❑ Each transition is triggered by an event, and the transition occurs only if the [*condition*] is met and the action is successful.

What the Diagram Shows

Upon receiving the create event, the **Order** transitions from the initial state into state **Unpicked**.

When an allocateStock event occurs the **Order** will return to the Unpicked state if the [stock not available] condition is true, otherwise – if the [stock available] condition is true and the removeItem action completes – then it will transition to state **Picked**. Alternatively the transition from state **Unpicked** may be to state **Canceled** if a cancel event is received.

The order may transition to state **Delivered**, from state **Picked**, upon receiving a deliver event. It may transition to state **Invoiced**, from state **Delivered**, upon receiving an invoice event.

When **Canceled** or **Invoiced**, that's the end of the line for this **Order**, so there is a notional transition to the **end** state.

Only those transitions shown on the diagram are allowed. Thus for example it is impossible to move an order to state Canceled once it has been picked, because none of the states Picked, Delivered, or Invoiced has an outward transition to state Canceled.

Static Structure Diagram

The sequence diagrams, collaboration diagrams, and statechart diagrams that we've encountered in the previous two sections are termed **dynamic diagrams**. They represent the dynamic model, which is the model showing how our system will behave over time.

We also need a static model, showing the persistent relationships and dependencies between classes and components. Out first static model will be the **Static Structure diagram** (Visio terminology), which is otherwise more commonly known as the **class diagram**.

Here is a sample class diagram with the important UML elements labeled, followed by a description of those elements.

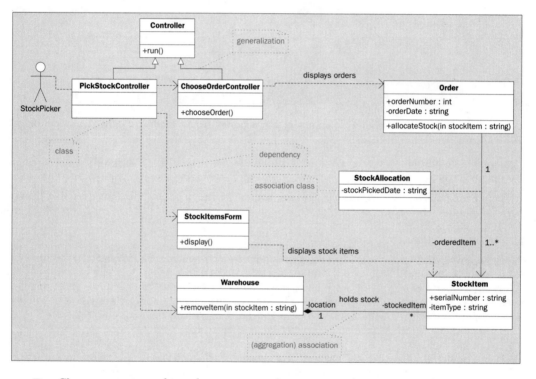

- ❑ **Class** represents an object class as a rectangle comprising three segments that show the **class name**, the **member attributes**, and the **member operations**.

- ❑ **Generalization** is an inheritance relationship between a super-class and one or more subclasses.

- ❑ **Dependency** shows that one class depends (maybe temporarily) on the functionality of another class, but is otherwise not linked up to instances of the other class in any persistent sense.

- ❑ **Composition** shows that instances of one class may be linked to instances of another class persistently in an owner-owned kind of relationship. The composition, which is a special form of association, may be adorned with **roles** and **multiplicities**.

❑ **Association** is a more general form of linkage between class instances, which does not imply an owner-owned relationship. The association may be adorned with an **association class**, instances of which occur only for each link between the two associated classes.

What the Diagram Shows

PickStockController and ChooseOrderController are specializations of a generalized class called Controller. In our design, all controller classes will be subclasses of the Controller super-class.

The PickStockController class depends on the ChooseOrderClass class, the StockItemsForm class, and the Warehouse class. Look back at the sample sequence diagram to see how the PickStockController calls operations of those other classes.

The ChooseOrderController depends on the Order class by virtue of the fact that it displays orders.

A Warehouse instance owns aggregate StockItem instances according to the following aggregation:

1 (multiplicity) Warehouse (class) location (role) holds stock (association name) of * (many multiplicity) stockedItem (role) StockItems (class).

Each Order instance is associated with one or more (1..*) StockItems, with linked stock items taking the role of orderedItem. For each such link there arises a StockAllocation instance that holds the date that the stock was picked and allocated.

The static structure diagram (class diagram) shown here as an example does not contain the complete set of classes for the entire application, but rather those classes that are relevant to the Pick Stock use case. As such, it represents View of Participating Classes (VOPC) for that use case.

Component Diagram

An application will be delivered or deployed typically not as individual classes or even a package of classes, but rather as one or more deployable components – executables or libraries – into which the classes or packages have been collected.

For a Java application, these components would likely be JAR files. For a .NET application the components will be executables (.EXE) and libraries (.DLL) corresponding to the solution structure within Visual Studio .NET.

Here is a sample component diagram with the two component types described overleaf:

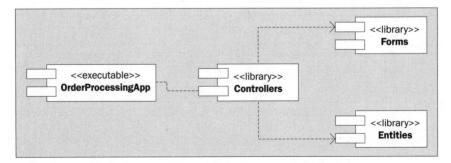

❑   <<executable>> represents a .EXE file, a program that you would actually run.

❑   <<library>> represents a .DLL file, a collection of classes that you might reference in a project.

The component diagram is a static diagram, just like the class diagram, because it shows how the application is organized rather than how it will behave over time.

What the Diagram Shows

Our application will comprise a main executable program, the OrderProcessingApp deployed as file OrderProcessingApp.exe. This program will depend on a library of control classes deployed as file Controllers.dll, which in turn will depend on two more component libraries: Forms.dll and Entities.dll.

We've hinted at the fact that components represent deployable collections of classes. For this example, the mapping of classes onto the <<library>> components will be:

❑   The Controllers <<library>> component realizes classes PickStockController and ChooseOrderController.

❑   The Forms <<library>> component realizes the StockItemsForm class.

❑   The Entities <<library>> component realizes classes Order, Warehouse, StockAllocation and StockItem.

Note that this is just one way in which classes may be mapped on to components, in this case according to the types of each class: form, control, or entity. You might instead decide to package classes onto components according to application subsystems, for example StockControl.dll (containing forms, controls, and entities relating to stock control functionality) and OrderHandling.dll (containing forms, controls, and entities relating to order handling functionality).

> **Visio for Enterprise Architects note – although you can't see in this diagram the classes that are mapped to each component, you can double-click any component in Visio EA to view and set the list of mapped classes as shown in the following figure.**

UML Component Properties

Categories:
- Component
- Attributes
- Operations
- Nodes
- ⇨ Classes
- Constraints
- Tagged Values

Choose the classes which are implemented in this component:

- ☐ ChooseOrderController
- ☑ Order
- ☐ PickStockController
- ☑ StockItem
- ☐ StockItemsForm
- ☑ Warehouse

[Select All]

[Deselect All]

[OK] [Cancel]

Deployment Diagram

The final UML diagram we'll look at is the deployment diagram, the purpose of which is to show the physical nodes on which the software components will actually be installed. Here is a sample deployment diagram for our hypothetical deployment platform:

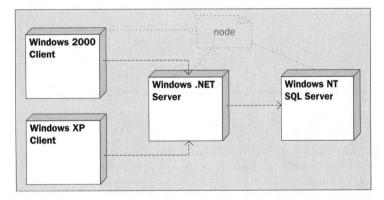

❑ **Node** is a run-time computational or physical resource – a software or hardware device on which software components may be deployed.

What the diagram shows

Our deployment platform will comprise a backend Windows NT server running a SQL Server database, with the `Entities.dll` component deployed to this node. There will also be a Windows .NET application server that services Windows 2000 and Windows XP clients.

Whether the `Forms.dll` component and the `Controllers.dll` component are deployed on the Windows .NET Server or on the clients themselves will depend on our choice of a thin- or fat-client architecture. For the sake of argument, we'll assume these components to be deployed to the Windows .NET Server. In either case, we'll deploy the main `OrderProcessingApp.exe` executable program directly on the client nodes.

> **Visio for Enterprise Architects note – although you can't see in this diagram the components that are deployed to each node, you can double-click any node in Visio EA to view and set the list of deployed components as shown in the following figure.**

Fitting the Pieces into the UML Jigsaw

As stated earlier, the problem with many UML books and training courses is that they often present the various diagram types in isolation. To make things worse, the examples are often disjointed and not relevant to any system that you're ever likely to build: a vehicle gearbox as the state diagram example, a telephone handset as the sequence diagram example, an insect classification for the class diagram. All of which leaves you wondering about the relevance of these modeling techniques and the relationships between the various techniques.

To address the issues of relevance and consistency of examples you will notice that all of the diagrams in the previous section relate to a common application, the **order processing application**, which is one that should be familiar to you, whatever your background.

Now, what of the relationships between the diagrams that we've alluded to? Well, each diagram shows a different aspect of the same application design so they should be taken, not individually in isolation, but as a **consistent** whole. The word consistent in that sentence is important because you affect the correctness and completeness of your design significantly by ensuring consistency between the diagrams.

The following figure shows how the various diagrams relate to each other at the macroscopic level. The Use Case Diagram represents the functionality requirements of the system from a user's – or a least a system analyst's – perspective. These use cases are realized as the object interactions of a Sequence (or Collaboration) Diagram and the use case participating classes may be represented as a Class (Static Structure) Diagram. For each class that is stateful in nature there may be a State diagram.

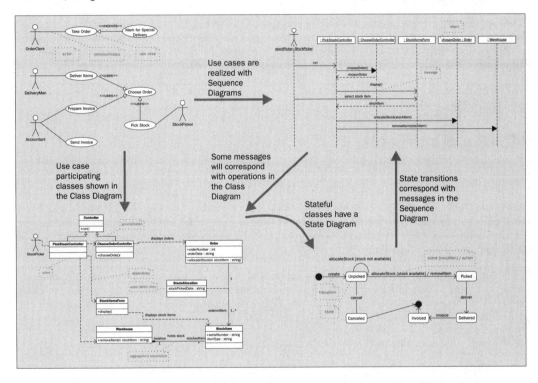

Don't worry if you can't read the detail in these four diagrams. You've seen them all before in this chapter and you can refer back to them. What is important is that you understand the significance of the arrows that show how the diagrams fit together.

Here's the consistency bit, which we've distilled into the following set of rules:

❑   Does every use case have at least one Sequence or Collaboration Diagram describing its realization? If not, the design is incomplete.

❑   Is every one of the classes of the Static Structure Diagram present on at least one Sequence (or Collaboration) diagram? If not, you might be missing a use case realization or even a whole use case because, effectively, the class is never used.

25

❏ For all stateful classes is there a corresponding Statechart Diagram? If not, the rules for allowable state changes will be ambiguous or unknown.

❏ For each event in a Statechart Diagram is there a corresponding message in a Sequence Diagram that provides a context in which the event actually occurs? If not, the state transition may never occur.

Depending on your approach to analysis and design, and the kind of application you're developing, those rules may be more or less important and you're unlikely ever to achieve 100% mutual consistency. So treat them not as revealed truth but as rules of thumb – I've found that they've certainly served me well in my development work.

The fact that the previous figure has arrows emitting from the Use Case Diagram – with none going in – suggests that as the starting point. That's true unless you draw some activity diagrams up-front, and it makes perfect sense to start with the diagram that represents the functional requirements doesn't it? However, the diagram to start with is not really a question of UML but a question of **process**.

We'll conclude this chapter by looking at the process side of things, just after a brief mention of the tools that support the modeling effort.

UML Modeling Tools

It's doubtful that anyone would be working with UML these days without the aid of a modeling tool, because these tools are to software design what a word processor is to writing.

In creating a chapter like this one, few authors would ever dream of writing out the words long-hand with pencil and paper. How would they delete unwanted paragraphs, rephrase sentences and insert the pictures without making the first draft a complete mess? – and how time-consuming would it be to write it all out again for the final draft?

Now make the analogy with UML diagrams and a modeling tool. How would you add an operation to a class on a static structure diagram, or change the order of events in a collaboration diagram, or change a relationship between an actor and a use case in a use case diagram without a significant amount of redrawing?

At this point, the following question might occur to you:

> *"OK, but we could just use a good drawing package to solve those problems. They're only diagrams, right?"*

Wrong! The whole point about a modeling tool is that besides allowing you to draw the diagrams, it actually understands the model you're creating. It knows that a line between two classes is an association or aggregation so an instance of one class must be linked to an instance of another class, perhaps via a member variable. It's this understanding of the model that allows the modeling tool to provide added value to your software development effort through code generation, documentation production, and model semantic checking.

Before the arrival of Visual Studio .NET on the software development scene, your choice of modeling tool would most likely have been one of **Rational Rose**, **Select Enterprise**, or **Together Control Center** – none of which cater specifically for UML in the context of .NET. The main contenders in the .NET modeling space are **Rational XDE** and **Visio for Enterprise Architects**.

Rational XDE has the Rational pedigree, some impressive .NET-related features, and tight integration with Visual Studio .NET; so it's well worth a look if you're from a Rational tools background. The main problem is that you may have to shell out on an expensive license on top of what you've already paid for Visual Studio .NET, and – on that subject – it actually won't run without the IDE.

Visio for Enterprise Architects comes bundled with the Visual Studio .NET (Enterprise Architect version) and/or an MSDN Universal Subscription, so you may already have it at no extra cost. It supports UML notation as well as the back-catalogue of other Visio diagram types. Code generation, reverse engineering, model semantic checking, and document production are supported, plus integration with the Visual Studio .NET IDE. All of which make this *not just a drawing tool*, or – more accurately – *no longer just a drawing tool.*

Process Essentials

UML is a notation not a process, but invariably you will use UML in the context of a software development process; so which one to choose?

As indicated already, you are not compelled to use any particular process. You could adopt a pure **Rapid Application Development** (RAD) approach, or join the growing band of practitioners adopting the **eXtreme Programming** approach. Just a few years ago you might have been tempted by the **Select Perspective** method, which was – and still is – biased towards component-based development and based on an **iterative-incremental** approach. In all cases there would be nothing to stop you using UML as the analysis and design notation.

To round off this chapter we'll focus in on two processes in particular, the **(Rational) Unified Process** and the **Microsoft Solutions Framework**; the former because has been devised by the authors of UML as the preferred partner process, and the latter because in this book we're interested in designing software for the Microsoft environment.

(Rational) Unified Process

The Unified Process has its roots in the Objectory method devised originally by Ivar Jacobson. It represents the unification of the process ideas of the three amigos, thus it is complementary to the Unified Modeling Language and is marketed by Rational Software as the Rational Unified Process (RUP).

In practical terms what you get when you purchase this product is a set of HTML pages describing the process, its roles, activities, and artifacts, along with a set of Microsoft Word templates that provide a starting point for those artifacts – not to mention a great deal of encouragement to buy the Rational Suite.

Three of the essential points of this process are that it is:

- ❑ **Use-case driven** – this ensures that the system we build will actually meet the requirements of the business.

- ❑ **Architecture-centric** – so we won't complete the analysis under the blind assumption that we can build the application on our chosen technical platform. Early on we'll do some technical prototyping.

❑ **Risk managed** – with an emphasis on tackling the tricky parts of the system – the architecturally significant use cases – at the beginning rather than at the end to reduce the likelihood of nasty surprises later on.

The fact that the process is use-case driven suggests that we start with the use case diagram(s). That's true to an extent, but not the whole story. We've already suggested that activity diagrams may add value early on by describing the workflow of the business, in essence the ordering of the use cases. There's a lot to be gained by producing a static structure diagram (class diagram) of fundamental business entities up front, to be called the **domain model**.

The point is that although the various diagrams will each have a lesser, or greater, impact as we move through various stages of the process, we won't simply be stepping through the diagrams in waterfall fashion. Rather, we'll analyze, design, and build the software as a series of **increments** via a set of **iterations**.

Within each iteration, any combination of diagrams may be valuable, those diagrams becoming more detailed as we go along. However, it goes without saying that as we approach implementation we'll have much greater need for component diagrams than for use case diagrams!

Though the Unified Process is iterative, not waterfall in nature, these iterations do fit into a series of distinct phases called **Inception**, **Elaboration**, **Construction,** and **Transition**.

❑ Inception is the initial phase in which you establish the business case for the project and determine the project scope.

❑ Elaboration is the phase in which you gather detailed requirements, undertake analysis and high-level design, define the architecture, and plan for construction.

❑ Construction is the phase in which you undertake the detailed design and build the software components themselves.

❑ Transition is the final phase in which you test the software, tune for performance, and train the users in preparation for going live.

The relationship between phases and iterations is shown in the following figure.

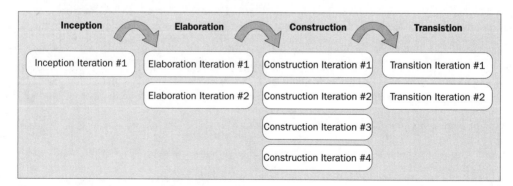

RUP .NET Developer's Configuration

Since we're dealing specifically with .NET application design in this book it's worth mentioning that the Rational Software web site (http://www.rational.com/products/rup/sample.jsp) describes a variant of the Rational Unified Process called RNDC, which is defined as the following:

> *"The RUP .NET Developers' Configuration (RNDC) is a straightforward, lightweight process configuration of the Rational Unified Process® that has been specifically customized to address the needs of the .NET software developer."*

There are two important aspects here.

Firstly, it's a customization of the Rational Unified Process specifically for the .NET development environment. Historically RUP has been biased towards Java software development and tools, with .NET now presenting some new technical challenges – and marketing opportunities – for customized version of the process.

Secondly, it's aimed specifically at software developers rather than all the team members defined by RUP. Presumably, no customization was required for technology-independent business analysts, but this also seems to reflect Rational's positioning of UML in the context of .NET. Experimentation with the new **Rational XDE** UML modeling tool shows this to be much more of a **developer tool** than Rational Rose ever was.

At the URL listed above is the RNDC roadmap, which provides a somewhat disappointing overview of the customized process. Under the headings Requirements Activities and Analysis Activities it simply states the following, which is at least consistent with the presumption that certain aspects of the process require no customization:

> *"Requirements activities are technology independent."*

> *"Analysis activities are technology independent."*

Under the heading Define an Initial Architecture, the reader is encouraged to use the .NET Framework – in particular Enterprise Templates – *"to create reusable reference architecture templates for .NET applications that can be tailored to support a certain application structure or a specific application domain"*

Finally, the RNDC roadmap references several concepts and guidelines such as *"Concepts: Microsoft .NET Architectural Mechanisms"* and *"Guidelines: Partitioning Strategies in Microsoft .NET"*. Unfortunately these additional references are not hyperlinked in the RNDC, which renders it not too useful in itself. For a complete picture – with hyperlinks to all the required content – we need to look into the RUP .NET Plug-in.

RUP .NET Plug-in

The vanilla Rational Unified Process may be enhanced by applying various plug-ins for:

❑ Compatibility with alternative approaches, such as eXtreme Programming

❑ Technologies such as IBM Websphere and, of course, .NET

You can find general information about the .NET Plug-in at URL http://www.rational.com/tryit/rup/seeit.jsp and, more usefully, you can step through a slide-show presentation at URL http://www.rational.com/demos/viewlets/rup/msnet/MSNET_Tour_viewlet.html.

In that presentation you will see that this plug-in contains detailed information in the form of workflows, roadmaps, guidelines, and links to relevant information on the **Microsoft Developer Network** (MSDN) and **Rational Developer Connection** web sites.

Microsoft Solutions Framework

The **Microsoft Solutions Framework (MSF)** is a process-methodology for development in a Microsoft environment. In effect, we can view MSF to be a potential substitute for the Rational Unified Process, perhaps one that is more relevant to the Microsoft tools we'll be working with.

A Framework not a Process

We've referred to the MSF as a process, to justify a comparison with RUP. In fact, it's a framework incorporating a **Process Model** (the process), a **Team Model**, and a **Risk Management Model**. Let's start with the process model.

The process model is described as **phase-based, milestone-driven, and iterative**. We've taken the liberty of incorporating iterations within the four phases of the core process – **Envision**, **Plan**, **Develop**, and **Stabilize** – to come up with the following figure.

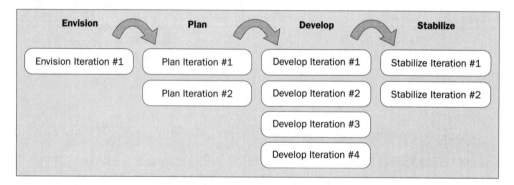

You should be experiencing some déjà vu now, and if you're not you should look back at the RUP process described previously. For Envision (MSF) read Inception (RUP), for Plan (MSF) read Elaboration (RUP), for Develop (MSF) read Construction (RUP), and for Stabilize (MSF) read Transition (RUP).

The process model is not the only area of similarity between the MSF and RUP. As mentioned above, the MSF includes a Risk Management Model and earlier we described RUP as being a risk-managed process, and where the MSF incorporates a Team Model this corresponds with RUP roles and activities.

A sensible conclusion then is that whichever process you start off with – RUP or MSF – the underlying concepts and approach are similar enough to allow a degree of compatibility or a change of mind later on. Indeed the MSF datasheet proclaims the following:

> *"[MSF] ... can easily coexist with virtually any other process framework or provide sufficient structure where no methodologies are in place."*

Summary

In this chapter we've introduced the Unified Modeling Language in terms of what it is (an analysis / design notation) and what it is not (a software development process). We said that the notation represents a synthesis of three predecessor methods – Object Modeling Technique (OMT), the Booch Method, and Object-Oriented Software Engineering (OOSE) – with contributions from some others.

In terms of why you might use UML at all, we offer four main reasons:

❑   Establishing a blueprint from the application

❑   Estimating and planning the time and materials

❑   Communicating between teams, and within the team

❑   Documenting the project

The remainder of the chapter was divided into two main sections, *End-to-End UML Modeling* dealing with the UML notation and *Process Essentials* dealing with the companion process(es). Let's now review the modeling and process sections.

Modeling Summary

In this section, we looked at seven UML diagram types:

❑   Activity diagrams

❑   Use Case diagrams

❑   Sequence diagrams

❑   Collaboration diagrams

❑   Statechart diagrams

❑   Component diagrams

❑   Deployment diagrams

Each kind of diagram was annotated with the UML metatypes such as **actor**, **use case**, **class**, **dependency**, **association,** and so on.

Each diagram represented a different view of exactly the same application, so that you could relate the diagrams to each other with the help of the *What this diagram shows* sections. We consider the relationships between the diagrams to be so important – and all too often ignored – that we placed further emphasis on this point in the *Fitting the Pieces into the UML Jigsaw* section.

Finally, we suggested that you will almost certainly be doing UML modeling with a dedicated modeling tool, and that doesn't just mean a good drawing tool. Visio for Enterprise Architects represents such a modeling tool, no longer just a drawing tool, that we set out as the preferred tool on which the rest of this book has been based.

In the main, Visio terminology has been used *in this chapter* so as to avoid confusion when you come to use the tool. Other modeling tools may use slightly different terminology and, in fact, the UML terms themselves have changed slightly over the years. To help with the transition to – or from – other books and tools, here is a summary of this chapter's Visio UML terms and the alternative terminology that you may encounter:

Visio Terminology	Other Terminologies
Static Structure Diagram	Class Diagram
Package	Category
<<uses>>	<<import>>
State	Activity (on Activity Diagram), State (on Statechart)
Statechart Diagram	State Transition Diagram
Transition (fork)	Synchronization (start)
Transition (join)	Synchronization (end)

Process Summary

As to which software development process you should adopt, two were picked out two for discussion. The Unified Process, because it's the natural companion for the Unified Modeling Language, and the Microsoft Solutions Framework, because it's the Microsoft process offering. What these have in common with each other – and with other good object oriented software processes, such as the Select Perspective – is that they are:

❑   Iterative and incremental

❑   Use-case driven

❑   Focused on Risk Management

You also have a choice of **eXtreme Programming**, traditional **waterfall**, or **RAD**, and as the UML notation is independent of the process, ultimately the choice is yours.

In the next chapter, to complete our foundations for working with Visio for Enterprise Architects, we'll take a tour of the Visio environment and look at some of the available diagram features relevant to the software developer.

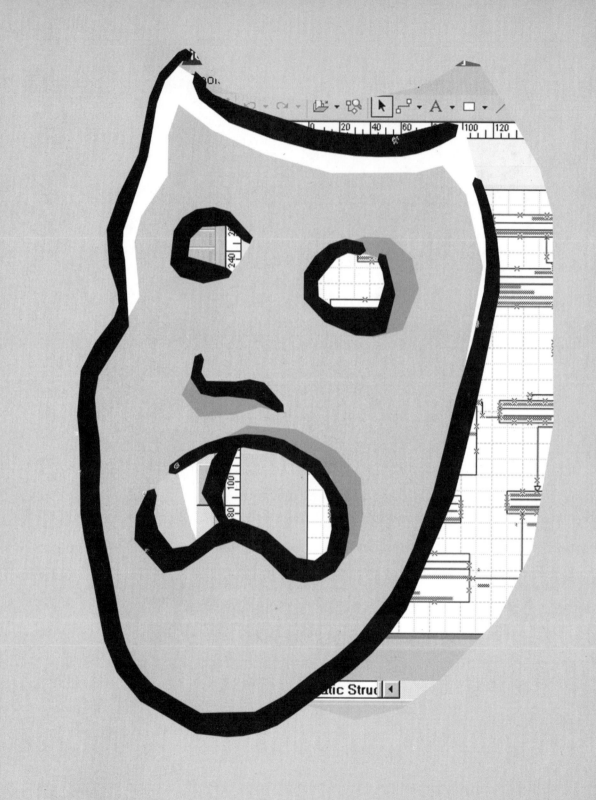

A Tour of Visio

This book focuses on using Visio to support the software development process. Throughout the book, you'll find examples of using Visio to diagram various aspects of software and software designs. In most cases, those diagrams will be built using the UML. Since Visio is central to the material covered in the following chapters it makes sense to take an early look at the features and capabilities of the product and point out various aspects of Visio that aid software development. Therefore, the purpose of this chapter is to illustrate Visio as a software-diagramming tool and to provide examples of how developers can use Visio help design and document their applications.

Visio Background

Fundamentally, Visio is a diagramming package. When most business software users hear the name Visio, they think flowcharts. That's certainly understandable – Visio cut its teeth as a product building business flowcharts and similar diagrams. The makers of Visio smartly expanded the basic flowcharting capabilities of the application by addressing specific industries or domains and, in particular, common charting or diagramming tasks occurring within those industries. For instance, Visio can create a diagram of an entire web site by tracing hyperlinks from one page to another when given a starting page. Visio can also generate a database diagram from existing database tables. Visio also has built-in support for generating organizational hierarchy charts and building plans like space layout diagrams. Visio even supports automation, giving COM developers the ability to include diagramming and flowcharting capabilities within their applications.

The point is this – Visio is a powerful application that has found many uses in a variety of places. As developers we can benefit from the functionality others already enjoy. In addition to support for UML diagrams, Visio also supports building a variety of other software-oriented diagrams including Windows User Interface diagrams, COM and OLE diagrams, and Data Flow Diagrams.

Before we delve into detailed software diagrams let's look at some basic Visio operations – how to create and manipulate simple diagrams and work with some common Visio functions. After that, we'll examine some of the more technical, software development-oriented Visio tools.

Beginning Visio – A Simple Diagram

Many developers are already familiar with Visio or have enough experience with similar packages that we don't need to spend a lot of time reviewing how to produce simple diagrams. Since the balance of this chapter heavily depends on the reader's ability to interact with drawing shapes and lines, and use other Visio tools, we do need to spend a little time reviewing the basics of creating a simple flowchart diagram and doing some common tasks like saving, printing, etc. Let's start with a quick tour of the Visio environment.

The Visio Environment

Fortunately, Visio follows most of the standard Windows UI rules in terms of how menus, pop-up menus, dialog boxes, and shortcut keys behave. For instance, you can right-click just about anything in a drawing and see a list of tasks you can perform relating to that object – changing properties, and copying for example. If you have Visio installed on a machine, now might be a good time to start the application. Otherwise, we'll try to provide enough screenshots to help point out useful items and make things clear.

The main working view in Visio is very similar to the following. We use "very similar" because each user has quite a bit of control over such things as whether certain UI elements are visible, and where they are positioned. So, let's take a look at what we see when we start drawing in Visio. The screenshot below shows the basic look of the UI when we start a new Basic Flowchart diagram:

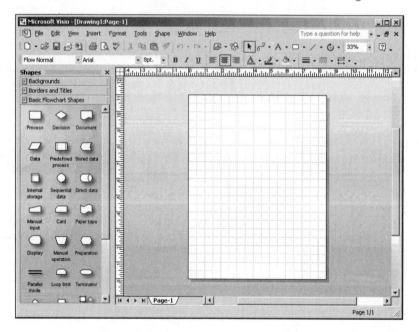

The first thing to notice is the familiar (dare we say 'comfortable'?) look and feel of the UI. The main menu is spread across the top of the form over the top of a number of toolbars, with the choice of which toolbars are visible up to you. In this screenshot, we have the Standard and Formatting toolbars visible.

Obviously, the main portion of the UI is designed for drawing. The white page lined with horizontal and vertical grid lines represents, by default, a single printed page – this grid can be switched on or off, and a snap feature can be set so that objects snap onto the grid lines, and of course the grid line spacing can be adjusted. Visio calls this area the drawing page. It's size and orientation are entirely up to you via page properties found in File | Page Setup.

Arranged vertically along the left side of the UI are groups of drawing shapes. Shapes and the lines that can connect them are the heart of any Visio drawing. Shapes can represent discrete, physical objects such as a piece of networking equipment or something more abstract like the relationship between types of data in a high-level database diagram. Shapes are also intelligent – we'll get into some of the more common shapes shipped with Visio shortly, and see examples of the shape intelligence. Shapes are organized into containers called **stencils**. In the screenshot above, there are three stencils – Basic Flowchart Shapes, Borders and Titles, and Backgrounds. Stencils are prearranged groups of shapes, generally oriented around a common theme or tasks that could include things as simple as basic flowcharting or as complicated as UML activity diagrams.

When multiple stencils are open for a drawing, you can switch between them by clicking on their name bar in the stencil list. In the following screenshot, we've clicked on the Backgrounds stencil. Notice how the display has changed from our original screenshot.

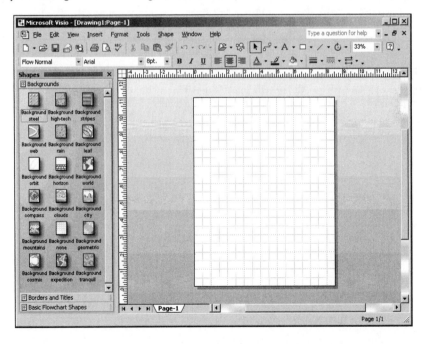

One other quick comment about the basic Visio environment before we dig into shape and line details –
Visio groups multiple pages together into one drawing using the **Page Tab** on the lower left of the main
drawing window. Notice in our screenshots there exists one tab labeled **Page-1**. Visio gives us the
ability to create multiple pages and store them in one drawing file. To add a new page either select
Insert | New Page from the main menu or right-click on the **Page Tab** and select **Insert Page**. You'll
see a dialog box for the new page that looks like the following screenshot.

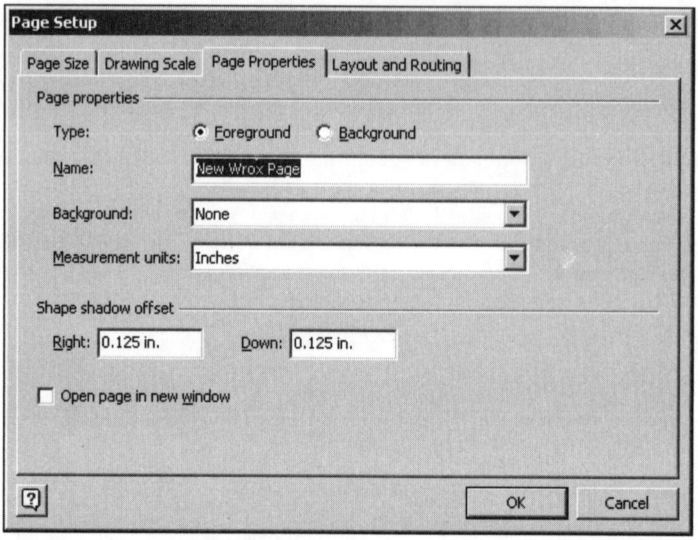

Notice the highlighted page name. Pressing the **OK** button adds a new page to the drawing document
named **New Wrox Page**. Also, notice that other page properties are available when you create the new
drawing page. We won't review the details here, but you have the option of including many pages
within a single drawing that all have different page properties – such as size, or orientation.

With the addition of our new page, the drawing environment now looks like this:

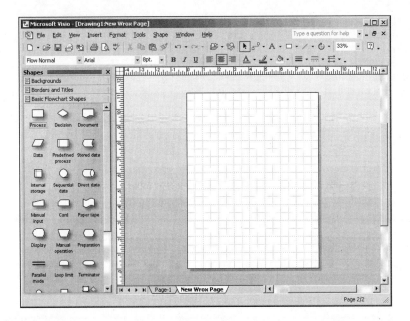

There certainly is a multitude of properties, options, and functions related to the basic Visio drawing environment – more than a chapter of this scope could ever hope to cover. In the previous few pages we looked at a few of the most common drawing environment items that you'll most likely need to use. In the next section, we'll review working with the core components of any drawing – **shapes** and **connectors**.

Shapes

Shapes are merely drawings that represent something else. As we've already discussed, the things shapes represent can be as simple as a piece of equipment like a chair or as complex as some concept in a software design. Lines called connectors represent relationships between shapes. In Visio, there are many shapes available for your diagrams. At least in the author's experience, new Visio users spend a lot of time opening shapes and their stencils just to see what shapes are available for different drawing purposes.

Using our simple flowchart example, let's look at how we get a shape onto the drawing page and what we can do with the shape once it's there. From the Basic Flowchart Shapes stencil, let's draw a Process shape. We don't really draw the shape on the form; we drag it from the stencil to the drawing page. Using the mouse, click on the Process shape – it's the first shape in the stencil in the first row. With the mouse button still clicked down, drag the Process shape onto the drawing page and position it somewhere in the middle of the page. It will look something like this:

Wow, a box! So what's the big deal about this? Well, as simple boxes go, it's not too exciting. However, what we're about to discover is that the simple box is actually a **Process** shape that has custom properties specific to that shape type. That means the shape has some intelligence. It knows what it was designed to do, what properties it can expose to the diagram builder and even rules about what other kinds of shapes it can be connected to. If you right-click on the **Process** shape (its border will display green handles when you've selected it) and select **Properties** from the pop-up menu, you'll see a dialog box like this:

Our little box has gotten smarter. Notice the **Cost**, **Duration**, and **Resources** boxes into which we can type information. That data will be saved with the shape. Since this is only a simple flowchart shape there really aren't that many properties, but the potential for building complicated shapes and properties that are domain-specific should be obvious. As we'll see in chapters throughout the book, these shape properties come in very handy for complicated software diagrams, such as UML diagrams.

Let's examine a few other shape features before we move on. One of the most common tasks is putting some kind of text within the shape. The name or a short description of the process our shape represents would be appropriate here. If you highlight the shape – click on it to display a dashed green border with a number of small square handles – and type the words Process One, Visio will zoom in on the shape, and show a blinking cursor as you start to type. Depending on the size of your display and whether you have the Visio UI maximized, your application will now look something like this:

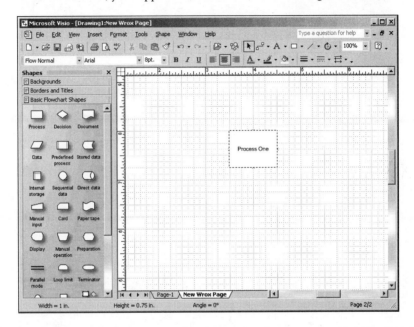

At this point we have a single shape on our drawing page and some custom data for that shape's Cost, Duration, and Resources. We also have some text inside the shape to identify it. To make the drawing useful at all we probably want to connect the shape to other shapes. Since our little example is a simple flowchart, let's create a flowchart consisting of four steps – Process One, Process Two, Process Three and Process Four. If we drag three more Process shapes onto the drawing page and give them the appropriate text, our drawing page will look like the following screenshot with a little shape repositioning. Notice too that the zoom factor in the upper right corner changed to 100%.

Connectors

From the titles of our shapes, the order of this flowchart is clear, but to make it perfectly clear in other, more complicated drawings, we need lines. Lines are called **connectors** in Visio. On most stencils, including the Basic Flowchart Shapes stencil we've been using, there is a connector called the Dynamic Connector – it's very useful.

Scroll down the stencil until you find it. In this stencil, it's in the second to last row in the middle column. Drag the connector onto the drawing page just like the shapes. Visio will draw a line with a couple of ninety degree breaks and an arrowhead at one end that looks like this (obviously, wherever you dropped the connector has an impact on what your Visio UI looks like):

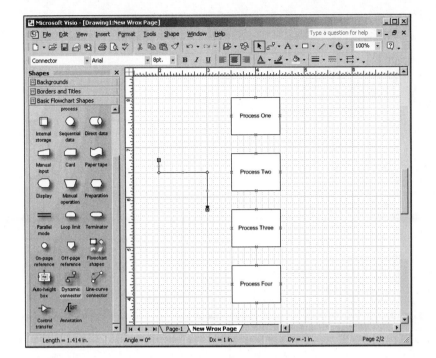

To connect two shapes together using the **Dynamic Connector**, click on one end of the line with the mouse pointer and hold it down. Drag that end to one of the connection points on the shape. If you look closely at the shape **Process One** you'll notice four connection points – one on each side of the rectangle. If you drag the end of your connector to one of those connection points, it turns red and repositions the end of the line to be flush with one side of the shape. Once a connector line and the shape are associated this way, the end of the line is said to be glued to the shape. Here's what it looks like (you won't see the red color of the glued endpoint, but notice the slightly larger connection point now that that they've been glued):

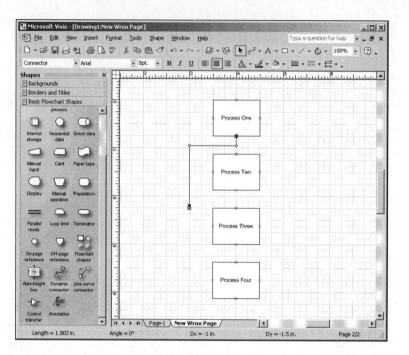

The same process is repeated with the other end of the connector line to glue that end to the Process Two shape. Now we have two shapes with a single line connecting them. Even though it's an extremely simple diagram, there's no doubting what relationship exists between Process One and Process Two. Nor is there any confusion about what happens after Process One.

If you repeat the same process with all the shapes, you'll get a diagram that looks something like this:

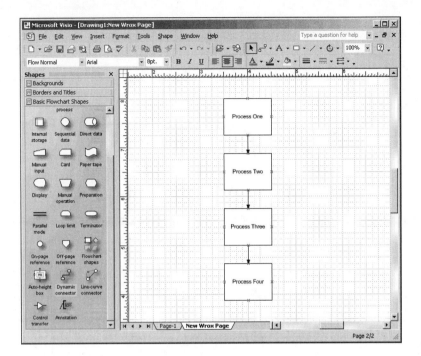

Since the shapes and their connectors are glued together, we can drag shapes all around the drawing page and their connectors will retain their relationships.

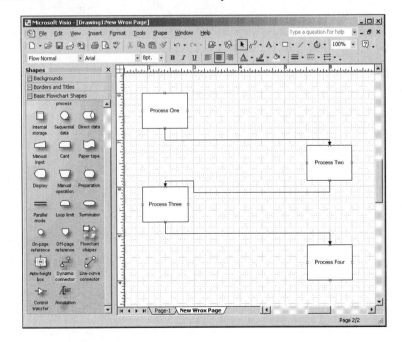

Again, this is a simple diagram, but the idea that Visio makes drawing complicated diagrams easy should be clear.

Here are a few more comments about connectors before we continue. Firstly, you have quite a few options regarding the end points, size, and color of your connectors. In the drawing, right-click on one of the connector lines and select Format | Line. You'll see this dialog:

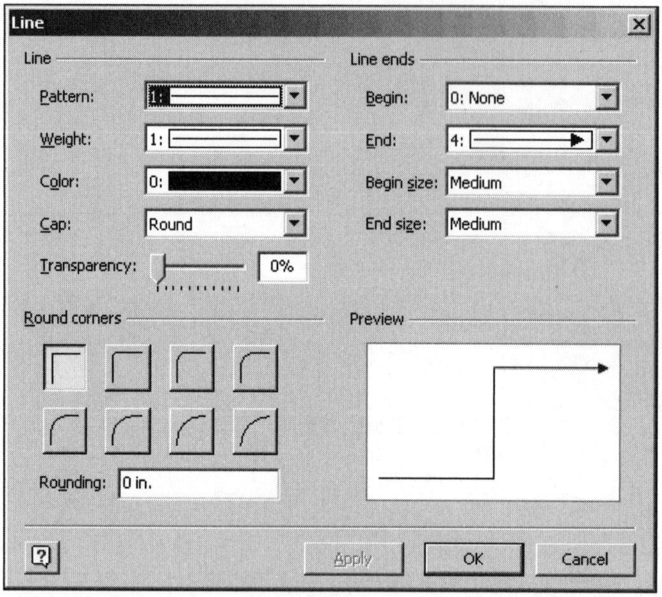

Using this dialog it's not only easy to change the beginning and end of the line – what kind of arrow, if any, but it's also easy to change the connector line pattern, thickness (**Weight**), and color as well as several other line properties. Additionally, depending on what type of connector you choose in your diagrams, Visio can smartly reroute how connections are drawn so the diagram looks its best. In other words, if you drop a shape in the middle of a group of connectors, those connectors will reroute themselves around the diagram automatically. For instance, dropping a tall process shape into the middle of our diagram we just used to illustrate glued connection points will have the following effect:

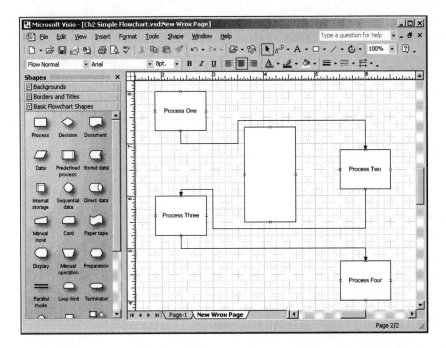

Notice how the connectors were automatically rerouted around the new shape. That's a handy feature and more times than not Visio does a good job at redrawing connector paths. Sometimes, however, it's necessary to tell Visio not to reroute when you move shapes around. To do that right-click on the connector for which you want to disable rerouting and select **Never Reroute**. Now Visio will allow other shapes to be drawn over top of your connector without moving it.

Common Visio Software Diagrams

Now that we've had a quick look around the Visio environment, we're ready to tackle some of the interesting software-oriented diagram templates shipped with Visio. There are many basic shapes and templates for some common diagramming tasks included with Visio. In addition to software development, Visio contains ready-made templates for a variety of diagramming applications. Not surprisingly, most of them are technical or engineering oriented. Here are the software diagrams available in Visio for Enterprise Architects:

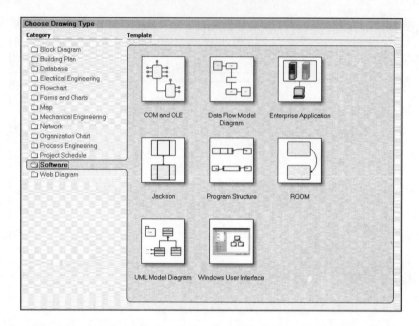

For our purposes in this chapter, we'll be focusing on a set of **Software** diagrams that includes the following templates:

- ❑ **COM and OLE** – diagrams illustrating COM and OLE interfaces

- ❑ **Data Flow Model Diagram** – diagrams showing the interaction between data producing and consuming processes and data stores

- ❑ **Enterprise Application** – diagrams illustrating enterprise applications using shapes that represent mainframes, PCs, etc.

- ❑ **Windows User Interface** – diagrams that contain common Windows UI controls for creating screenshot simulations

We'll also take a look at the following template from the set of **Database** diagrams:

- ❑ **Database Model** – diagrams that illustrate the structure and relationships of database objects including tables, views, triggers, etc.

In the next chapter we'll begin our detailed look at the UML diagrams, and revisit the database model diagrams in Chapter 8. Now, however, let's take each of the above diagram templates one at a time and describe the basics of creating diagrams of each type.

Creating COM and OLE Diagrams

Windows developers will probably grasp the intent of a COM and OLE diagram immediately. The purpose of such a diagram is to illustrate the relationship or interaction of a group of COM and OLE objects by using shapes that represent interfaces, processes, and process boundaries, among other things. We'll get into the details of the most common shapes used in these diagrams in a moment, but first let's take a look at a quick example to help with the discussion. Notice that the shapes in the diagram below are somewhat self-describing. Using our software development background we can probably read this diagram without any previous exposure to this type of diagram.

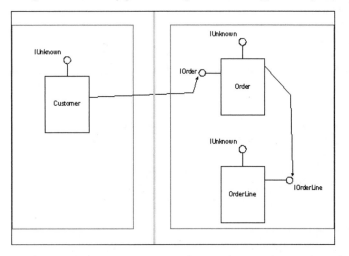

If you surmised that this is a simple representation of an application that works with customer and order data you are correct. Each of the two boxes represents a boundary of some sort. The thicker line between them represents a process boundary. On one side of the process boundary in a component of some sort is an object called Customer that uses another object in another component called Order. Within that component, within the same process, the Order object uses the OrderLine object. So even without much background in COM and OLE diagrams, we can read and derive something meaningful from the diagram. Let's take a closer look at the common shapes in this template and how you can use them in your own diagrams.

❑   COM Object – the COM Object shape is represented by a rectangle with the familiar lollipop shapes indicating the interfaces exposed by the object. Since, in the Windows COM world, every object has to implement the IUnknown interface, the shape defaults to one interface named IUnknown when you drag it onto a new diagram. We've already seen the COM Object shape in our earlier example; here is the default shape as seen immediately after it's dragged onto the Visio drawing page.

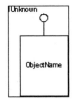

❏ **References** – The COM and OLE diagram gives you the ability to express two types of references – a Standard Reference and a Weak Reference. A typical reference, called just **Reference** by Visio, represents a typical reference from one `Object` to another. The shape that represents a **Reference** is a common Visio connector with a slightly bent starting shape. A Weak Reference is very similar to the standard **Reference**. The only distinction between the two is the temporal nature of a Weak Reference – it's a reference between COM objects that is only temporary. A Reference is drawn with a solid black line; the Weak Reference is drawn with a similar shape, but the line is dashed.

❏ **Vtable** – Vtable is a contraction of the more impressive sounding Virtual Function Table. They are included in the COM and OLE diagram because Vtables are such an important part of COM programming. If you think of a COM interface as a set of methods exposed by a particular component then you'll probably understand a Vtable. All of the methods (function pointers in COM and C++ terminology) of an object's interface are arranged together in one list or table. A **Vtable** shape is included in the diagram stencil to help add some detail to the diagram. Including the **Vtable** shape in a diagram helps add detailed information where it may be useful.

The shape itself is easy to use. It literally is a series of smaller, rectangular shapes grouped together. Each rectangle represents a function or method supported by the interface. When you drag the shape onto the drawing page, you'll be prompted to specify how many rows you want in the `Vtable`.

If, as in this screenshot, you select 4 (the maximum is 16), Visio will draw a **Vtable** shape consisting of four rectangles grouped together. You can then click on each region inside the **Vtable** and add your method details.

❏ Interface – we've already seen the interface shape in action. It's represented by what some call a lollipop – a straight line with a small circle sitting on the end. Since all COM objects do their work via one interface or another, a properly constructed COM and OLE diagram will rely heavily on this shape.

It is possible, of course, for an object to have many interfaces. Visio makes creating such an object easy. After dragging a **COM Object** shape onto the drawing page, new interfaces can be added by dragging the **Interface** shape onto the drawing. If you drag the tail of the **Interface** shape over top of the **COM Object,** the two will connect themselves automatically.

A `Customer` object that gets used by various business components for `Shipping`, `Billing`, and `Order Entry` might have different interfaces for each purpose. In that situation, we could draw the object and its interfaces like this:

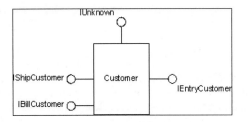

❏ Process Boundary – since one of the benefits of a COM and OLE diagram is illustrating the interaction between objects, we need to account for situations when those objects may be implemented in different processes. Crossing a process boundary is an expensive operation and has other implications, so making the process boundary clear in the diagram is an important issue. In our diagram, we represent the process boundary by a thicker, solid line. The shape's orientation is vertical by default, but once on the drawing page it can be arranged just like any other Visio line.

❏ Boundary – in addition to process boundaries, there are other boundaries worth noting in your diagram. Typically, they are logical or physical boundaries that exist within the same process and shouldn't be confused with the **Process Boundary** shape. The **Boundary** shape is just a large box drawn with a dashed black line (the printed screenshots don't show the dashed line, you'll have to take my word for it). As an example, consider the following diagram:

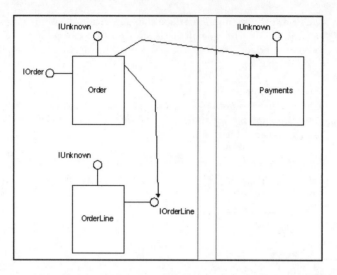

The Order object in this diagram is most likely implemented within one physical component and the Payments object is probably implemented in another component. Although the **Boundary** shape doesn't contain implementation details, it does make clear the separation between the Order and Payment objects.

There are several benefits to these kinds of diagrams:

❑ Object relationships are immediately clear regardless of whether the reader is familiar with the diagram notation.

❑ The interfaces exposed by COM objects are included in the diagram and can be specified in some detail using the **Vtable** shape.

❑ Process boundaries can be immediately identified by the diagram reader, helping point out expensive cross process operations.

❑ Physical or logical boundaries can be illustrated, helping to bring out any design structure or architecture that may be important to grasping how sets of objects work together.

Creating Data Flow Diagrams

Data Flow diagrams are used to illustrate the flow of data from one process to another. They don't really offer much detail about particular processes like running a credit check or creating an inventory record; rather they are good at making the flow of data through a multi-step process easy to understand. Visio ships with a variation of the Data Flow Diagram (DFD) using the **Gane-Sarson** notation. It's unlikely that any experience you've had with DFD's will vary greatly from the notation included in Visio.

DFD's consist of processes, data stores, and the flows of data between them. Processes are any activity that transforms data. Data stores are any place information resulting from a process transformation can be stored. Data flows are a notation illustrating the movement, or flow, of data from a data store to a process.

Let's have a look at an example first, and then dig into the details of how the diagram is constructed. Consider a simple order processing system for an online merchant. To properly create and fill orders there's quite a bit of information that has to be gathered, recalled from, or written to a database. We won't cover the entire process from beginning to end, of course, but it will serve as a decent example for our DFD discussion. The steps in an order entry application might be listed as follows:

❑ Customer calls service center with a particular product purchase request.

❑ Service center rep retrieves product information from database and answers any questions the customer has.

❑ Service center rep retrieves the customer's personal information from database.

❑ Service center rep updates any changes in customer information.

❑ Service center rep creates order.

❑ Call is ended.

The diagram depicting this series is steps are rather simple.

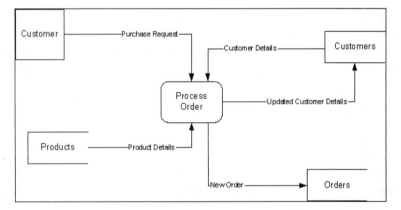

Notice how data flows from the shape representing the **Customer** into the **Process Order** step. Data flows from the **Products** and **Customers** data stores for looking up product and customer details. The primary flow of data out of **Process Order** is into the **Orders** data store – a new order is created. Each of the shapes used in a DFD is rather simple. Let's have a look at the four shapes.

❑ **Interface** – in the example above, our customer was represented by an **Interface** shape. In a DFD, external references are called Interfaces. **External** means any source of data outside of the system the diagram is modeling. Interfaces can be people like our customer or other systems and applications such as a Purchasing System. The shape itself is a simple square with the name of the interface in the middle.

❑ **Process** – as we've mentioned before, Processes are activities that modify data somehow. In a diagram, there can be dozens of processes or there can be just a few. The process shape is drawn as an oval with the name of the process written inside.

❑ **Data Store** – data stores are drawn as an open-ended rectangle. They represent any store of data – database, file, document, etc. For the purposes of the DFD, the physical details of a data store are irrelevant. The point is to illustrate how data flows in and out of the Data Store and what Processes use or create that data.

❑ **Data Flow** – a Data Flow is a simple line in a Visio DFD. It is, however, the key to the entire diagram. The DFD template contains a connector labeled Data Flow that behaves like other Visio connectors.

There are some rules governing how these shapes can be connected and the DFD template in Visio enforces them.

❑ All processes have to have at least one input data store and at least one output data store.

❑ Processes cannot be connected together directly via a Data Flow.

❑ All data flows must to lead to a data store.

If you violate these rules, Visio will let you know. The DFD template is built with some intelligence indicating what's allowed in a drawing and what isn't. In fact, you'll get error messages if you mess something up. For instance, if we add a process to our example DFD for processing credit cards and we don't give it an output Data Store, Visio will write an error message to the Output window as this screenshot illustrates:

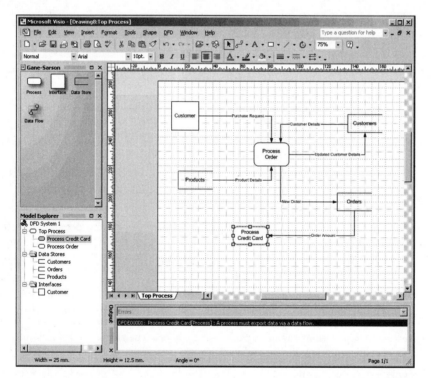

Notice the new **Process Credit Card** shape near the bottom of the diagram. On your screen, the color of the shape's line is now a bold red, indicating some error. In the **Output** window is written the message:

Process Credit Card[Process] : A process must export data via a data flow.

Any other error you might generate by violating DFD rules will always be written to the Output window.

Let's cover one last point regarding the DFD before we move on. In the screenshot above, there's a new docked window in the lower left of the Visio UI. It's labeled Model Explorer and quite literally, that's what it is – a tree-view-based explorer listing every process, interface, and data store in the diagram. For complicated diagrams, it's a handy feature. We'll see similar devices in other diagram templates. The UML diagram template in particular has a nice Model Explorer, and we'll see much of it as we progress through the book!

Creating Enterprise Applications

Sometimes it is necessary to describe how an application will be implemented or deployed and give some indication of the types of machines that will either host application server components or run client components. The Enterprise Application diagram template was designed with this scenario in mind. Distributed applications with complicated and varied deployment platforms are good candidates for Enterprise Application diagrams.

The diagram itself is built from a template consisting of a series of shapes designed to look like hardware you might encounter in many larger applications – mainframes, servers, workstations, laptops, among others. The diagram also contains a few shapes we've already seen like the Boundary and Interface from the COM and OLE diagram. Enterprise Application diagrams get their complexity from the scope of the applications they are illustrating. The building blocks of the diagram itself are very simple. For that reason we'll take an example and discuss its construction rather than taking each shape one at a time.

Consider a distributed application designed to support a mobile sales staff. Sales personnel will be working from the road placing orders, looking up product data, and checking on shipping status for various customers. This type of application is very common in larger manufacturing companies. If we include the mobile sales staff, represented by laptops and an internal group of users represented by workstations, we can illustrate how this application will be deployed and the various platforms it requires.

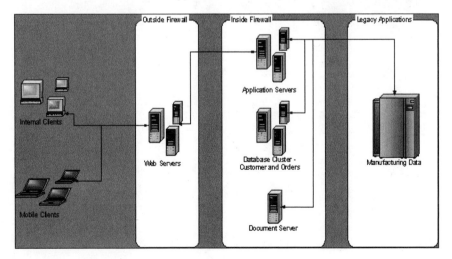

Notice that the level of detail pertaining to each platform or group isn't high. We can, however, take away from this diagram an understanding of the types of machines involved in this application and their relationships to one another. Of course, there are many important pieces of information missing, like communication protocols, but that isn't the intent of Enterprise Application diagrams. You could always add that level of detail, but the primary purpose of this diagram is to communicate the big picture.

Windows Interface Diagrams

One of the more interesting diagram templates shipped with Visio is the Windows Interface Diagram. The purpose of this diagram is to prototype Windows interfaces before development. During the early stages of most development projects, it's very useful to present UI designs to user groups for feedback. Not only does UI prototype generate good feedback on UI layout and usability, but the process also forces users to think about their needs in terms that are more realistic. Instead of some abstract idea of what an application might look like when the software is finally delivered, users armed with prototype UI layouts will have thought through how they intend to use the software and hopefully have identified problem areas and made suggestions for improvements.

Some developers use VB itself for laying out sample Windows forms. It certainly is quick. There are a couple of problems with prototyping UIs with VB, though. First, users and developers see those prototypes as actual working software and may be less likely to tear it up, since it's a real program regardless of how little functionality it may contain. Second, developers seem to build more functionality into their prototypes making them harder to walk away from once the prototype stage is complete. Effective prototypes are generally throwaway pieces of code. Otherwise, they aren't prototypes and their importance as a design and development tool is minimized.

OK, hopefully the case is made for prototyping your UI designs. So how do we do it? The Windows UI template included with Visio contains just about any UI control you can think of for building interface prototypes. Sticking with the pattern of showing an example and breaking it down, here's what a UI prototype development in Visio might look like:

After just a few minutes of working with the Windows UI template in Visio, we can produce a simple Windows form, professional enough to include in documentation sent to clients or presented to user groups for review and comments. Also, we won't have opened any IDE or other rapid application development package to do it. In addition, when changes are requested, we can quickly and easily add and remove UI items and reposition existing items. This diagram template has the potential for saving quite a bit of design and development time depending on the UI requirements of your applications and involvement of your user groups.

Having seen a simple example, let's have a look at some of the UI diagram shape in more detail. We won't cover them all, of course, just the most common and more interesting shapes. Let's consider the simple Windows Form shape first.

Windows Form Shape

If you are working on designing dialog boxes, the Form shape is probably where you'll start with each form you layout. Although it's not necessary to place all UI controls into a Form shape container like our first example above, doing so helps create a realistic look and feel for your prototypes. To create a simple Windows form, start Visio and select File | New | Software | Windows User Interface. Your Visio application will look like this – notice the large group of shapes in the stencil that is added to your new drawing.

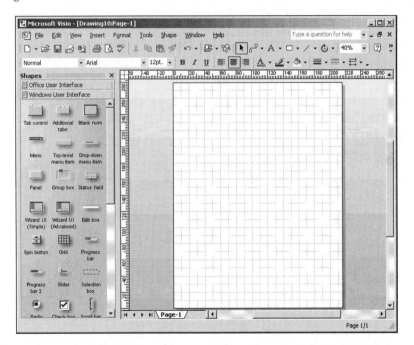

Now, grab the Blank Form shape (first row on the Windows User Interface stencil, third column) and drag it onto the drawing page. You'll get a Windows form with an editable caption – it says Enter Title Here by default. Double-click on the caption area of the form and type Sample Windows Form. You should then have a form that looks like this:

Sample Windows Form

Now that you have a form going, you can add all kinds of UI controls to the form. There are, however, a few controls that you might want to pay attention to that are common to most Windows forms – form buttons, status fields, etc. Let's have a look at a few and see how we can dress up our simple form before we start adding items like text boxes and combo boxes.

A very common UI control you'll likely find on a Windows form is a button to minimize, maximize, or close the form. The standard buttons on the upper right of many forms. Visio let's you drag a Windows button onto the drawing page and select which type of button it represents – **Restore, Minimize, Maximize, Close,** or **Help.** Let's add a **Close** and a **Help** button to the sample that we just started creating. From the stencil, find the shape labeled **Windows buttons.** Click and drag that shape onto the drawing page. Try to drag the shape onto the upper right corner of the **Form** shape so that the connector turns red, indicating the button will be docked onto the **Form** shape. When you release the dragged shape, you'll see this dialog:

Custom Properties

Button Type : Close

Prompt
Select button type.

Define... OK Cancel

If you want a **Close** button, as we do now, just press **OK** and Visio will create a new Windows button with a small X: (⊠). Now, create another Windows button to represent **Help.** Drag the **Windows buttons** shape back onto the existing form and try to arrange it close to our **Close** button – they will dock together. When the **Custom Properties** box appears this time, select the **Help** button type. If all goes well, you'll have a form resembling this screenshot:

Other common Form-related UI controls are the **Corner Resize** and **Status Field** shapes. The **Corner Resize** (also known as the **Grip**) is the angled shape you find on forms that allow resizing. The user will click and drag the **Corner Resize** control and make the form's height and width change. It's easy to add – the control is found near the bottom of the stencil in the next to last row. Similar to the Windows buttons, drag the **Corner resize** to the lower right corner of the sample form we've already created and drop it when the connector points of the control turn red.

Now let's add some **Status** fields across the bottom. These regions are generally used to display application information like page numbers, current line position, or any other application information that may be useful to the user at a quick glance; Microsoft Word uses Status fields as well as do most other Microsoft applications. To create the Status field, locate the **Status field** shape on the stencil (third row, third column), drag it onto the sample form, and drop it near the bottom of the form. Again, Visio will help you out by docking for **Status field** shape onto the Windows Form shape if you get it close. Our example Form now looks like this screenshot:

You can resize the Status field controls to be as wide or as narrow as you like, depending on your application's needs.

So, we've got some of the basics of building a Windows form done, but how about adding some more exciting UI controls? The template in Visio supports quite a few commonly used UI controls that we'll probably be using in our applications:

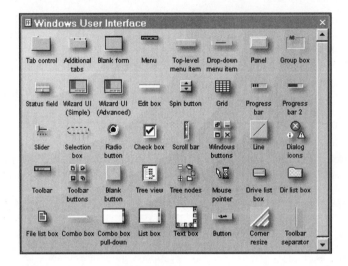

Let's start with the Menu controls and their Visio shapes.

In the Windows UI diagram in Visio, standard Windows menus are represented by a few shapes – the Menu itself, a Top-level menu item, and a Drop-down menu item. By combining the three shapes we can mimic just about any application menu we need to. Let's start by adding the Menu shape to the form we've been building. Make sure you have Visio running and have a Windows User Interface drawing open. We'll be adding to our Sample Windows Form we've been building in this section, so locate that if you've been following along.

In the stencil for this drawing in the second row, first column, is a shape that represents a Windows menu. It's really just a long, resizable rectangle shaded to match the standard Windows form color. Click and drag the Menu shape onto the sample form and try to dock it near the top of the form, below the title bar. The upper left and right corner of the form (not the title bar) supports docking so if you get one end or the other of the Menu shape close, you'll see a connection point turn red when it's lined up enough to be docked. Depending on how wide your form is, you may have to shorten the length of your Menu shape. If all goes well, you'll have a form with an empty menu.

To add top-level menu items, find the shape in the stencil labeled Top-level menu item. These are dockable shapes that will contain menu names like File, Edit,View, etc. Drag the shape onto the Menu shape already on the form and dock it on the left side of the Menu shape. Watch where you dock the top-level menu item – there are several connecting points available in the drawing now. Click on the newly added top-level menu item and type the word File. You'll see a form that looks like this screenshot:

Add a few more top-level menu items and you've got a good looking Windows form complete with many common form-level UI controls.

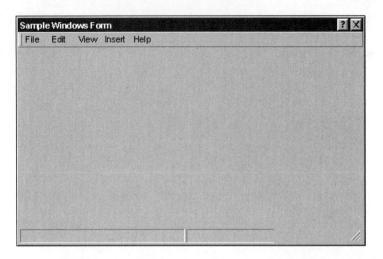

If you are interested in illustrating some of the menu items themselves (what you see when the menu is expanded when you click on the top-level menu item), locate the **Drop-down menu item** shape on the stencil (next to the **Top-level menu item** shape). Drag that shape immediately below the **File** top-level menu item already on the form. Since the first menu item on the **File** menu is commonly **New**, click on the **Drop-down menu item** and type the word **New**. Add a new **Drop-down menu item** shape below the **New** menu item and label it **Open**. Add others for **Save**, **Save As…** and **Exit**. You'll now have a form that looks like this:

Interestingly the Drop-down menu item isn't resizable the way the **Top-level menu item** shape is, but the drop-down items do have some properties that may be useful. Right-click on any of the drop-down items you just added and select **Menu Item Properties**. You'll see a dialog like this:

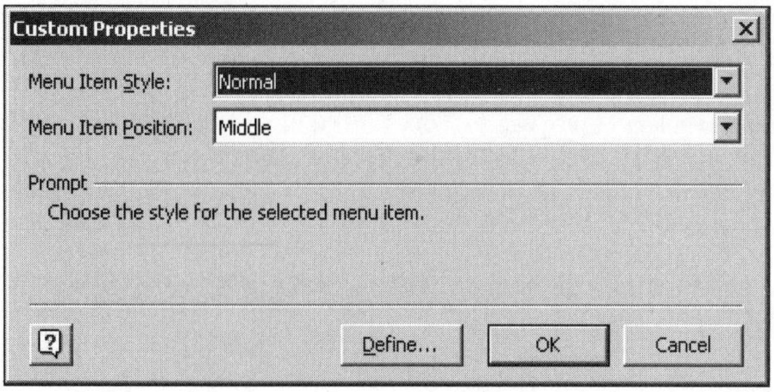

The **Menu Item Style** dropdown contains several values that might be useful depending on how much detail you need in your menu items. The values include:

- **Normal** – a standard menu item with no extra formatting.

- **Checked** – a menu item that can be preceded with a check mark that could indicate some option is turned on.

- **Radio** – a menu item that can be preceded with a radio button-like circle that may indicate an option or setting is activated. This style is very similar to the **Checked** style.

- **Cascading** – a menu item that explodes into a set of related sub menu items. The sub menu is represented by a small black arrowhead displayed on the right of the menu item.

- **Separator** – a menu item used to segregate other menu items into logical groups. Visio creates a sunken, beveled line similar to the menu separators you see in many other Windows applications.

Another common UI control that's useful to diagram before building is a **Tab** control. Fortunately, the UI template in Visio supports prototyping tab controls also. In fact, it's the first control listed in the stencil. To build a **Tab** control, drag the **Tab** shape onto the drawing page. At this point, we're still using the **Sample Windows Form** we've been building up to this point. The **Drop-down menu** shapes have been removed to free up some room on the form itself. When you've dropped the `Tab` control you can resize it to be somewhat centered on the form. Now, click on the **Tab Control** and type it's name – we'll use **Main** for our example.

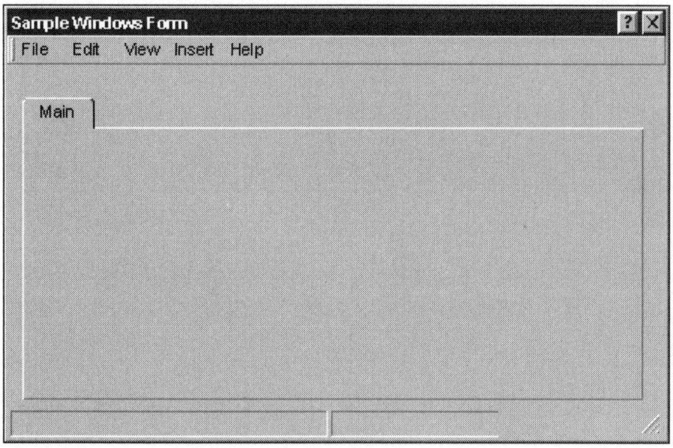

If your tab control consists of more tabs, you can drag the shape labeled Additional tabs and dock it immediately to the right of the Main tab you just created – name it Options. Notice that the Options tab is slightly lower than the Main tab. That's how Visio indicates which tab is active. If you right-click on the Options tab you can select Move Tab to Top. Both tabs will be the same size so you need to right-click on the Main tab and select Move Tab to Back. Now the Options tab is active. You can add controls to the body of the tab control to represent what's visible when the Options tab is clicked. The screenshot below shows the active Options tab with three fictitious options represented by checkboxes.

The last item we'll discuss in this section is the Wizard control that the Visio Windows Interface stencil supports. Clearly there are more UI controls available in the template, but most of them, such as text boxes or radio buttons, are familiar to most developers already in terms of their usage and placement.

The Wizard UI shape is incredibly useful. We've all used wizards at one time or another in Windows, and it's likely most of us have built them as well. So we all know that a wizard is generally multi-step process controlled by three buttons – Back, Next, and Cancel. Some kind of content for data entry or other purposes is displayed in the body of the wizard form. As you move through the wizard, the Next buttons takes you to a following page, while the Back button takes you to a previous page, and the Cancel button exits the wizard. Building a good wizard isn't exactly simple, so working out the details of what data is displayed on which pages of the wizard is a good idea. Let's have a look at a hypothetical wizard UI.

For starters, drag the Wizard UI (Simple) onto the drawing page. You see the shell of a standard Wizard UI with three main regions. There's one on the left of the form shaded green used to display information or graphics that generally don't change with each Back or Next button click; a main working area that contains text and other UI controls that change with each Back and Next button click; and an area for buttons on the lower left of the form. You can add text to either of the regions above the buttons by clicking on the region and typing. It does take some trial and error, though, to get the right region. The Wizard UI shape itself is actually a grouping of several other shapes so you'll probably have to experiment to get it right. We can add some text to the regions by first selecting the Text tool from the standard toolbar:

Now if we add some text to both regions, it can look like this:

Of course, you can also drag any shapes onto the Wizard UI you find necessary.

Since the buttons at the bottom of the form are so important for controlling the behavior of the wizard, the Visio template comes with some extra functionality for controlling how the buttons are drawn. In the course of running the Wizard both the **Back** and **Next** buttons may or may not be enabled. For instance when a user is on the first step in the wizard, there's no point in enabling the **Back** button – there's nowhere to go. To disable the **Back** button, right click on it and select **Disable** Button. The button will be displayed on the form as if it was a disabled Windows application button. The same can be done to the **Next** and **Cancel** buttons.

We also have the ability to set the default button on the wizard form. In Windows, a darker line drawn around the button usually indicates defaults. The default button is executed when the user presses the *Enter* key. To set the **Next** button as the default on the first page in a wizard, right-click on it and select **Selected and Default** from the pop-up menu. With the **Back** button disabled and the **Next** button set as the default button, our wizard now looks like this screenshot:

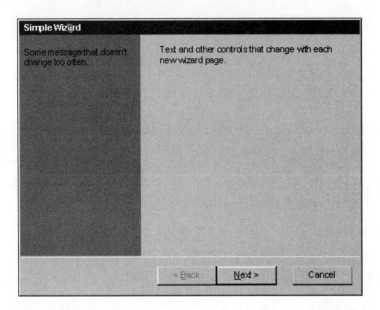

Creating Database Model Diagrams

The last Visio diagram we'll review in this chapter is the one I've personally used the most – database model diagrams. These diagrams show tables and their relationships and, optionally, table details like fields, indexes, foreign keys, and other information. In practice, it seems that creating and distributing data models is a common task in the course of building a software application. I won't speculate on why but I imagine that it's easier to illustrate table relationships graphically in a diagram than it is to describe verbally. You may find in your own work that you spend more time on building database model diagrams than any other type of diagram.

Visio can build database model diagrams from scratch or it can reverse engineer an existing database model and produce a diagram after the database has already been created. As a design tool, it's very useful; as a documentation tool, it's also very useful. Let's have a look at building a simple data model, then we'll run through reverse engineering an existing SQL Server database.

Creating a Simple Data Model

Let's build a simple data model used to track customers and their orders for a hypothetical web application. The core of the data model will be a `Customer` table. We'll also need an `Order` table for storing order details, an `OrderItem` table to store what each order contains, and a `Product` table used to store product details like name and price.

Here's a listing of the tables and their contents:

- ❑ `Customer` – `CustomerID, Name, Address, Phone`
- ❑ `Order` – `OrderID, CustomerID, OrderDate, Amount`
- ❑ `OrderItem` – `OrderItemID, OrderID, ProductID, Price`
- ❑ `Product` – `ProductID, Name, Price`

It's a simple data model that is somewhat normalized. That's not the focus of this section so I won't make any normalization comments, other than this one: Price is duplicated in OrderItem and Product in case the main product price changes after an order has been created.

Let's start with a brand-new Visio diagram. If Visio is running close all open diagrams and select File | New then select Database | Data Model Diagram. You'll get an empty drawing page that looks similar to this screenshot:

In the stencil, there are really just two main working shapes in this template – Entity and Relationship. The others aren't unimportant, but these two do most of the work. The Entity shape represents tables. To create a new table in the diagram, drag the Entity shape onto the drawing page. By default, Visio will display the new table and populate a docked Window underneath the drawing page with table information. If you don't see a Database Properties window near the bottom of the Visio form, right-click on the Entity shape you just created and select Database Properties. You should see something similar to the following screenshot (notice the page zoom setting has also changed here):

In the Database Properties Window, we can adjust quite a few properties of this table. Calling the Window Database Properties is a little misleading. We are actually looking at the properties of a single table. Notice the list of categories in the listbox on the right. As you click on Categories, the remaining region to the right of the window will change.

Let's start by naming the table Customer. To add fields click on the Columns line in the Categories list box and you'll see the Properties window change to include a grid.

You can add fields by typing directly into the grid in the first row or you can press the Add button. Add a new field called CustomerID, make it required, and set its type to VarChar. The default size is 10 and that's fine for our purposes now. If you want to change the size, or other characteristics of the field, you can press the Edit button and get a dialog that looks like this:

Size and data types are on the **Data Type** tab, by the way. You can explore the other options in this dialog.

Continue accepting the defaults Visio gives you and add the rest of the **Customer** fields so you have a grid that looks similar to the following:

The last step is to identify a **Primary ID** for this table. In our case, that's easy – the **CustomerID** field. Click on the **Primary ID** line in the **Categories** list box. Select the **CustomerID** from the list of available columns and add it to the Primary ID columns. Your window will look like this:

Now have a look at the Entity shape we first dragged onto the drawing page. It is populated with a table name, a list of fields, and the primary key field is identified by a bold underline with a PK beside it. Repeat the same process for the remaining tables and you'll get a drawing page that looks like this:

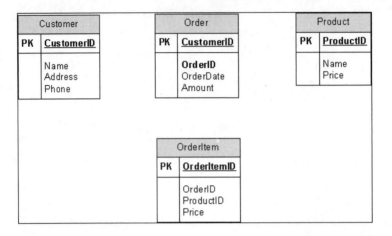

Now that the tables are defined, we have to relate them together. In Visio, it's simple. The second of our most commonly shapes is the relationship. As you might expect, the relationship shape represents actual database relationships – one to one, one to many, and many to many.

Let's draw a relationship between Customer and Order first. By definition, a Customer can have many orders, but an Order record can only belong to one Customer. Click and drag the Relationship connector onto the drawing page. Drag the end of the connector with the arrowhead into the middle of the Customer table. The table should become highlighted in red. That means you've connected the line to the Entity shape so they'll move together. You've also started giving the template information on how to build the relationship. Click and drag the other end of the line into the middle of the Order table. The same thing should happen – a red highlighted Entity shape. Without actually connecting the shapes together with the Relationship connector, what we're about to discuss won't work correctly. Make sure you've got the connector drawn correctly – to confirm this, select the connector and check that both ends are colored red, indicating they are glued. You should have something that looks like this:

Our two tables are basically the same. The only difference is the FK1 listed in front of the CustomerID field in the Order table. That indicates the CustomerID field is a foreign key back to the Customer table. That relationship will tell us which customer a particular order belongs to.

Repeat the same process for the rest of the tables and you'll end up with a group of tables and relationships that looks like this:

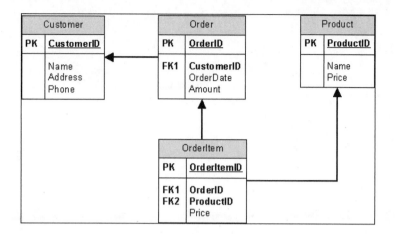

It's common to have to correct what Visio does when naming foreign keys. The application does a reasonably good job, but don't trust it blindly.

Always review what Visio has created for you!

In Chapter 8 we'll take a deeper look into the database modeling, and see how to actually generate database tables from these diagrams, and also how to reverse engineer database structures into diagrams like the above.

Summary

In this chapter, we have had a quick orientation of the Visio environment, and seen some of the software diagrams that it provides – Visio has many, many other diagrams, but we'll only be focusing on a subset of those here, and in subsequent chapters.

We began the chapter with a simple Visio diagram, looking at setting page properties, shapes, and connectors. We saw that shapes are organized into containers called stencils, and that shapes possess an intelligence, which we shall see more of whenever we work with Visio. It is this intelligence that gives Visio its power as a diagramming tool.

We then moved on to look at some of the common software diagrams to get a better idea of what Visio can offer the developer, and also to provide an opportunity to become more comfortable with environment. We didn't, however, look at the UML model diagrams – we will begin our exploration of these diagrams in the next chapter.

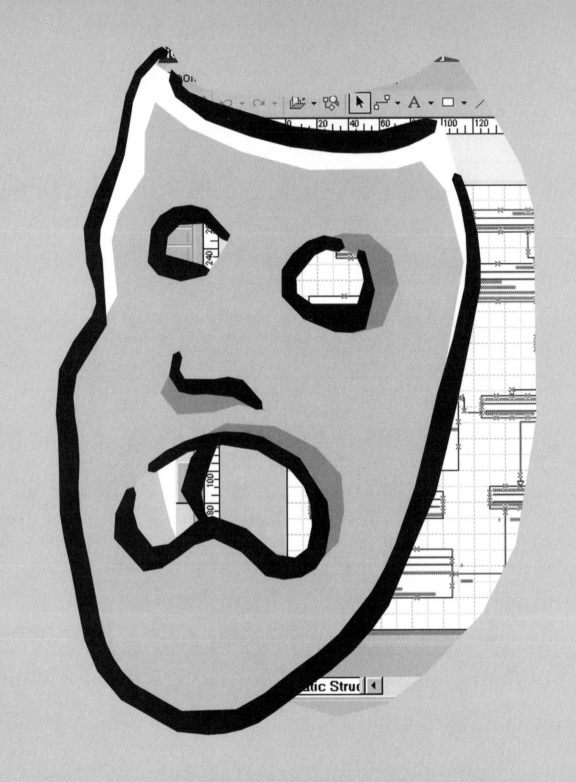

Diagramming Business Objects

The UML without business objects is like the Tour de France without bicycles. Without business objects, class diagrams, collaboration diagrams, sequence diagrams, and state chart diagrams hold little meaning. It's not until you begin designing and using business objects that you see a real need for the UML or modeling tools such as Visio or Rational XDE. However, once you begin using business objects, you'll be firing up your UML modeling tool on a daily basis to conceive, design, and understand the object model of your applications, which usually produces more flexible, extensible, and maintainable software.

Although much has been written about the benefits of business objects, many companies continue to create monolithic applications. A monolithic application is a piece of software with the user interface, business logic, and data access inextricably bound together. This is what you find in most of the .NET sample code shown in books, magazine articles, and on-line resources.

In this chapter, we are first going to learn what business objects are and why you should use them. If you are going to climb the business object learning curve, you should have compelling reasons to do so. Although business objects can be one of the more difficult concepts for developers to grasp, once you "get it" and begin using business objects in your applications, you'll never go back again.

In this chapter we will also cover:

- ❑ Using Visio for object modeling
- ❑ Defining data-access base classes for your .NET applications
- ❑ Defining a business object base class
- ❑ How to derive business classes from use cases

❑ Working with abstract and concrete classes

❑ Thinking about data during object modeling

❑ Using sequence diagrams to model the flow of messages between objects

What is a Business Object?

A business object is an object usually representing a real-world person, place, or thing. Business objects allow you to represent both the attributes and behavior of these entities. For example, if you are creating a point-of-sale invoicing application, you may have business objects representing real-world entities such as a customer, an invoice, a payment, an inventory item, and so on. Business objects allow you to create a one-to-one correspondence between real-world entities and objects in your computer system.

Object Modeling Compared to Data Modeling

If you're familiar with data modeling, this concept of modeling entities shouldn't be too foreign. As shown in the following image, when you model data, you often create data tables representing attributes of real-world entities. Using the point-of-sale invoicing application as an example, you may have customer, invoice, payment, and inventory tables that represent real-world entities.

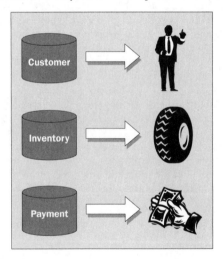

During data modeling, you design tables with fields that represent the properties or attributes of real-world entities. For example, a customer table may have fields for a customer's name, mailing address, e-mail address, phone number, and so on. An inventory table represents the properties of a real-world inventory by means of description, quantity-on-hand, price, and other fields.

However, modeling the attributes of a real-world entity is only half the story. Entities also have *behavior* that can be modeled. For example, customers can change phone numbers, buy loads of inventory and become 'preferred' customers, or not pay their bills and be put on credit hold. Inventory can be sold, ordered, back ordered, and change in price. Business objects allow you to encapsulate both the attributes and behavior of real-world entities.

Modeling Attributes and Behavior

Business objects model the *attributes* of real-world entities because they encapsulate an entity's data. As shown in the following image, all data manipulation in your application should take place via business objects. This image shows a user interface, possibly a Windows Forms client accessing application data using business objects. The Customer Business Object accesses the Customer data, the Inventory Business Object manipulates the Inventory data, and the Payment Business Object manipulates the Payment data.

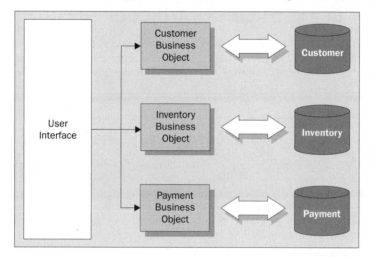

You can add data manipulation methods to your business object classes. For example, a Customer business object might have a method called `GetCustomerByPk` that accepts a customer primary key value and returns a `DataSet` containing the specified customer. An Inventory object might have a method called `GetInventoryByPartNumber` that accepts a part number and returns a `DataSet` containing the specified part. You can also add methods to your business objects that manipulate and save data to the back-end database.

Business objects model the *behavior* of real-world entities because you can add methods to them representing real-world actions. For example, you can create a `PutOnCreditHold` method for a Customer business object that performs a series of actions to put a customer on hold. When you want to place a customer on credit hold, you simply call this method. You can add a `ChangePrice` method to an Inventory object that you call (passing a part number and the new price) whenever an inventory item's price changes. Later in this chapter, we'll be taking a closer look at how to decide which methods should be added to a business object.

Building Monolithic Applications

As mentioned earlier, the alternative to using business objects is creating monolithic applications. Many software applications are still created this way today. Sometimes the reason that they are created this way is that developers believe it's easier – and on some levels, it is! In other cases, upper management may not be willing to make an investment in analysis and design. Regardless of the reason, monolithic applications are extremely inflexible. Whenever change comes along, and it always does, you have to spend countless hours tearing out code (and your hair!) to implement new technology.

Building Component-Based Applications

There are many benefits from building component-based applications with business objects, which we'll cover in the next section. As you realize these benefits over time, you will begin to understand why we can say with confidence that you will never go back again to building monolithic applications.

Benefits of using Business Objects

We mentioned a few benefits of using business objects in this chapter's introduction, but we're going to dive a bit deeper to provide a rationale for using business objects in your application. Building applications with components initially adds a degree of difficulty to your software development, so it's good to establish compelling reasons for doing so. To do this, we'll first look at the alternative – building monolithic applications.

Flexibility – Write Once, Reuse Everywhere

When building a Windows Forms desktop application, many developers have it in the back of their mind they also need to provide access to the application via the Internet. However, if you build a monolithic application, where the majority of your application logic is tucked away inside the methods and event handlers of a Windows Form, when that user interface goes away (replaced by a Web browser) all your application logic goes with it. How can you access application logic that is stuck in the methods of a Windows Form from an ASP.NET application? The answer is you can't.

In contrast, as shown in the following image, if you place application logic in business objects, these objects can be accessed from a Windows Forms application, a Web Forms application, or a Web Service.

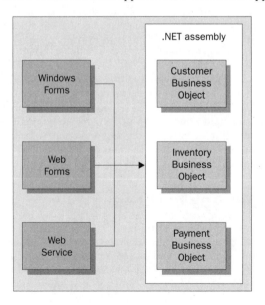

Data-Access Flexibility – Write Once, Change Once

Will your application access SQL Server data, Oracle data, or something completely different? The answer to this question might change mid-development or maybe even after your application is deployed. Most of the .NET sample code published in books and magazines places data-access code in the user interface. However, the .NET Framework uses a different set of classes (.NET Data Providers) to access different kinds of data, so if your application data changes, and your data-access code is scattered throughout the user interface, you've got quite a code change on your hands.

In contrast, if all data access takes place through your business objects, you only have one place you need to change your data access code – in the business object. In reality, good business object design dictates that your business objects should have data-access classes that you can switch in and out depending on the type of data you need to access.

Normalizing Application Logic – Write Once, Period!

Good database designers know how to normalize application data. The term "normalize" refers to eliminating redundancies in data. But have you ever thought about normalizing your application logic? If you ever get an opportunity to look at code written by teams of developers, you'll often find the same application logic repeated several times over in a single application. When you place application logic in the user interface, there are no checks and balances preventing you from creating the same logic repeatedly.

Again, business objects come to the rescue. When you place your application logic in business objects, it's far less likely you will create two methods that do exactly the same thing. When all forms in the application use the same business objects, developers have a common repository for application logic.

Where's the Code? – Write It and Find It

Have you ever played "Where's the code?" If you've built monolithic applications, I'm sure you have. When application logic is scattered throughout the user interface, it can be very difficult to debug and maintain. In a monolithic application, you can spend countless hours hunting through hierarchies of user interface controls to find the code you're searching for.

In contrast, if you place your code in business objects, you lift it out of the 'weeds' and logically segregate it into business components making it easier to debug and maintain. If you have a bug in the invoicing portion of your application, you can be quite sure the problem code is in the Invoice business object. If you need to modify the way you handle inventory, it's a safe bet the code you're looking for is in the Inventory business object – and if you've named your business object methods well, it makes it even easier to determine where the code resides.

Designing Complex Software

Although last in the list, this benefit is not least in importance. When you elevate your programming by using business objects, it can help you better conceive and design complex software systems. In a monolithic application, something known as a **semantic gap** exists. This gap is the breach between your software system and the real world. Monolithic systems do not have objects that correspond to real-world entities, thereby creating this gap.

In a component-based application, business objects bridge this gap. Because you can create business objects that represent real-world entities, it is easier to solve real-world problems. I have a number of clients who struggled with thorny conceptual problems for weeks or months, without coming up with a solution. The simple act of creating business objects and manipulating these on class and sequence diagrams helped solve these thorny issues each time.

Designing a Component-based Application

Now that we've covered the basics of business objects, we're going to design a simple component-based application that implements business objects. First, we'll create business object and data access base classes from which we can derive all of our application-specific business objects. After that, we'll take some "already built" use cases for a simple library application, and create business objects that implement the use cases. During this process you'll see how thinking about data early on can help to prove and solidify your object model.

Business and Data-Access Base Classes

Later in this chapter we're going to create business objects that are specific to a particular application. However, before we get to that point, we need to design business objects and data-access base classes to use for deriving our application-specific business objects.

Although the .NET Framework class library contains many great classes, there is no business object base class. This means you'll have to roll your own or buy a third-party business component. In either case, there is some important functionality you should expect from a business object base class.

As mentioned earlier, a business component should be able to access different types of data. A good way to accomplish this is by placing all data access logic in data-access classes rather than in the business object itself. When a business object gets a request for data, it can pass the call to a data-specific data-access object that contains the actual data-access logic. We can create a family of data-specific classes for accessing SQL Server, Oracle, and so on. This allows us to attach the data-access classes we need to the business object at run time.

We'll take you step by step through the process of modeling these data access classes in Visio to show you how it's done. We'll go into greater detail creating these first classes, but later in the chapter we'll assume you are familiar with the process described here.

To begin, launch Visio and create a new **UML Model Diagram**. This opens a new, blank diagram in the Visio IDE and displays a new **Top Package** node under the **Static Model** node of the **Model Explorer** as shown in the following image.

The Model Explorer displays your UML model as a hierarchical tree view. As described in the next section, folders in this tree view can correspond to a namespace hierarchy. You can add diagrams, sub-packages, subsystems, classes, interfaces, data types, actors, and use cases diagrams to a package. Each of these elements is represented by a different icon in the tree view. You can right-click on these elements to delete, rename, and edit them, or you can drag and drop them on various diagrams.

In the next section, we will create packages representing namespaces in .NET.

Creating Namespace Packages

In .NET, namespaces provide a means for categorizing your classes and creating unique class names. In Visio, packages perform a similar function. Packages, represented as folders in the Model Explorer, can be used to represent namespace hierarchies. In the case of our data-access classes, we'll create a package structure representing a `Wrox.UMLDotNet.Data` namespace. According to Microsoft's naming convention, the first part of a namespace should be your company name (we'll use `Wrox` for this example), the next part should be your product (this book, `UMLDotNet`), and then any additional name segments to further categorize your class. To create this package structure in Visio:

1. Right-click the **Top Package** node and select **New | Package** from the context menu. This launches the **UML Package Properties** dialog shown in the following image.

2. In the **Name** text box, enter **Wrox**, and then click **OK**. This adds a new **Wrox** package node beneath the **Top Package** node.

3. Right-click the new **Wrox** package and perform the same steps to add a new **UMLDotNet** node.

4. Add a new **Data** package beneath the **UMLDotNet** package. This time add the following text to the **Documentation** box:

The Wrox.UMLDotnet.Data package contains a family of data access classes used to access a variety of data using .NET managed data providers.

Documentation is critical to a good object model. Regardless of how descriptive your package, class, and member names are, you need to document your intent for those who read and interpret your model. Although your design may seem self-evident at that time you create it, a few weeks or a few months later I guarantee that good comments will save you hours of rethinking and head scratching!

5. When you're done, click OK, and the packages in the Model Explorer look like the following diagram.

Creating an Abstract Data-Access Class

Because there are a variety of ways to access data, it makes sense to model an abstract data access base class defining an interface for a family of data access classes. We can then model concrete subclasses that access specific kinds of data.

To create a new class belonging to the Wrox.UMLDotNet.Data namespace, add the class to the Wrox | UMLDotNet | Data package in Visio:

1. Right-click the Data package in the Model Explorer, and select New | Class from the context menu. This launches the UML Class Properties dialog that allows you to specify a variety of class attributes.

2. As shown in the following image, enter DataAccessBase in the class Name text box. To specify that the class is abstract, select the IsAbstract checkbox. You can also enter a description of the class in the Documentation box.

3. When you're finished, click OK to close the dialog.

When the dialog closes, look in the Model Explorer and you will see a new DataAccessBase class node as shown in the following screenshot. We can see that the classes added to a package belong to the namespace represented by the package hierarchy.

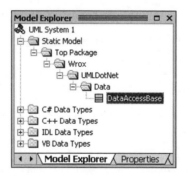

Creating a Class (Static Structure) Diagram

Next, let's create a new class diagram beneath the Top Package node to display the classes we create. Class diagrams are a type of static structure diagrams that provide visual representations of your classes. They allow you to model class attributes, operations, associations, interfaces, and dependencies.

1. Right-click the Top Package node and select New | Static Structure Diagram from the context menu (a class diagram is a type of static structure diagram). This creates a new static structure diagram and opens it in the Visio IDE. It also adds a new Static Structure-1 node beneath the Static Model node as shown in the following diagram.

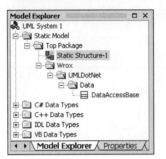

2. Rename the class diagram node to **Business and Data Classes** by right-clicking the **Static Structure-1** node, selecting **Rename** from the context menu, and entering the new name in the node edit box. You should see the new title of the class diagram displayed in the Visio title bar.

3. I usually turn off grid lines and connection points on the document to make it easier to see the class in screenshots. If you want to turn these off too, from the Visio main menu, select **View | Grid**, and then **View | Connection Points**. When you turn these off, the corresponding menu items are unchecked.

4. Drag the **DataAccessBase** class from the **Model Explorer** and drop it on the class diagram. It should look like the following image:

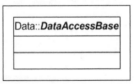

A few things to note – the class name is shown in italics. The UML specification dictates that abstract class names be displayed in italics. The **Data:** prefix indicates this class is found in the **Data** package.

This is a good time to save your Visio UML Model. Select **File | Save** from the menu to display the **Save As** dialog. Specify the name you want to give this file and the directory where you want to save it. If this is the first time you've saved the diagram, a **Properties** dialog displays prompting you to specify information about your model. In the **Summary** tab, you can specify information such as a title, subject, author, manager, and company. You can also specify a relative path for hyperlinks and how you want to display a preview of the model. The **Contents** tab displays each page of the model and the master shapes on them. For more information on this dialog, click the **Help** icon at the bottom left corner of the dialog. For now, just change the **Title** to **My Sample Model**, and then click the **OK** button.

Adding Operations to the Class

Now let's add a few basic operations to the `DataAccessBase` class. An operation in a UML class is implemented as a method in a real-world .NET class, as shown in the table earlier in this chapter. In Visual Basic .NET, operations that do not return a value are implemented as subroutines (`Sub`), whereas operations that *do* return a value are implemented as `Functions`. In C#, there is only one kind of method – methods that do not return a value simply return `void`.

This isn't a study in data access, so we won't go into too much detail here. We'll just add a few operations allowing us to retrieve and save data in a `DataSet`. Both operations will accept a database key used to look up database connection information in a configuration file:

❏ `GetDataSet` – Accepts a SQL command string parameter and a database key. Returns an untyped `DataSet`.

❏ `SaveDataSet` – Accepts a `DataSet` parameter and a database key. Returns an integer indicating the number of records updated.

In a production data access class, we would also add a number of methods to delete records, work with stored procedures, and typed `DataSet` objects. For this example, the two methods shown above are sufficient.

Now let's add these two operations to our abstract `DataAccessBase` class. The implementation of these operations is different for each concrete subclass (there is different code in the methods of each subclass), so we'll make them abstract. This also guarantees any future subclasses will implement these operations, because .NET compilers enforce implementation of inherited abstract methods.

The UML Class Properties Dialog

In Visio, you add a new operation to a class by using either the **UML Class Properties** dialog or the **UML Operation Properties** dialog (discussed in the next section). To launch the **UML Class Properties** dialog, you either right-click the **DataAccessBase** node in the **Model Explorer** or right-click the class on the static structure diagram and select **Properties** from the context menu. When the dialog appears, select the **Operations** item in the **Categories** pane on the left and the **Operations** grid is displayed on the right as shown in the following screenshot – from here we will be able to add new operations to a class.

Here is a description of each column in the **Operations** grid:

Column	Description	Default Value
Operation	The name of the operation.	operation1
Return Type	This column contains a combo box listing all classes in your model as well as the basic C#, C++ .NET, IDL, and VB.NET data types.	<None>
Visibility	This column's combo box has three options – public, protected, and private. There are two visibility options missing – internal and protected internal in C#, and the equivalent Friend and Protected Friend in VB.NET, so unfortunately, there is no way to specify these options.	public
Polymorphic	Specifies if the operation can be overridden by subclasses. Select this checkbox if the operation is virtual in C# or Overridable in VB.NET.	unchecked
Scope	There are two options in this column – classifier and instance. Classifier is equivalent to static in C# and Shared in VB.NET. Instance is the same as instance methods in both C# and VB.NET.	instance

The UML Operation Properties Dialog

Although this dialog can be used to add new operations, it doesn't include entry fields for some very basic operator information such as a description and parameters. This is where the UML Operation Properties dialog comes to the rescue. To launch this dialog, click the New button from the UML Class Properties dialog, which adds a new record to the Operations grid, and then click the Properties button. As you can see in the following image, this dialog allows you to specify more information than the previous dialog to better define your class operations.

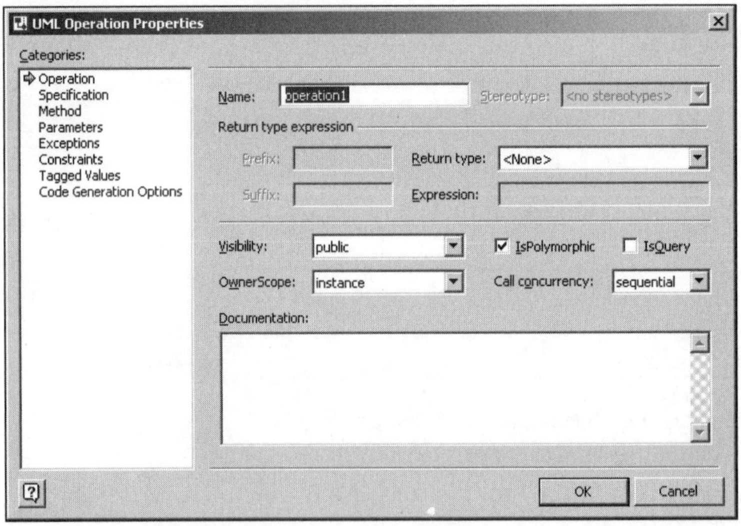

Here is a description of each entry field in this dialog (some of these fields are the same as those in the **Operations** grid described previously):

Column	Description	Default Value
Name	The name of the operation.	operation1
Stereotype	Operation stereotype. You can add your own custom stereotypes that appear in this combo box by selecting **UML I Stereotypes** from the main menu.	\<no stereotypes>
Prefix	Allows you to specify a language-specific prefix to further identify an operation return type. This box is disabled if the operation return type is set to \<None>.	
Suffix	Allows you to specify a language-specific suffix to further identify an operation return type. This box is disabled if the operation return type is set to \<None>.	
Return Type	This combo box lists all classes in your model as well as the basic C#, C++ .NET, IDL, and VB .NET data types.	\<None>
Expression	A read-only field that displays the concatenated prefix, return type, and suffix values you have specified.	
Visibility	This combo box has three options – **public, protected,** and **private**. There are two visibility options missing – internal and protected internal in C#, and the equivalent Friend and Protected Friend in VB .NET, so unfortunately, there is no way to specify these options.	public
IsPolymorphic	Specifies if the operation can be overridden by subclasses. Select this checkbox if the operation is virtual in C# or Overridable in VB .NET.	unchecked
IsQuery	Specifies if the application of the operation changes the state of its element. Select this checkbox if running the operation changes the state of an object. For example, a Contract business object may have an Accept method that changes the state of the contract from 'pending' to 'accepted'.	unchecked
OwnerScope	There are two options in this combo box – **Classifier** and **Instance**. **Classifier** is equivalent to static in C# and Shared in VB .NET. **Instance** is the same as instance methods in both C# and VB .NET.	instance

Table continued on following page

Column	Description	Default Value
Call Concurrency	There are three options in this combo box – Concurrent, Guarded, and Sequential. Concurrent describes how an operation acts in the presence of multiple threads of execution. The Concurrent setting means multiple concurrent calls can occur at the same time and proceed concurrently. The Guarded setting specifies multiple calls can be made from concurrent threads, but only one call is processed at a time and others are blocked until the current operation completes. The Sequential setting means only one thread can execute in the operation at a time.	sequential

Follow these steps to add a new `GetDataSet` operation to the `DataAccessBase` class:

1. Enter GetDataSet in the Name field. When you enter this name, it is immediately displayed in the Model Explorer.

2. Navigate to the Return type combo box. If you open the list, you see a list of all classes in the model, as well as .NET data types. At this point, the only custom class you'll see is the `DataAccessBase` class. As mentioned earlier, this method is intended to return a `DataSet`, however, because the `DataSet` class is not in the model, select <unspecified> from the list.

3. Leave Visibility set to public. Check the IsPolymorphic checkbox, because an abstract operation must be polymorphic. Leave the IsQuery checkbox unchecked.

4. The OwnerScope combo box is equivalent to the Owner combo box on the previous dialog. Leave it set to instance.

5. Leave the Call concurrency combo box set to sequential.

6. Add the following text to the Documentation box:

Retrieves a DataSet containing a result set for the specified SQL SELECT string.

> **You should always specify a description for all classes and members so developers using your classes can know your intent!**

Specifying Operation Parameters

Now let's add parameters to the operation. Previously, we determined this method accepts two string parameters–a SQL SELECT string and a database key.

1. In the Categories pane, select Parameters. This displays the Parameters grid on the right side of the dialog as shown in the following image.

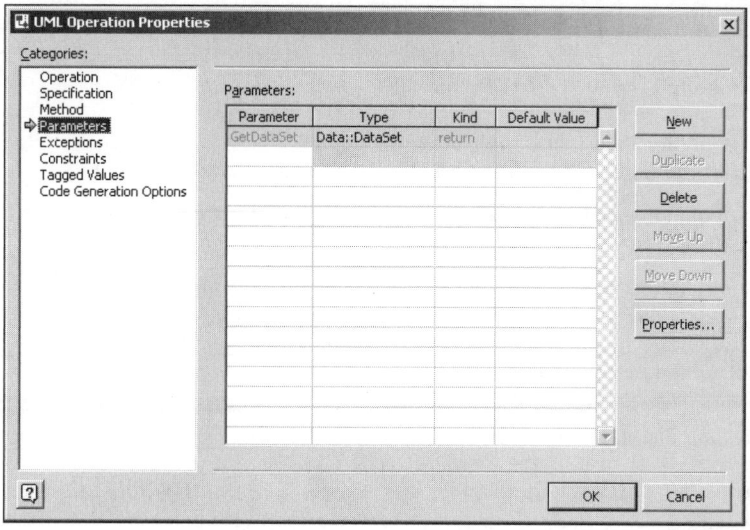

The **Parameters** grid allows you to view and specify operation parameters. You may be surprised to see a parameter already shown in the grid. If you look in the **Kind** column, you can see that this is the return value that we specified for this operation.

2. Click the **New** button to add a new parameter to the grid, and then click the **Properties...** button to edit the new parameter record. This launches the **UML Parameter Properties** dialog as shown in the following image, from which we can specify operation parameters.

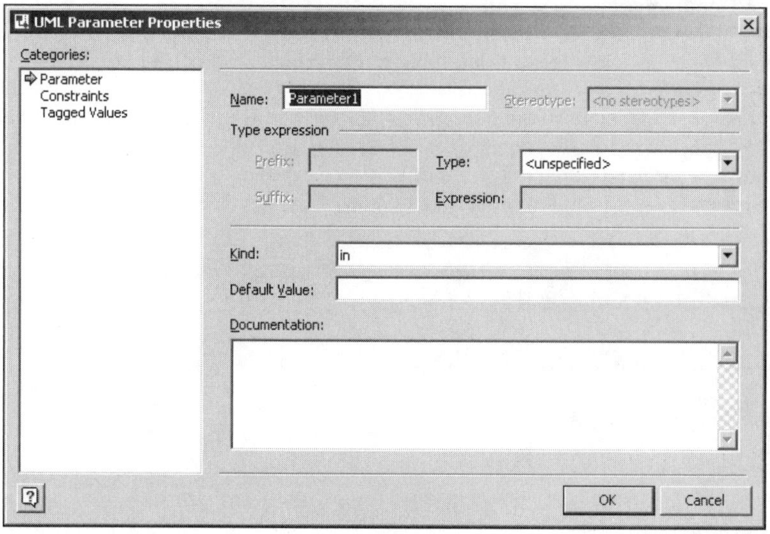

3. In the **Name** textbox, enter **command** as the name of the parameter.

4. In the Type combo box, select one of the string data types.

In the Kind combo box, there are three choices – in, out, and inout.

❑ The in option means that if the parameter value is changed in the method, the change does not affect the caller. This is also known as passing a parameter by value.

❑ The out option specifies the parameter value is passed from the method back to the caller. This is similar to C#'s out parameters.

❑ The inout option means the parameter is passed by the caller, can be changed by the method, and the caller sees this change. This is also known as passing a parameter by reference.

Leave the Kind combo box set to in.

5. In the Documentation box, enter Specifies a SQL SELECT command to be executed.

6. Click OK to close the dialog. This takes you back to the UML Operation Properties dialog, displaying the new parameter in the Parameters grid.

7. Add another parameter to the operation by clicking the New button, and then clicking the Properties button.

8. In the UML Parameter Properties dialog, set the Name to databaseKey.

9. In the Type combo box, select one of the string types.

10. In the Documentation box, enter:

Specifies a lookup key for the database in the application configuration file

and then click OK to close the dialog.

You should now see three parameters for the operation as shown in the following image. Note that both the operation return values and parameters are displayed:

Parameter	Type	Kind	Default Value
GetDataSet	Data::DataSet	return	
command	C#::string	in	
databaseKey	C#::string	in	

Marking an Operation as Abstract

As we mentioned earlier, the `GetDataSet` method is supposed to be abstract. To mark it as such, select **Method** in the **Categories** pane to display the controls shown in the following image.

This brings up the question of what the difference is between an operation and a method. When you implement classes in code, *methods* are added to the class for every *operation* specified in the class model.

> **When it's on a diagram, it's an operation; when it's implemented as code in a real-world class, it's a method.**

The following table shows how different basic UML class elements map to .NET code:

UML Element	C#	VB .NET
Class	Class (a.k.a. Type)	Class (a.k.a. Type)
Operation	Method	Subroutine or Procedure (see the entry for "Return value" below)
Attribute	Field	Member variable
Parameter	Parameter	Parameter
Return value	Return value	Return value. Operations that do not return a value are implemented as Subroutines. Operations that return a value are implemented as Procedures.

Unlike concrete operations, abstract operations have no corresponding concrete method, just a method signature, which includes the method name, its parameters, and their types.

The **Has** method checkbox is selected by default, indicating that the operation selected in the **Operation** name combo box will have a corresponding method in the realized class. Because this is an abstract operation that will not have a corresponding method containing code, let's uncheck this box. When you clear this checkbox, the **Language** and **Method body** fields are disabled indicating there is no code associated with this operation. If this box is unchecked, when you generate code from the class, the resulting method is marked as `abstract`.

Click **OK** to close the UML Operation Properties dialog, and then click **OK** again to close the **UML Class Properties** dialog. The visual representation of your `DataAccessBase` class should look like the following image:

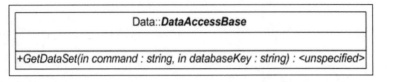

Notice the `GetDataSet` method is shown in italics per the UML specification for abstract operations. The class diagram shows the `GetDataSet` operation signature, including the parameter names and their types. In the next section, we'll take care of the method return value being marked **unspecified**.

Adding .NET Base Classes to the Model

There isn't a `DataSet` class in our model, so we weren't able to specify the `GetDataSet` operation returns a `DataSet`. If you don't have .NET base classes in your model, you're not able to specify the base classes from which your custom classes are derived, and you can't specify parameters and return values that are .NET base class types. Although we discuss an interesting way around this problem in Chapter 5, for the purposes of this chapter, let's address this problem by adding a `DataSet` class to our model. The `DataSet` class belongs to the `System.Data` namespace, so we need to add **System | Data** packages to the **Top Package** node in our diagram.

1. Right-click the **Top Package** node and select **New | Package** from the context menu. This launches the **UML Package Properties** dialog.

2. In the **Name** text box, enter **System**, and then click **OK**.

3. Right-click the **System** package and add a new **Data** package beneath it.

4. Right-click the **Data** package and select **New | Class** from the context menu.

5. In the **UML Class Properties** dialog, enter **DataSet** in the **Name** text box and click **OK** to save changes.

When you're done, your model tree should look like the following diagram.

Now that we have a `DataSet` class, we can go back into the definition of the `GetDataSet` method and specify a return value of `DataSet`. The easiest way to do this is to expand the **DataAccessBase** node in the Model Explorer, and double-click the **GetDataSet** operation. This launches the **UML Operation Properties** dialog with the `GetDataSet` operation ready for editing. In the **Return type** combo box, select **Data::DataSet**, and click **OK** to close the dialog.

Adding the SaveDataSet Operation

Now, let's add our second `SaveDataSet` operation to the `DataAccessBase` class. This time, we'll launch the **UML Operation Properties** dialog directly, without first going through the **UML Class Properties** dialog. To do this:

1. In the Model Explorer, right-click the **DataSet** class node and select **New | Operation** from the context menu. In the **Name** text box, enter **SaveDataSet**.

2. In the **Return type** combo box, select the integer data type of your target programming language. For example, if you're going to implement your classes in C#, select **C#::int**, or if using C++, select **C++:int**, or if Visual Basic .NET, select **VB::Integer**. In this example, let's select **C#::int**.

3. In the Documentation box, enter:

Saves the passed DataSet and returns an integer specifying the number of rows updated.

4. In the Categories pane on the left, select **Method**, and then uncheck the **Has method** checkbox, indicating the operation is abstract.

5. Now select **Parameters** in the **Categories** pane, and then click the **New** button. This adds a new record to the **Parameters** grid. Click the **Properties** button to launch the **UML Parameter Properties** dialog.

6. Set the parameter **Name** to **ds**, the **Type** to **DataSet**, and the **Documentation** to **DataSet to be saved**, and then click the **OK** button to close the dialog.

7. Click the New button and Properties button again to add another parameter to the operation named 'databaseKey', of the type 'string', and with the description:

Specifies a lookup key for the database in the application configuration file.

8. When you're done, click OK to close the dialog.

Your `DataAccessBase` class on the class diagram should now look like the following image. Note the full signature of class operations is displayed:

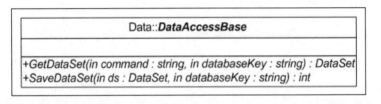

If you expand the GetDataSet and SaveDataSet operation nodes of the DataAccessBase class in the Model Explorer, you'll see three parameters listed under each as shown in the following diagram. The GetDataSet and SaveDataSet parameters represent the return values of their respective operations.

Personally, I think this is a bit confusing; because return values are not truly parameters, they should be displayed with a different visual cue.

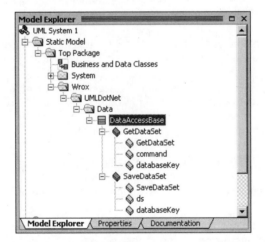

If you double-click a parameter node (or right-click the node and select Properties from the context menu), it launches the UML Parameter Properties dialog allowing you to view or edit the parameter's properties. You can easily add new parameters to an operation by right-clicking the operation node and selecting New | Parameter... from the context menu. You can also delete a parameter by right-clicking it and selecting Delete from the context menu, or by selecting the parameter and pressing the *Delete* key.

Creating Concrete Subclasses

Now that we have an abstract data access class, we can create a few concrete subclasses. We'll create these classes in quick succession and then show you how to make them subclasses of the DataAccessBase class. You create these classes using the **UML Class Properties** dialog that is launched by right-clicking the **Top Package I Wrox I UMLDotNet I Data** package in the **Model Explorer** and selecting **New I Class** from the context menu. Set the following name and description for each of these classes (you can accept all other default settings):

Name	Description
DataAccessSql	Accesses SQL Server data using the SQL Server .NET Data Provider classes.
DataAccessOracle	Accesses Oracle data using the Oracle .NET Data Provider classes.
DataAccessOleDb	Accesses any data for which there is a classic OLE DB provider, using the OLE DB .NET Data Provider classes.

Now we can specify that these new classes are derived from the DataAccessBase class. To do this, drag and drop each of these classes onto the class (static structure) diagram. Next, make sure the **UML Static Structure** stencil is open as shown in the following diagram – this stencil contains shapes you can use on your static structure diagrams. Now drag and drop a **Generalization** shape (a line with a single, solid arrow head) onto the diagram for each subclass. In Visio, when you want to add two or more instances of the same shape to a diagram, just drag and drop the first shape, and then press *Ctrl+D* for each additional shape you want to add.

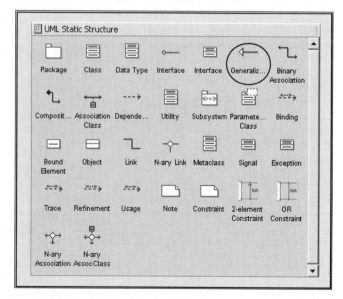

For each **Generalization** shape, connect the arrowhead to the bottom of the DataAccessBase class, and connect the other end of the arrow to the top of a concrete subclass. When you're done, your class diagram should look like the following image.

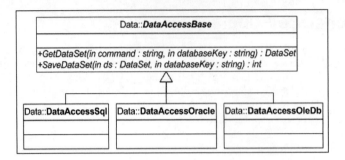

Now we have three concrete data-access classes to use for accessing different types of back-end data. Depending on the type of data that a business object needs to access, it can instantiate one or more of these classes. These classes act as wrappers for the different .NET data provider classes, giving us some important advantages. First of all, these classes encapsulate the complexity of ADO.NET classes, by allowing us to call higher-level methods that sweat the details of ADO.NET for us behind the scenes. Since our data access classes are all derived from the DataAccessBase class, it also allows the business object to reference any concrete data-access class the same way – by treating it as if it is of the type DataAccessBase. This allows us to have generic code throughout our business object rather than SQL Server, Oracle, or OLE DB-specific code.

Each of these new concrete subclasses inherits the GetDataSet and SaveDataSet operations declared in the DataAccessBase class, and this is reflected in the Visio model. To see this, right-click the DataAccessSql class node and select Properties from the context menu to launch the UML Class Properties dialog. In the Categories pane, select Operations. We haven't added any custom operations to the DataAccessSql class, so there are no operations listed in the grid. However, at the bottom of the Operations grid is a tab selector (similar to Excel's worksheet selector) that lists all of the classes in the DataAccessSql hierarchy. If you select the DataAccessBase tab, you see the GetDataSet and SaveDataSet operations belonging to the DataAccessBase class displayed in the grid as shown in the following image:

Operations:

Operation	Return Type	Visibility	Polymorphic	Scope
GetDataSet	Data::DataSet	public	☑	instance
SaveDataSet	C#::int	public	☑	instance

◄ ► DataAccessSql   **DataAccessBase** ◄ ►

Creating a Business Object Base Class

Now that we have a family of data access classes, we're ready to create a business object base class. One of the first things we need to decide is the .NET type to use as the base class for our business object class.

Choosing a .NET Type for Your Business Object Class

A great candidate for our business object's base class is the `MarshalByRefObject` type, because classes derived from this type can be accessed remotely. When creating n-tier applications, assemblies containing business objects are often placed on application servers and accessed from workstations. Using `MarshalByRefObject` gives our business objects this functionality.

Based on this, we need to add the `MarshalByRefObject` class to our Visio model:

1. In the Model Explorer, right-click the Top Package | System package and select New | Class... from the context menu to launch the UML Class Properties dialog.

2. In the Name text box, enter MarshalByRefObject.

3. In the Documentation box, enter the description of this class found in the .NET Help file:

Enables access to objects across application domain boundaries in applications that support remoting.

4. Click OK to save changes, and close the dialog.

If you'd like, you can add all classes in the hierarchy for `MarshalByRefObject` as well as the `DataSet` class we added earlier. The `MarshalByRefObject` class derives directly from `System.Object`. You can add the `Object` class directly to the **System** package in the Visio model. The `DataSet` class derives from the `System.ComponentModel.MarshalByValueComponent`, which in turn derives from `System.Object`. To add this class to the model, you need to add a **ComponentModel** package below the **System** package (representing the .NET `System.ComponentModel` namespace), and then add a `MarshalByValueComponent` class to the package. After you've added these classes, your **System** package should look like the following image:

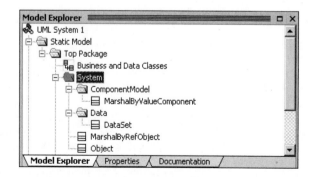

You can also add a new static structure diagram to the Visio model (named something like .NET Base classes) where you specify the generalization relationships between these classes. You can add this diagram to the model by right-clicking the Top Package node and selecting New | Static Structure Diagram from the context menu. This diagram should look like the following image:

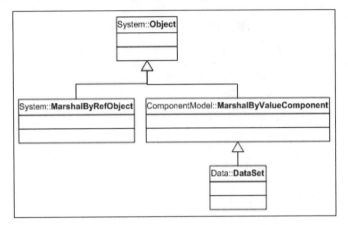

Although we've added these .NET base classes to our model to show how it's done, rather than creating your Visio UML models from scratch, you should create them from a Visio model that already contains most of the common .NET base classes.

You can create such a template model yourself – in Chapter 5, where we look at reverse engineering code with Visio, we see how to create limited models of the .NET base classes.

Creating the BusinessObject Class

Now we're ready to create our business object base class.

1. Create a new package named Business in the Visio model below the Top Package | Wrox | UMLDotNet package, and specify the following in the Documentation box:

The Wrox.UMLDotNet.Business namespace contains business object and related classes.

2. Add a new class named BusinessObject to the new Business package. When creating the class, accept all the default settings in the UML Class Properties dialog, and give it the description Business object base class.

3. Drag and drop the new BusinessObject class from the Model Explorer onto the Business and Data Classes static structure diagram.

4. Drop the MarshalByRefObject class on the diagram and specify that BusinessObject is derived from MarshalByRefObject by adding a generalization relationship between the two. If you have System.Object in the model, you can also drop this class on the diagram. If you've already specified that MarshalByRefObject is a subclass of System.Object in the .NET Base Classes diagram, then a generalization object is automatically added to the diagram when you drop System.Object onto it.

When you're finished, the static structure diagram should look like this (not including the data-access classes):

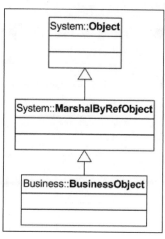

Specifying a Composition Relationship

Now we can use the class diagram to specify the association between the business object and the data-access classes. There are many associations between classes that can be modeled in the UML. One such relationship is aggregation, which is a whole-part relationship. This sort of relationship exists between our business object and data-access classes – but with a special twist. In this aggregation, there is strong ownership between the business object and data-access class – the data-access class lives and dies with the business object class. This special form of aggregation is known as **composition**.

To define a composition association between the business object and data-access classes, drag a **Composition** shape from the **UML Static Structure** shapes stencil, and drop it on the class diagram. Attach the diamond to the business object class and attach the other end of the composition shape to the DataAccessBase class. When you're finished, your diagram should look like the one shown in the following image (we've left out the BusinessObject class hierarchy):

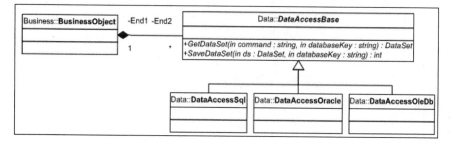

In the UML, a filled-in aggregation diamond indicates composition. The default one-to-many multiplicity, indicated by the 1 (one) and asterisk (*), is exactly what we need for the BusinessObject and DataAccessBase classes.

> The -End1 and -End2 text strings are placeholders for roles that can be specified for associated objects. In this context, we don't need to specify roles, so we'll remove them.

97

To do this, double-click the aggregation shape to launch the UML Association Properties dialog as shown in the following screenshot:

Normally, you don't need to give the association or its end points names, so we'll leave the association name set to its default value, and we'll simply remove the end-point role names. To clear the names, remove the End1 and End2 text from the records in the Association Ends grid. You can also click the Properties... button and edit each association end point individually in the UML Association End Properties dialog that provides access to additional properties as shown in the following image:

Regardless of the method you choose to remove the end points, when you click OK to save changes from the UML Association Properties dialog, the end-point names are no longer visible in the class diagram.

Adding Overloaded BusinessObject Operations

Now we're ready to specify some basic data-access operations for our business object base class. We will add GetDataSet and SetDataSet operations to the BusinessObject class corresponding to methods of the same name on our data-access classes. When these methods are called on the business object class, the business object passes the call to an associated data-access class. Because we have a family of data-access classes, we can vary the type of data we work with by using different concrete data-access classes. For example, if we want to access data in an Oracle database, the business object passes the call to an instance of the DataAccessOracle class. If we want to access data in a SQL Server database, the business object passes the call to an instance of the DataAccessSql class.

In the business object class, we'll create a few different implementations of the GetDataSet and SaveDataSet methods that provide an opportunity to learn how overloaded methods are modeled in a UML class diagram.

Adding the GetDataSet Operations

Now we're going to add several operations to the BusinessObject class, so let's launch the UML Class Properties dialog. There are four ways to launch this dialog:

❑ Double-click the BusinessObject node in the Model Explorer.

❑ Right-click the Business Object node in the Model Explorer and select Properties from the context menu.

❑ Double-click the BusinessObject class located on the class diagram.

❑ Right-click the BusinessObject class located on the class diagram and select Properties from the context menu.

As a refresher, here are the basic steps for adding a new operation:

1. Select Operations in the Categories pane of the UML Class Properties dialog. Click the New button, and then click the Properties... button to launch the UML Operation Properties dialog.

2. Change operation property values and click OK to save changes.

And the steps for adding parameters to an operation:

3. Select Parameters in the Categories pane of the UML Operation Properties dialog. Click the New button, and then click the Properties... button to launch the UML Parameter Properties dialog.

4. Change parameter property values and click OK to save changes.

With this knowledge in hand, add three operations named `GetDataSet` to the `BusinessObject` class. These operations should all return a `DataSet` and their visibility should be set to **protected**. Also, specify the operation description, parameters, and parameter descriptions (shown in parentheses) listed in the following table:

Name	Description	Parameters
GetDataSet	Retrieves a `DataSet` containing a result set for the specified SQL `SELECT` string.	`command : string` (SQL command to be executed)
GetDataSet	Retrieves a `DataSet` containing a result set for the specified SQL `SELECT` string and database key.	`command : string` (SQL command to be executed) `databaseKey : string` (Database Key)
GetDataSet	Retrieves a `DataSet` containing a result set for the specified SQL `SELECT` string and database key. Results are stored in the specified `DataTable` name.	`command : string` (SQL command to be executed) `databaseKey : string` (Database Key) `tableName : string` (DataTable name)

In this section, we've added three overloaded `GetDataSet` operations to the `BusinessObject` class. These operations allow us to retrieve data by passing a SQL `SELECT` string and optionally, a database key and table name.

Adding the SaveDataSet Operations

Now add three overloaded operations named `SaveDataSet` to the `BusinessObject` class. These operations should all return an integer and their visibility should be set to **protected**. Also, specify the operation description, parameters, and parameter descriptions (shown in parentheses) listed in the following table:

Name	Description	Parameters
SaveDataSet	Saves the passed `DataSet`.	`ds: DataSet` (DataSet to be saved)
SaveDataSet	Saves the passed `DataSet` into the database specified by the database key.	`ds : DataSet` (DataSet to be saved) `databaseKey : string` (Database key)
SaveDataSet	Saves the passed `DataSet` into the database specified by the database key. Data is saved from the specified `DataTable` name.	`ds : DataSet` (DataSet to be saved) `databaseKey : string` (Database key) `tableName : string` (DataTable name)

When you're done, the `BusinessObject` class located on the class diagram should look like the following image:

Business::**BusinessObject**
#GetDataSet(in command : string) : DataSet #GetDataSet(in command : string, in databaseKey : string) : DataSet #GetDataSet(in command : string, in databaseKey : string, in tableName : string) : DataSet #SaveDataSet(in ds : DataSet) : int #SaveDataSet(in ds : DataSet, in databaseKey : string) : int #SaveDataSet(in ds : DataSet, in databaseKey : string, in tableName : string) : int

Both the `GetDataSet` and `SaveDataSet` operations have overloads allowing you to pass a database key and a table name. Typically, in a .NET application, we store database information in an XML configuration file, which allows us to retrieve database information such as connection strings. If we have more than one database in our application, the database key allows us to specify which database we want to retrieve information for from the configuration file. The table name parameter specifies the name of the `DataTable` you want to work with.

The sharp sign (#) indicates these operations are protected. The reason we have protected these methods is so consumers of our business objects cannot call them directly. For example, if we make the `GetDataSet` operations public, it provides an opening for consumers of the object to pass any SQL `SELECT` command conceivable and return secure data stored in the database. Later we'll add higher-level public methods to the business object passing predetermined SQL `SELECT` strings to these operations. In a more robust data-access model, we would also provide methods that allow us to call stored procedures. However, for this simple model our existing methods will suffice.

Adding Attributes to the BusinessObject Class

Next, we are going to add two attributes to the `BusinessObject` class – `DatabaseKey` and `TableName`. These attributes hold default values in cases where the database key and table name are not specified in calls to the `GetDataSet` and `SaveDataSet` operations. For example, if a call is made to the overload of `GetDataSet` that has only a single `command` parameter, default database key and table name values can be retrieved from the `DatabaseKey` and `TableName` attributes.

> **Don't let the term "attribute" throw you. UML attributes are not the same as .NET attributes. Attributes in a UML class map to fields in a C# class and member variables in a Visual Basic .NET class, as shown in the table earlier in this chapter.**

You add new attributes to the `BusinessObject` class using the **UML Attribute Properties** dialog. If you are adding only one attribute, you can launch this dialog by right-clicking the **BusinessObject** class in the **Model Explorer** and selecting New | Attribute from the shortcut menu. However, we want to add two properties, so we'll launch this dialog from the **UML Class Properties** dialog.

To do this, double-click the **BusinessObject** class node in the **Model Explorer**. In the **Categories** pane of the **UML Class Properties** dialog, select **Attributes**. Click the **New** button, which adds a new record to the **Attributes** grid, and then click the **Properties** button to launch the **UML Attribute Properties** dialog shown in the following image.

The following table describes some of the more important entry fields in the UML Attribute Properties dialog and how they relate to .NET languages such as C# and Visual Basic .NET:

Entry Field	Description
Name	Attribute name.
Type	The attribute type.
Visibility	There are three choices – private, protected, and public. Again, there are two visibility options missing – internal and protected internal in C# and the equivalent Friend and Protected Friend in VB .NET. As discussed earlier, there are no equivalent visibility options in Visio.
Multiplicity	Specifies the number of data values the property can store. Typically, this is one (1), but if you have a property that holds more than one value (such as an indexer), you can choose a different option.
InitialValue	The initial value of the attribute.
Changeable	The Changeable combo box contains three options – none, frozen, and addOnly. The default selection is none, which means there are no restrictions on changing the value. The frozen option specifies the value of the attribute cannot be changed. This is equivalent to a read-only property in C# and Visual Basic .NET. The addOnly option applies to attributes with a multiplicity other than one (1). It specifies values can be added to the attribute, but cannot later be removed or changed.
OwnerScope	The instance option is equivalent to instance properties in C# and VB .NET. The classifier option is the same as static in C# and Shared in VB .NET, and these actually do map to static and Shared when generating code from the model.

1. In the Name textbox, enter DatabaseKey.

2. In the Type combo box, select one of the string data types.

3. Set the Visibility to protected because this attribute does not need to be accessed by clients using the BusinessObject class, but should be accessible by classes derived from it.

4. In the Documentation box, enter the following:

The default database key used to look up database information from the application configuration file.

5. Click OK to save changes.

Now follow the same steps outlined above and add a second protected string attribute named TableName, with the following documentation:

The default DataTable name of DataSets manipulated by the business object.

When you're done, click OK to save changes, and then click OK to close the UML Class Properties dialog. The BusinessObject class located on the class diagram should now look like the following image:

Business::**BusinessObject**
#DataBaseKey : string
#TableName : string
#GetDataSet(in command : string) : DataSet
#GetDataSet(in command : string, in databaseKey : string) : DataSet
#GetDataSet(in command : string, in databaseKey : string, in tableName : string) : DataSet
#SaveDataSet(in ds : DataSet) : int
#SaveDataSet(in ds : DataSet, in databaseKey : string) : int
#SaveDataSet(in ds : DataSet, in databaseKey : string, in tableName : string) : int

Use Cases for a Simple Library System

Now that we have defined our business object and data-access base classes, we're ready to look at the use case diagrams we will use to derive our application-specific business objects. In a normal project lifecycle, use cases are created before we begin object modeling. In this chapter, we haven't created any application-specific business objects – just our base classes, so we're still playing by the rules.

Use cases are an extremely important aspect of UML modeling. They allow developers to understand software systems from the user's perspective, and cause the whole system architecture to be driven by what the user wishes to do with the system – which, unfortunately, doesn't often happen!

The use cases in our example describe a simple software application for a library. This example is a variation along the classic theme of use case examples and works well because it's simple enough to model in a chapter this size, but has enough meat on its bones to demonstrate many aspects of the UML. In our simple library system, media is borrowed and returned. Late fees are assessed as follows: Three dollars per day for overdue DVDs, two dollars per day for magazines, and one dollar per day for overdue books. A borrower is not allowed to check out media if they have any overdue media, if they already have five items checked out, or if they have accrued more than fifty dollars in fines.

The following image contains a high-level overview use case diagram containing most of the main use cases in this application:

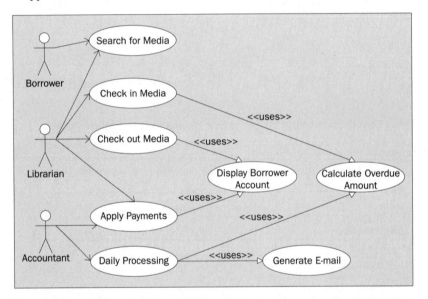

As you can see in this diagram, there are three actors – the Borrower, Librarian, and Accountant. The Borrower (as you might imagine) represents people who borrow media from the library. In our application, media consists of books, magazines, and DVDs. As with most library systems, the only action the Borrower can perform is to search for media.

The Librarian searches for media, but also performs a few additional actions. A Librarian checks in media, checks out media, and applies payments for fines to a Borrower's account. The Accountant performs two main actions. They apply payments to a Borrower's account, as well as run daily processing. This daily processing procedure is run each evening to generate e-mails warning borrowers of unreturned media and overdue fines.

Notice our use case diagram identifies three "uses" relationships, indicating places where application functionality is reused from multiple use cases. Both the Check in Media and Daily Processing use the Calculate Overdue Amount use case. Check Out Media and Apply Payments use the Display Borrower Account use case.

We won't perform object modeling on all these use cases, but we'll pick a few key use cases so you get a feel for how it's done.

Modeling the Check Out Media Use Case

The first use case we'll model is "Check Out Media". Here is a more detailed explanation of this use case:

1. The Librarian enters the Borrower's ID. This is either entered manually or scanned from a library card.

2. The system responds by displaying the borrower's account. The Display Borrower Account use case is implemented here. Here is the description for this use case:

   The system displays the borrower's account. This information includes the number of items they can borrow, unpaid fines, and a list of media checked out. The "checked out media" list includes due date and special indication for overdue media.

   Here are the business rules for checking out media: the Borrower can only check out items if they have no overdue media, less than five articles checked out, and outstanding fines less than fifty dollars.

3. The Librarian enters the media ID. This is either entered manually or scanned from the media bar code.

4. The system responds by marking the media as "checked out". This step can be repeated for the total number of items a borrower can check out.

Deriving Classes from Use Cases

Now we're ready for the hard part – deriving business classes from use cases. Part of the problem is that use cases are not object-oriented. They simply represent a list of everything users can do with the computer system. We need to examine the description of the use case and derive business classes from it.

When using techniques such as CRC cards (which are *not* part of the UML), we are encouraged to look at the nouns in the use case description as possible candidates for use cases. Here's a list of some of these key nouns (ignoring nouns that are obviously attributes of other entities such as Borrower ID and Media ID):

- Librarian
- Borrower
- Media
- Fines

This process can actually get you pretty far, but I've found from experience it doesn't take you far enough. If you start out with this list of entities, you start going down a particular path, and have to backtrack and rework your object model. Although reworking or refactoring your model is part of the process, we can get ourselves closer to a working object model by thinking about data.

Thinking about Data

Why does thinking about our application's data help us in our object modeling efforts? As we mentioned earlier in this chapter, when we data model we often create tables representing real-world entities. Due to this relationship, you will often create a business object for each main table in your application, so thinking about data early is a wise decision.

Although you want to start thinking about data, you don't want to get 'married' to a particular data model this early on. Use your data model to help you think things through, but don't set it in stone. Be willing to let your business object's behavior influence the data model. I have found data modeling helps shake the bugs out of an object model. Even if you wait to model data until after you've first tried to create your object model, you can test your model by creating test data, which you access from your business classes. In other cases, you may have a data structure you are forced to work with. In this case, you simply can't ignore the data structure. However, a good object model can help hide the flaws in an otherwise imperfect data model.

So, let's start thinking about the structure of the data we need for our application. The following diagram shows a Visio data diagram containing tables we've started to flesh out for our library application:

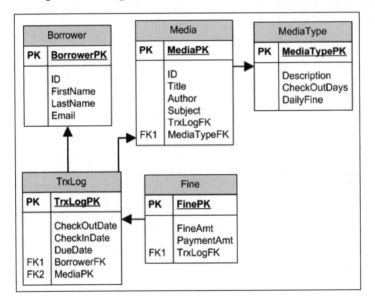

The first table in this diagram is the **Borrower** table. This is an easy place to start because our use case specifically mentions a `Borrower ID`. Notice the **Borrower** table has both a primary key field (`BorrowerPK`) and an ID field (`ID`). Most database designers agree it's important for all tables in your application to have a system-generated primary key used to uniquely identify each record in addition to any 'business' keys you may have. In this table, the `ID` field corresponds to the Borrower ID mentioned in the use case. This is the value manually entered by the Librarian or scanned from the Borrower's library card. However, the primary key is used when linking Borrower records to records in other tables. For good measure, we've also added a few obvious fields such as `FirstName`, `LastName`, and `Email`. We'll talk about the `TrxLogFK` foreign key field in just a bit.

Media is another easy table. Obviously, we need to have a record of each media item borrowers can check out. Again, we have a situation where there is both a `primary key` field and an `ID` field. Again, we've added some obvious fields such as `Title`, `Author`, and `Subject`. There is also a foreign key pointer field (`MediaTypeFK`) to the `MediaType` table. Rather than storing the media type information directly in the `Media` table, we normalize our data by storing the information in a separate `MediaType` table.

The `MediaType` table contains a description of the type of media (magazine, book, DVD), the number of days it can be checked out, and the daily fine if the item is overdue.

The Transaction Log table (**TrxLog**) isn't as obvious. Our use cases specify we need to keep track of checked out media, whether or not it's overdue, as well as any unpaid fines. The easiest way to do this is to create a transaction log containing a record of each media check out/check in, including the media ID and the borrower ID. Although this information could be stored in the `Media` table, placing it there does not allow us to maintain a history, because these fields are overwritten the next time the media is checked out/in. The `DueDate` field provides a place where the media due date is stored. Although this information can be calculated dynamically, persisting it to the transaction record allows our system to account for any changes we make to the check out period rules. If the due date is calculated and saved when an item is checked out, even if the business rules change before the item is returned, we can still determine the correct due date for each piece of media.

The `Fine` table contains fines applied to specific transaction log records. The `TrxLogFK` field is a foreign key pointer to the `TrxLog` table. The `FineAmt` field contains the amount of the fine and the `PaymentAmt` field contains any payment amount applied to this fine. I guarantee this accounting solution will bring tears to you financial wizards, but this simple solution works fine for our example.

Creating a Sequence Diagram

Now that we have a basic idea of our data structure (and are agreeable to changing it as further analysis and design dictates), we're ready to create business object classes implementing the functionality of our "Check Out Media" use case. The main tool for achieving this is the sequence diagram. You can create a sequence diagram for each use case in your model, allowing you to model the behavior and collaboration between business objects in your application.

Creating a sequence diagram is a dynamic process that involves the following steps:

❑ Reading through the steps of your use case.

❑ Creating business objects that carry out the use case.

❑ Adding business objects to the sequence diagram, and deciding which objects should carry out each responsibility.

❑ Adding messages between objects on the diagram. A message sent to an object in a sequence diagram creates a new operation on the receiving object.

To create a new sequence diagram, right-click the **Top Package** node in the Model Explorer and select **New | Sequence Diagram** from the shortcut menu. This opens a new, empty sequence diagram in Visio and adds a node named **Sequence-1** to the **Model Explorer**. Right-click this node, select **Rename** from the shortcut menu, and change the name to **Check Out Media**.

107

Changing the Drawing Page Orientation

By default, the sequence diagrams drawing page orientation is the same as your printer paper orientation (either landscape or portrait). I prefer to use landscape orientation for my sequence diagrams to give myself a little breathing room on the horizontal axis. If you want to do this, select File | Page Setup... from the menu, which launches the Page Setup dialog as shown in the following image:

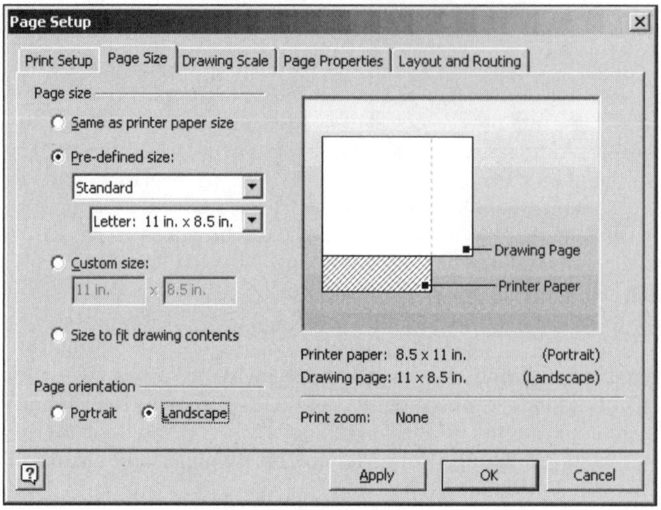

Select the Page Size tab, and under Page size select the Pre-defined size option. Then, under Page orientation, select Landscape. If your printer paper orientation is set to portrait, this will be shown in the image to the right of the Page Size tab. When you're done, click OK to save changes and close the Page Setup dialog.

Adding Use Case Text to the Sequence Diagram

Before we get into the meat of the sequence diagram, let's first add some initial basic elements. I often find it helpful to add a description of the use case I'm modeling to the sequence diagram. Although this is a bit unconventional, it doesn't break the rules of the UML, but it provides a great reference when creating a sequence diagram and later understanding it.

1. Double-click the Check Out Media use case node in the Model Explorer, which launches the UML Use Case Properties dialog as shown in the following image. Select all the text in the Documentation box and press *Ctrl+C* to copy it to the clipboard. Press Cancel to close the dialog.

2. Select the sequence diagram by clicking somewhere on its design surface, and then pressing *Ctrl+V* to paste the text onto the diagram.

3. Change the font size of the text block (I usually set it to 10 points), and then resize the textbox so it forms a tall, thin rectangle on the right side of the diagram as shown in the following image.

109

Adding the Actor and UI Placeholder

The next step in creating our sequence diagram is adding the actor to the diagram and a user interface `placeholder` class. Adding these elements to a sequence diagram gives your sequence diagram context. It allows you to show how the user interacts with the computer system, and how the business objects within your application respond.

Since we didn't build the use case diagram in this chapter, we need to create a `Librarian` actor we can use in our sequence diagram. To do this, follow these steps:

1. First add a Use Case package to contain the new `Librarian` actor by right-clicking the Top Package node, and selecting New | Package from the context menu.

2. In the UML Package Properties dialog, enter Use Cases in the Name text box, and then click OK to save changes.

3. Right-click the new Use Cases package and select New | Actor from the context menu, which launches the UML Actor Properties dialog as shown in the following image.

4. In the Name text box, enter Librarian, and then click OK to save changes and close the dialog. When you're finished, you should see the new Librarian actor in the Model Explorer as shown in the following image.

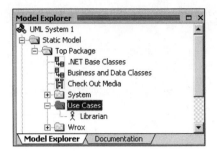

Next, follow these steps to add the Librarian actor to the diagram:

5. Make sure the UML Sequence stencil is selected as shown in the following image:

6. Drag an Object Lifeline shape from the stencil and drop it on the top of sequence diagram to the immediate right of the use case text. This displays a shape named Object1 with a lifeline beneath it as shown in the following image.

> Object1
>
> 1. The Librarian enters the Borrower's ID. This can either be entered manually, or scanned from a library card

7. Right-click Object1 and select Properties from the shortcut menu, which launches the UML Classifier Role Properties dialog shown in the following image.

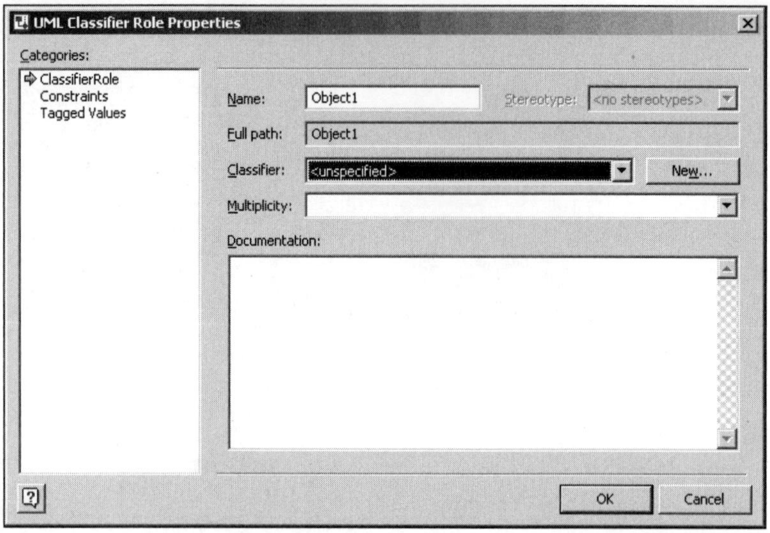

8. In the Classifier combo box, select Use Case::Librarian, and then click OK. This displays the Librarian actor shape on the diagram.

9. By default, the Librarian actor shape displays the object name (Object1) rather than the name of the class. Let's change the shape and diagram settings to display the classifier instead. To do this, right-click the Librarian shape and select Shape Display Options... from the shortcut menu. This displays the UML Shape Display Options dialog shown in the following image.

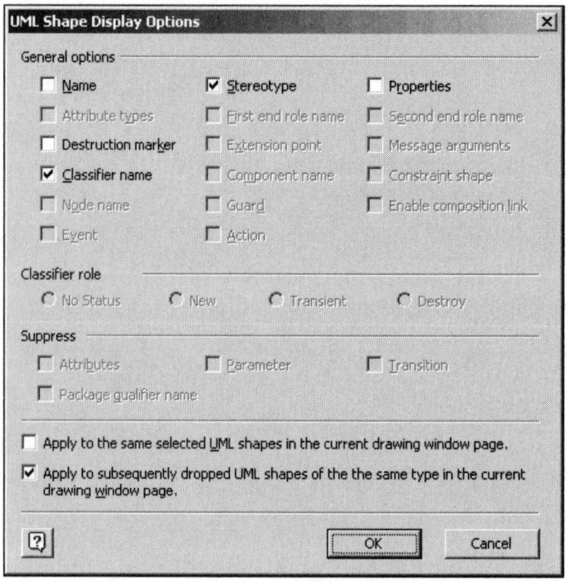

10. Clear the **Name** checkbox and select the **Classifier name** checkbox instead. Also select the **Apply to subsequently dropped UML shapes of the same type in the current drawing window page** checkbox. This ensures all shapes we drop on the diagram from this point on also use these settings. Click **OK** to close this dialog.

When you're done, the Librarian actor shape should look like the following image:

Next, we need some way to represent the user interface on our sequence diagram. In a simple system, the easiest way to do this is to create a single class that represents our application's user interface. This class acts as a placeholder for all user interface elements in our application. We can add this user interface placeholder class to our diagram and send messages to it from the actor that represent actions the user takes when interacting with the user interface. If your application is more complex and has many forms, you might want to create create a different concrete user interface class for each form. This is a simple model, so we'll just create one class named UI to represent the entire user interface.

1. Right-click the **Top Package** node in the **Model Explorer** and select **New | Class** from the shortcut menu. In the **UML Class Properties** dialog, set the **Name** to UI and enter the following description in the **Documentation** box: User interface placeholder.

2. Click **OK** to save changes and close the dialog.

3. Drag another **Object Lifeline** shape from the **UML Sequence** stencil and drop it on the sequence diagram to the immediate right of the Librarian actor shape. Double-click the shape, and in the **UML Classifier Role Properties** dialog's **Classifier** combo box, select **Top Package::UI**.

4. Click **OK** to save changes and close the dialog.

When you're done, the sequence diagram should look like the following image – adding both an actor and user interface placeholder to your sequence diagrams provides a context for understanding your application's business object interaction. It allows you to see how specific business objects respond to a user's interaction with the computer system.

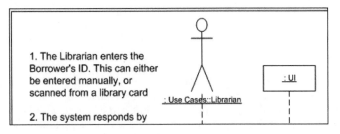

Adding Messages Between Objects

Now we're ready to add our first message between objects. Although this isn't a true message because our UI placeholder isn't a real class, this will give you a feel for how it's done.

1. Lengthen the object lifelines beneath the Librarian and UI objects. To do this, click on the lifeline and then drag the yellow diamond at the end of the lifeline towards the bottom of the diagram.

2. Drag an Activation shape from the UML Sequence stencil onto the lifeline a little below the Librarian shape as shown in the following image. You may need to move the Activation shape up or down slightly to properly glue it to the object lifeline. You'll know it's properly connected when the shape turns from red to black. You can also see any semantic errors and warnings listed in Visio's Output window. Also, notice we've left some space between the bottom of the Librarian description and the top of the Activation shape. This provides room for the message text, which we'll be adding soon.

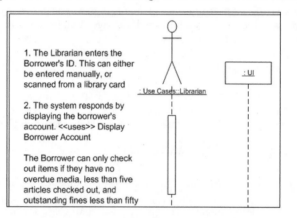

3. Drag another Activation shape from the UML Sequence stencil and drop it on the UI object's lifeline. Make sure the activation box tops line up on the horizontal axis. You may need to move the UI shape up or down a little to make this happen. You can move the UI object by clicking on it and then pressing the up and down arrow keys. Again, the Activation shape is not properly glued to the lifeline until its border turns black.

4. Drag a Message (call) shape from the UML Sequence stencil onto the diagram, (the one with the straight, solid message line and solid arrow head) as shown in the following image.

Connect the end of the message without the arrow to the top of the Librarian's Activation shape. Then connect the end of the message with the arrow to the top of the UI object's Activation shape. You'll know it's properly connected when the message arrow turns from red to black. When you're done, your diagram should look like the following image:

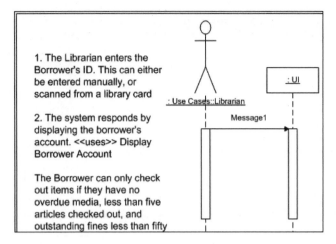

5. Now we're ready to specify the message sent from the Librarian to the user interface. Double-click the message shape. This launches the **UML Message Properties** dialog, which in turn immediately launches the **UML Operation Properties** dialog as shown in the following image.

The second dialog is launched because the UI class does not have any operations from which to choose. Any operation you add in the UML **Operation Properties** dialog is automatically added to the class receiving the message call – in this case, the UI class.

6. In the **Name** text box, type **Enter Borrower ID**. Because this isn't a real operation (UI isn't a real class, only a placeholder), we can put spaces in the operation name.

7. Click OK to close the UML Operation Properties dialog, and then press OK again to close the UML Message Properties dialog.

When you're done, your diagrams should look like the following image:

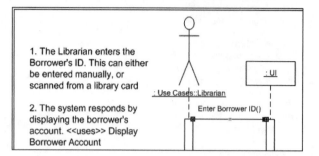

If you're familiar with other UML modeling tools, it may seem odd to manually add Activation shapes to the diagram. At first, I thought this was an unlikable feature of Visio. However, after using it for a while, I came to appreciate its benefits. When I manually add activation shapes to the diagram, I have complete control over their position and size. In tools such as Rational Rose, although the activation boxes are automatically added for me, I usually spend countless hours resizing and moving shapes while Rational Rose is being "overly helpful", auto-sizing and moving shapes where I don't want them!

As we've mentioned, when you specify an operation on a message shape, Visio automatically adds the operation to the class of the object receiving the message. If you look at the UI class in the Model Explorer, you'll see it has a new operation named Enter Borrower ID as shown in the following image:

```
Model Explorer                                    □ ×
🚲 UML System 1
└─📁 Static Model
   └─📁 Top Package
      ├─🖳 .NET Base Classes
      ├─🖳 Business and Data Classes
      ├─🎛 Check Out Media
      ├─⊞ 📁 System
      ├─⊞ 📁 Use Cases
      ├─⊞ 📁 Wrox
      └─⊟ 🔲 UI
           └─◈ Enter Borrower ID
  Model Explorer ╱ Properties ╱ Documentation ╱
```

Creating Business Object Classes

So far, we've modeled Step 1 of the Check Out Media use case that involves the Librarian entering the Borrower ID. Now, we'll add business objects to the diagram modeling the system's response.

The next step in the use case says the system responds by displaying the borrower's account, and then refers us to the Display Borrower Account use case. Here is the full text of this use case:

> *The system displays the borrower's account. This information includes the borrower's name, the number of items they can borrow, unpaid fines, and a list of media checked out. The "checked out media" list includes due date and special indication for overdue media.*

If we examine our application's data structure, we'll find this information is stored in a few different tables. For example:

- ❏ The borrower's name is stored in the `Borrower` table.

- ❏ A list of items they have checked out can be retrieved from the `TrxLog` table (joined to the `Media` table for the media description).

- ❏ The number of items they can check out is calculated by subtracting the number of items checked out from the total number allowed (five).

- ❏ As described in our business rules, borrowers can't check out items if they have more than fifty dollars in outstanding fines. The `Fine` table contains the information we need to calculate this information.

Using our basic rule of thumb of usually creating a business object for each main table in our application, we should create three new business objects to implement this part of the use case:

- ❏ `Borrower` business object
- ❏ `TrxLog` business object
- ❏ `Fine` business object

Let's create each of these now – then we'll add them to the diagram as we need them.

1. In the Model Explorer, right-click the **Top Package | Wrox | UMLDotNet | Business** node, and select **New | Class** from the shortcut menu.

2. In the **UML Class Properties** dialog's **Name** textbox, enter **Borrower**.

3. In the **Documentation** box, enter the following:

Borrower business object – maintains information regarding people who borrow items from the library.

Click **OK** to close the dialog.

4. Add another new class named `TrxLog`, and specify the following description:

Transaction Log business object – maintains information captured each time media is checked in or out.

5. Add a third new class named `Fine`, and specify the following description:

Maintains information regarding fines applied to a borrower for overdue media.

Next, drag and drop each of these three classes onto the **Business and Data Classes** class diagram. Afterwards, create a **Generalization** relationship between each class and the `BusinessObject` class as shown in the following image:

```
┌─────────────────────────────────────────────────────────────────────────────────┐
│                          Business::BusinessObject                                  │
├────────────────────────────────────────────────────────────────────────────────┤
│ #DataBaseKey : string                                                             │
│ #TableName : string                                                               │
├────────────────────────────────────────────────────────────────────────────────┤
│ #GetDataSet(in command : string) : DataSet                                        │
│ #GetDataSet(in command : string, in databaseKey : string) : DataSet               │
│ #GetDataSet(in command : string, in databaseKey : string, in tableName : string) : DataSet │
│ #SaveDataSet(in ds : DataSet) : int                                               │
│ #SaveDataSet(in ds : DataSet, in databaseKey : string) : int                      │
│ #SaveDataSet(in ds : DataSet, in databaseKey : string, in tableName : string) : int │
└────────────────────────────────────────────────────────────────────────────────┘
```

```
┌──────────────────┐  ┌──────────────────┐  ┌──────────────────┐
│ Business::Borrower│  │ Business::TrxLog │  │ Business::Fine   │
├──────────────────┤  ├──────────────────┤  ├──────────────────┤
│                  │  │                  │  │                  │
└──────────────────┘  └──────────────────┘  └──────────────────┘
```

Adding the Borrower Object to the Sequence Diagram

Now we're ready to take a closer look at the second step in the use case and assign responsibilities to business objects that carry out the use case.

The first thing we'll do is use the `Borrower` business object to retrieve the borrower's name. To do this, we must send a message from the UI object to the `Borrower` business object. Follow these steps to add the `Borrower` class to the diagram and send a message to it:

1. Select the "Check Out Media" sequence diagram.

2. Drag an **Object Lifeline** shape from the **UML Sequence** stencil and drop it onto the sequence diagram, to the immediate right of the UI object.

3. Double-click the new shape, and in the **UML Classifier Role Properties** dialog's **Classifier** combo box select **Business::Borrower**.

4. Click **OK** to save changes and close the dialog.

5. Resize the **Borrower** object's lifeline so it's about the same size as the other objects' lifelines.

6. Next drag an **Activation** shape from the **UML Sequence** stencil and drop it on the **Borrower** object's lifeline. Place the top of the activation shape a bit lower than the top of the UI object's activation shape as shown in the following image (from this point on, I'll leave out the use case text to save space).

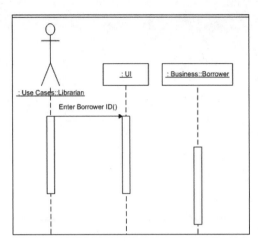

This causes the message passed from the UI object to the Borrower object to be lower in the horizontal plane, indicating the ordering, or sequence of the message.

Adding a Message Call to the Borrower Object

Now it's time to add a message call from the UI class to the Borrower business object. The Librarian interacts with the user interface by entering the borrower ID. The user interface now makes a call to the Borrower business object which has the responsibility of validating the specified borrower.

1. Drag a Message (call) shape from the UML Sequence stencil and drop it onto the sequence diagram. You may find it easiest to attach the arrow end to the top of the Borrower object's activation shape first, and then attach the other end to the UI object's activation shape.

2. Double-click the new message to launch the UML Message Properties dialog. The Operation combo box contains a list of all operations defined in the Borrower class and any operations it inherits from base classes. If you open the combo box list, you'll see it contains a list of operations inherited from the BusinessObject class as shown in the following image.

As you can see, it's impossible to tell which overload you are selecting, because the operation signature isn't shown. Microsoft may well address this in a future release of Visio.

3. We don't want to use either the GetDataSet or SaveDataSet operation, so click the New button to create a new operation.

4. We need to create an operation to retrieve information from the Borrower table for the specified borrower ID. It's best to provide descriptive operation names that are self-documenting. Although you may initially shy away from longer operation names, you'll find being able to figure out what an operation does simply by reading its name is a great time saver. With this in mind, enter GetBorrowerByID in the operation Name textbox.

5. In the Return type combo box, select Data::DataSet.

6. In the Documentation box, enter the following:

Returns a DataSet containing the specified Borrower's information.

7. In the Categories pane, select Parameters. Click the New button, and then the Properties... button to launch the UML Parameter Properties dialog. Create a new parameter named borrowerID, and specify its type as string. In this example, we're using a string ID, which may be implemented as a GUID (Globally Unique Identifier). In your applications, you can use any ID type you wish, such as an integer.

8. Click OK to close the UML Parameter Properties dialog, click OK again to close the UML Operation Properties dialog, and then click OK once more to close the UML Message Properties dialog.

When you're done, the diagram should look like the following image:

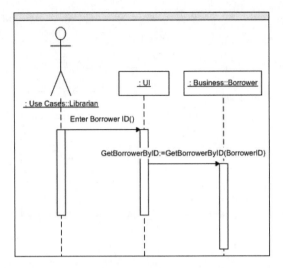

Notice the message text is GetBorrowerByID:=GetBorrowerByID(BorrowerID). The first reference to GetBorrowerByID in this text string indicates that the operation returns a value. This is somewhat unusual for a modeling tool, and I think, undesirable.

Although the UML allows you to add return messages to sequence diagrams to indicate a value has been returned from an object, you typically don't need to do so unless something out of the ordinary is returned, because message returns are assumed.

Resizing the Activation Shapes

In a sequence diagram, the height of an activation box indicates the lifetime of the associated operation. At this point, let's shorten the Borrower.GetBorrowerByID() activation, because the method is called, returns a value, and finishes execution. To do this, select the activation shape and drag the bottom of the shape up as far as Visio allows.

We have a few more operations to call from the UI object, so lengthen both the Librarian and UI object activation shapes a bit. When you do this, it may move one or both sides of the Enter Borrower ID message. If this happens, just move the message back to the top of the activation shapes. When you're finished, your diagram should look something like the following image:

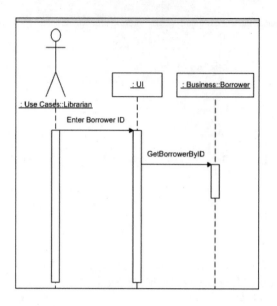

Retrieving Checked-Out Media

Next, we need to get a list of media checked out by the current Borrower. The TrxLog object is capable of giving us this information. In addition to this "media checked out" list, our use case also says we need to determine how many items a borrower can check out. There are two main criteria we must check – the number of items already checked out (they can borrow a maximum of five items), and outstanding fines (they can't check out media if they have more than fifty dollars in outstanding fines). We'll have to enlist the help of the Fine business object to calculate these fines.

We know we'll need both the TrxLog and Fine objects, so let's add both of these to the diagram now.

1. Drag an Object Lifeline from the UML Sequence stencil and drop it on the top of the sequence diagram to the right of the Borrower object.

2. Double-click the new object and in the UML Classifier Role Properties dialog, specify the class of the object as Business::TrxLog.

3. Click OK to save changes and then lengthen the object's lifeline.

4. Drop another Object Lifeline on the diagram to the right of the TrxLog object, and specify the class of the object as Business::Fine.

5. Click OK to save changes and then lengthen the object's lifeline.

Now we'll add messages to the diagram starting with a message from the UI object to the TrxLog object. We'll also add a call to the Fine object to determine outstanding fines for the specified Borrower.

Although we *could* make individual calls to each object from the UI, we can encapsulate the process by making a single call to the TrxLog object, and have the TrxLog object call the Fine object to determine the amount of outstanding fines. Based on the number of items checked out, and the amount of overdue fines, the TrxLog object can calculate the number of items the Borrower can check out, and return this value in an output parameter. With this solution, the TrxLog and Borrower objects collaborate to fulfill a responsibility.

The following steps show how to model this:

1. Drag and drop an Activation shape on the TrxLog object's lifeline. Position the top of the activation shape so its top is aligned with the bottom of the GetBorrowerByID() activation shape.

2. Drag and drop a Message (call) shape onto the diagram, attaching the arrowhead to the top of the TrxLog object's activation shape and the other end of the message shape to the UI object's activation shape.

3. Double-click the new message shape and then click the New button in the UML Message Properties dialog to add a new operation named GetBorrowerCheckedOutMedia. Specify the return type as Data::DataSet, and specify the description as:

Returns a DataSet containing all checked out media for the specified Borrower.

4. In the Categories pane, select Parameters. Click the New button, and then click the Properties... button to add a new parameter named borrowerID of the type string.

5. Add a second parameter named amtCanBorrow. Specify its type as integer, and in the Kind combo box, specify that it is an output parameter (out). In the Documentation box, enter the following:

Specifies the number of media the specified borrower can check out.

6. Click OK three times to save changes and close all dialogs.

When you're finished, your sequence diagram should look like the following image:

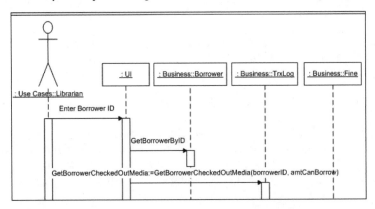

Now we need to add a call to the `Fine` method from within the `TrxLog`'s `GetBorrowerCheckedOutMedia` to indicate this method also calculates fines to determine the number of media a `Borrower` can check out.

Calculating Fines

As we've mentioned previously, it's a good idea to think about data during object modeling. The following image shows the structure of the TrxLog and Fine tables:

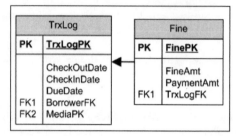

If you look closely at these tables, you'll see there isn't a direct way to get the total outstanding fines for a particular borrower. We could derive this information in a roundabout way by means of the `TrxLog` table, but because this is something we want to do often, we may want to denormalize the data so this information is more readily available. An easy way to do this is to save both the `TrxLog` foreign key pointer *and* a `Borrower` foreign key pointer in the `Fine` table. The Borrower key gives us what we need to retrieve outstanding fines for a specific borrower more easily. Assuming this structure, let's finish modeling this part of the sequence diagram

Please note that we're still working with our previous sequence diagram.

1. Drag an Activation shape from the UML Sequence stencil and drop it on the `Fine` object's lifeline. Place the top of the Activation shape a few steps lower than the top of the `TrxLog`'s activation shape.

2. Drag and drop a Message (call) shape on the sequence diagram. Attach the arrowhead to the top of the `Fine` object's Activation shape. Attach the other end of the message to the `TrxLog` object's `GetBorrowerCheckedOutMedia` activation shape.

3. Double-click the new message, and create a new operation named GetBorrowerOutstandingFines. Set the operation Return type to decimal, and in the Documentation box, enter the following:

Returns total outstanding fines for the specified Borrower.

4. In the Category box, select Parameters. Click the New button, and then click the Properties button to add a single parameter named BorrowerID of type string.

5. Click OK three times to save changes and close all dialogs.

6. Shorten the `Fine` object's activation shape to the smallest possible size. Resize the `TrxLog` object's activation shape so its bottom is aligned with the bottom edge of the `Fine` object's activation box.

When you're finished, your sequence diagram should look like the following image:

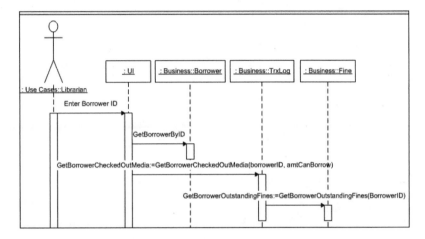

Displaying the Borrower Information

Now that we've returned the information we need from the `Borrower`, `TrxLog`, and `Fine` objects, let's add a message to the diagram indicating that this information is displayed to the user interface. The `UI` object needs to call a method on itself (also known as "local invocation"). Based on this, we're going to use a different message shape than we've used before.

1. Drag a "curved" Message (call) shape as shown in the following image from the UML Sequence stencil and drop it on the diagram.

Attach the message shape to the `UI` object's activation shape. This attaches both ends of the message shape to the activation shape as shown in the following image.

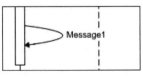

2. Double-click the new message shape, and in the UML Message Properties dialog, click the New button to add a new operation.

3. In the UML Operation Properties dialog, set the name of the operation to Display Borrower Account.

Remember; because UI is not a 'real' class, we can add spaces in operation names because they will never be implemented in code.

4. Click OK to save changes and close both dialogs.

When you model a reflexive message call like this, it's best to add an activation shape for the message. This allows you to make calls to other objects from within this message. Although we won't be making any calls from this message, let's add an activation shape to show you how it's done.

To add a nested activation shape:

1. If necessary, lengthen the UI object's activation shape to make room for the nested activation.

2. Drag an Activation shape from the UML Sequence stencil and attach it to the right side of the UI object's activation shape. Place the shape so its top edge touches the point where the message arrowhead meets the original activation shape.

3. Resize the new activation shape to the smallest possible size.

4. Attach the arrowhead of the Display Borrower Account message to the top right corner of the nested activation shape.

When you're finished, your diagram should look like the following image:

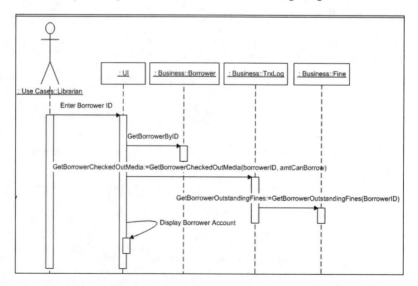

Checking Out Media

Now that the borrower's information has been retrieved and displayed, we're ready to model checking out media. If the GetBorrowerCheckedOutMedia operation returned zero (0) in its amtCanBorrow parameter, then the Borrower is unable to check out any media, and the user interface should enforce this. However, assuming the Borrower can check out one or more items, the Librarian interacts with the system again, and we'll use our business objects to respond accordingly.

The only business object we need to use when marking media as checked out is the TrxLog object. The Librarian either enters the Media ID by scanning, or manually enters it, and then this Media ID is passed to the TrxLog object, which marks the media as checked out.

Here's how we model this:

1. Lengthen the lifeline of the Librarian object to accommodate a new activation shape. Increase the size of the UI and TrxLog objects' lifelines to the same length.

2. Drag a new Activation shape from the UML Sequence stencil and attach it to the Librarian lifeline beneath the existing activation shape, but leave space between the bottom of the original activation shape and the new activation shape. This provides room for the display of the next message call we will add between the Librarian and the UI object.

3. Drag another new Activation shape to the sequence diagram and attach it to the UI object's lifeline. Align the tops of both new activation shapes.

4. Drag a new Message (call) shape from the UML Sequence stencil and attach the left side of the message shape to the top of the Librarian's new activation shape. Attach the arrowhead of the message shape to the top of the UI object's new activation shape.

5. Double-click the new message shape, and in the UML Message Properties dialog, click the New button to add a new operation.

6. In the UML Operation Properties dialog, specify the operation name Enter Media ID.

7. Click OK twice to save changes and close both dialogs.

When you're finished, your sequence diagram should look like the following image:

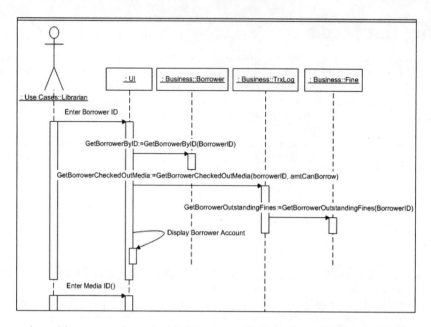

Now we need to add a message from the UI object to the TrxLog object. We'll pass the Borrower ID and Media ID so the TrxLog object knows what media is being checked out and to whom. We'll also pass the current or user-specified date to the TrxLog so it doesn't have to assume the check out date is today's date.

1. Drag an Activation shape from the UML Sequence stencil and attach it to the TrxLog object's lifeline. Position the activation shape so its top edge is lower than the Enter Media ID activation shape's top edge.

2. Drag and drop a Message (call) shape onto the sequence diagram. Attach the message shape's arrowhead to the top of the TrxLog's new activation shape. Attach the other end of the shape to the UI object's new activation shape.

3. Double-click the new message shape and click the New button in the UML Message Properties dialog to add a new operation named CheckOut. Leave the operation's return type as <None>, but in the Documentation box, enter the following:

Checks out the media for the specified borrower and date.

4. In the Categories pane, select Parameters. Add the following two string parameters to this operation named borrowerID, and mediaID.

5. Click OK three times to save changes and close all dialogs.

6. Resize the CheckOut message's activation box to the smallest size Visio allows. You can also shorten the Librarian and UI object's activation shapes accordingly.

Tweaking the Sequence Diagram

After performing the previous steps, resize the CheckOut message's activation box to the smallest size Visio allows. Also, shorten the Librarian and UI object's activation shapes accordingly.

Since the Borrower and Fine objects are not involved in the second half of the use case, shorten their lifelines so they line up with the bottom of the Enter Borrower ID activation box.

One other adornment we can add to the diagram is destructor shapes. When we're finished using an object, we usually destroy it. You indicate this in a sequence diagram by adding a destructor icon at the bottom of an object's lifeline.

To do this, right-click an object's lifeline, and select Shape Display Options... from the context menu. In the UML Shape Display Options dialog shown in the following diagram, just mark the Destruction marker checkbox, click OK to save changes, and close the dialog.

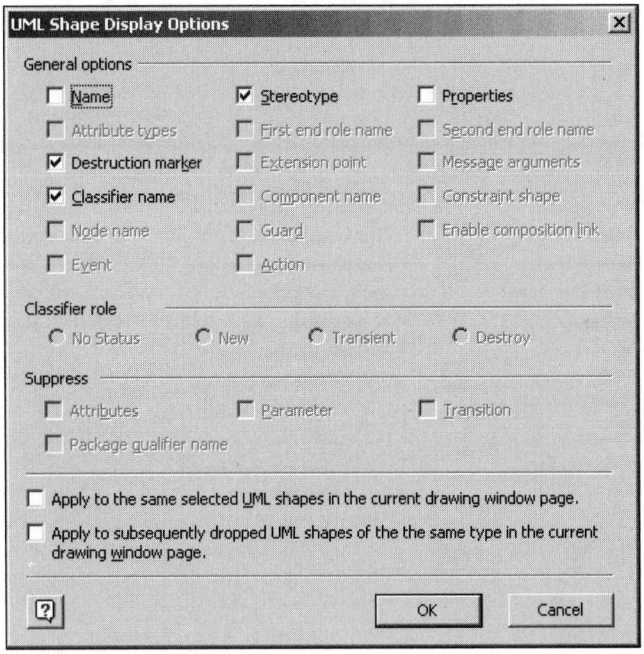

This places a large X at the bottom of the lifeline, as shown in the following image depicting our final sequence diagram:

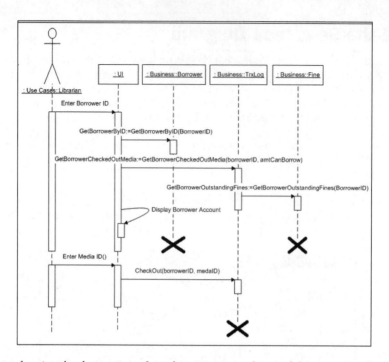

In addition to showing the destruction of an object, you can also model its creation. In our sequence diagram, all business objects are displayed at the very top of the diagram, which does not indicate a specific creation timeframe. If we want to model the creation of an object, we can add a method call that points directly at the object instance. For example, we could model the creation and destruction of the Fine object in our sequence diagram as shown in the following image.

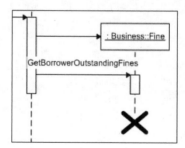

Summary

Although business object modeling is one of the more challenging aspects of analysis and design, it can also be the most rewarding. Business objects make your applications more scaleable and maintainable. They are also a great help in conceiving and designing complex software systems because they bridge the semantic gap by allowing you to model real-world entities. UML class diagrams and sequence diagrams are great tools for designing business objects that work well in both your Windows Forms and ASP.NET applications.

In addition to a high-level discussion of business objects, this chapter also discussed design principles for building business object and data-access base classes for your .NET applications. We learned how to use Visio to model the static nature of business objects in class diagrams and how different UML class adornments translate into elements of .NET classes. We also learned to model the dynamic nature of business objects in Visio sequence diagrams assigning responsibilities that carried out the functionality of use cases. Contrary to conventional wisdom, we also learned that thinking about data during object modeling can help us more quickly create a well-designed, working object model.

Once the dust has settled on your object model, you can begin implementing business objects in your .NET programming language of choice. The next chapter shows how Visio gives you a jump-start on your model by generating code from your object model.

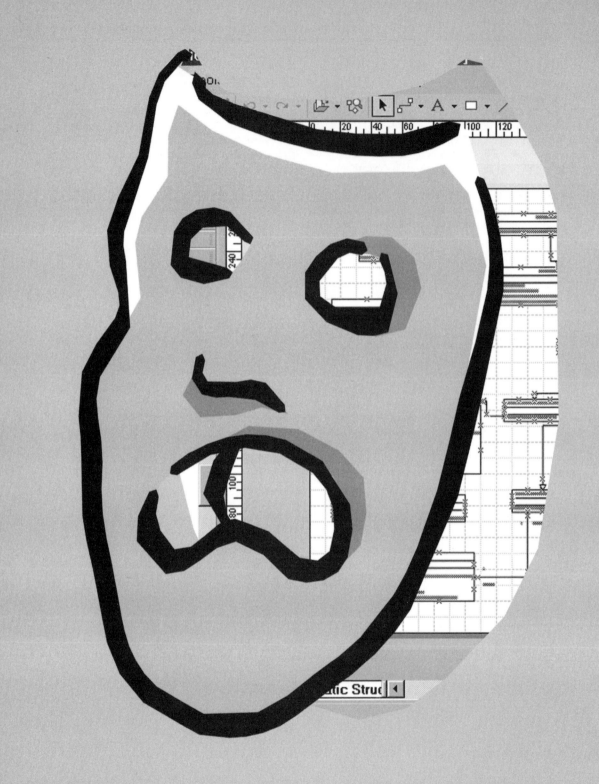

Generating Code from the Visio Model

The planning phase is over – you already have a full description of the static structure of your system, with classes, links, attributes and much more. Now, you are ready for the coding.

Visio for Enterprise Architects can generate skeleton source code from an existing UML diagram in C#, Visual Basic .NET, or C++. Moreover, Visio provides further options that give the developer greater control over the implementation of this source code.

We will begin this chapter with an overview of code generation, before moving on to look at the following topics:

- ❑ How to generate code from a UML model in Visio

- ❑ Templates for code generation – what they are, and how we work with them

- ❑ How to create a model that correctly maps to programming language and use specific .NET entities (like enumerations, delegates, events)

Overview of Code Generation

Code generation is an automated process of obtaining programming-language source code from a UML model.

Once you have properly described the static structure of your system, Visio can generate code skeletons from your models in one of three languages – C#, Visual Basic .NET, or C++. The current version of Visio works only with the static model of the system and does not support generating method stubs from activity or sequence diagrams.

Visio can generate the code for the classes and packages you specify from the whole static model, not only from the entities that reside on static diagrams, and can either generate the code into files, or place the generated code into a Visual Studio .NET project.

Furthermore, for each level of the model – class, attribute, or operation, Visio allows the developer a preview of the code that will be generated, and also to specify the language, code template, and the documentation produced.

With code templates, the developer is able to specify the structure of the source code generated by Visio. Code templates can be modified and customized, meaning that in-house coding styles can be enforced, resulting in standardized source code, and also extending the flat code generations options of the UML. We'll see more about this later in the chapter.

The completeness and correctness of generated code depends on the accuracy with which you have developed your model – an ill-defined model may not result in correct code generation. For example, you have the power to define the body of operations in Visio, so you have the power to do a 100% complete model in most cases.

It is worth remembering that although Visio allows you to enter code for the body of operations, when you write the body of, say, a method in a particular programming language, you make the model dependent on the programming language. Suppose you have created a 100% complete C# model, generate C# code from it, compile, run, and have fun. Now try to generate Visual Basic .NET code from it – all the code in the body of your methods, which you have carefully written yourself in C# will not compile in VB.NET of course.

Another important point to keep in mind with code generation is that UML is a *modeling* language and C++, Visual Basic .NET, and C# are *programming* languages, and each of them has its own flavor of syntax and structure. Thus you should be ready to sometimes modify the model in order to generate code into your favorite language.

Code Generation in Visio

To illustrate the process of code generation, let's begin by working through the construction of a simple diagram, and seeing the code generated for that. As we go through, we'll look at:

❑   Adding fields to a class, and their code generation options

❑   Adding methods to a class, and their code generation options

❑   Creating an interface, and adding properties to it

❑   Adding an implementation of the interface to a class

The Employee Class

Our example diagram will feature a class that will work with the employee details of a fictitious company. This class will contain information about the employee such as their name, ID number, hire date, and date of birth.

```
+-------------------------------------+
|              Employee               |
+-------------------------------------+
| -id : int                           |
| -hireDate : DateTime                |
| -salary : decimal                   |
+-------------------------------------+
| +FirstName() : string               |
| +LastName() : string                |
| +BirthDate() : DateTime             |
| +ID() : int                         |
| +Salary() : decimal                 |
| +HireDate() : DateTime              |
| +ChangeSalary(in amount : decimal)  |
+-------------------------------------+
```

We spent the last chapter looking at diagramming components from within Visio, so we should be familiar with the process, but as we shall see, the number of dialogs that open and close as we progress can become confusing, so its worth paying attention to the procedure again.

Since we're going to be using dates in our class, the first thing we'll do is add a `System.DateTime` structure. Right-click the **Top Package** node and select **New | Package** from the context menu. In the **UML Package Properties** dialog that is launched, enter **System** into the **Name** text box, and then click **OK**. Right-click this package, add a new class called **DateTime**, and set its **stereotype** to **struct**.

Now let's get on with creating the **Employee** class.

Right-click on the **Top Package** node and select a new class. Set the name of the class to **Employee**, and leave all the other options in the **UML Class Properties** dialog as they are:

Notice the **Code Generation Options** entry is the list of **Categories** – we'll see more of this as we go through.

Adding Fields

We'll begin by adding some fields to our **Employee** class by clicking on the **Attributes** entry in the list of **Categories**, and add the following attributes – they will be fields in our class.

> *Do not confuse UML attributes with .NET attributes here. A UML attribute for a class is the same as a class member in C# or VB.NET.*

Add the three fields id, hireDate, and salary as shown in the screenshot below. You may find it easier to widen the **Type** drop-down before you start trying to select the data types, in order to get a better view of the type names:

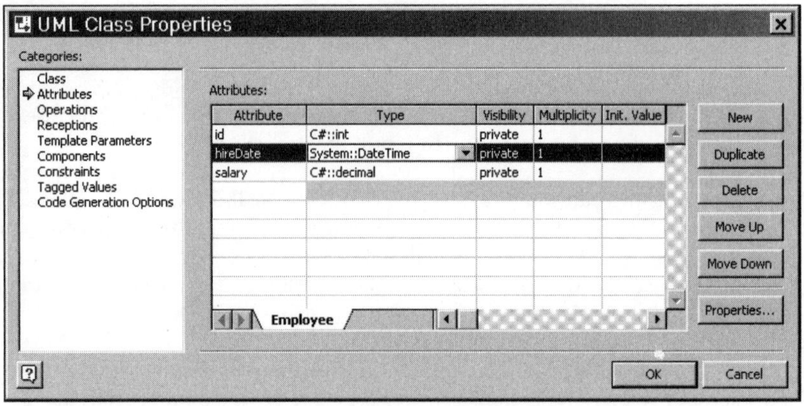

Note that we are already making an implicit choice of language for our eventual code here by selecting C# `int` and `decimal` types.

Previewing Code

Let's have a look at the skeleton code that will be generated from one of our attributes – select the `hireDate` attribute, and click **Properties** to go to its **UML Attributes Properties** dialog:

We explored the main options on this dialog in the previous chapter, looked at the default values for these options, and discussed how some of them mapped into code. Now we'll actually get to see this in action.

Select the Code Generation Options entry:

This rather bare dialog allows us to specify the code generation options for this particular attribute. From here we can specify the target language for this attribute, and also preview the code generated for this attribute. We'll talk about the Template drop-down later. For now, select C# as the Target language and click the Preview code button to see the code generated for our hireDate attribute:

If you click **Close** and return to the **UML Attribute Properties** dialog, then you can quickly experiment with some of the options on this page and preview the code generated to see the effect of these options.

Let's see the effect of the **OwnerScope** option – setting this to **classifier** produces a `static` member in C#, or `Shared` in VB.NET:

```
public static System.DateTime hireDate;
```

Setting **Changeable** to **frozen** produces a constant member:

```
private const System.DateTime hireDate;
```

Initial values can be set for attributes through the **InitialValue** field. Note that Visio simply places the text entered into this field directly into the generated code. For example, if your initial value is a string literal then you will have to include the quotes around it, as Visio will not add these for you, thus be wary when specifying such values from Visio.

Adding Properties

Now that we have some fields, let's add some properties to expose them – we will create properties that have get and set accessors automatically generated. To create properties, and other types of methods, we have first to define them as UML operations.

Select **Operations** from the list of **Categories** on the **UML Class Properties** dialog and click **New** to create a new operation. Click **Properties** to launch the **UML Operations Properties** dialog. Enter **ID** for its **Name**, and select its **Return type** as a C# int:

In the previous chapter, we looked at the meaning of the options available from this dialog – as we go through the chapter we'll see the effect of these options on the generated code.

To define ID as a property, select Code Generation Options from the list of Categories. This brings up a set of options that determine how the ID operation will map into code. From the Kind drop-down, select Property, and the Create Get Method and Create Set Method checkboxes will ungrey. ID is to be a read-only property – we only require a get accessor – so only check the Create Get Method checkbox:

From the Kind drop-down we can select from a list of operation types – the list of available types will depend on the target language chosen. Here are the types for C#:

139

Type	Description
Constructor	Defines a constructor – in the generated code, the constructor will always take the name of the current class, regardless of the operation name.
Destructor	Defines a destructor – in the generated code, the destructor will always take the name of the current class, regardless of the operation name.
Event	Defines an event – there are two checkboxes for adding the get and set event accessors.
Indexer	Defines an indexer.
Operator	Defines an operator for operator overloading in C# and C++.
Procedure	Defines a general method.
Property	Defines a property – there are two checkboxes for adding the get and set accessors.

For generation into Visual Basic .NET, Visio has no Indexer or Operator kind, and for C++ there is no Indexer, Property, or Event kind.

Visio will also adjust the kind of operation to fit the target language. This means that if you select C# as language and define an operation as an Operator, and later you are attempt to generate Visual Basic .NET code for this operation, Visio will automatically adjust this operation kind to Procedure.

Let's quickly check out the skeleton code that will be generated by clicking the Preview code button:

Note that if you attempt to add some code for the method body from the Method entry in the UML Operation Properties dialog, (we'll look at this in a moment) this code will only be entered into the get accessor, regardless of the presence of a set accessor.

That's our ID property done, so let's add two operations, Salary and HireDate with return types as below:

Operation	Return Type	Visibility	Polymorphic	Scope
ID	C#::int	public	☐	instance
Salary	C#::decimal	public	☐	instance
HireDate	System::DateTime	public	☐	instance

From the Code Generation Options dialog, set the Kind of Salary to Property, and check only its Create Get Method. For HireDate, set its Kind to Property and check both the Create Get Method and Create Set Method checkboxes.

Click OK to accept these values, and click OK on the UML Class Properties dialog.

> Remember that any changes you make from dialogs such as the **UML Operation Properties** dialog will not be committed unless you click **OK** from the **UML Class Properties** dialog. In other words, if you make a selection from the **UML Class Properties** dialog that launches another dialog, and you make some changes there and click **OK**, but then on returning to the **UML Class Properties** dialog you make a change you're not happy with and click **Cancel**, your changes will not be committed. This is important to bear in mind if you're finding that changes you thought you made on some dialog screens have not been persisted.

Drag an Employee class onto the page, and it should now look like this:

```
┌─────────────────────────────────┐
│           Employee              │
├─────────────────────────────────┤
│ -id : int                       │
│ -hireDate : DateTime            │
│ -salary : decimal               │
├─────────────────────────────────┤
│ +ID() : int                     │
│ +Salary() : decimal             │
│ +HireDate() : DateTime          │
└─────────────────────────────────┘
```

Adding a Method

Now let's add a public method to the Employee class – a simple method to modify the value of the employee's salary. This is accomplished again through the Operations entry in the list of Categories in the UML Class Properties dialog window. Click New to add a new operation, and select Properties to bring up the UML Operations Properties dialog for this new operation. Our method will be called ChangeSalary, and we will leave its Return type set to <None> – this method will not return a value. The screenshot overleaf shows this dialog for our method – note that we have also added some comments for the method in the Documentation field:

We can add parameters to the method through the **Parameters** entry in the list of **Categories**:

The name of the parameter is entered into the **Parameter** column, its type into the **Type** column, and in the **Kind** column we choose if the parameter is to be **in**, **out**, or **inout**.

The **Default Value** column allows a default value for the parameter to be specified – C# does not support default values for parameters, and any value entered here will not appear in code generated in C#.

Click **New** to add a new parameter, and then select **Properties** to open the **UML Parameter Properties** dialog:

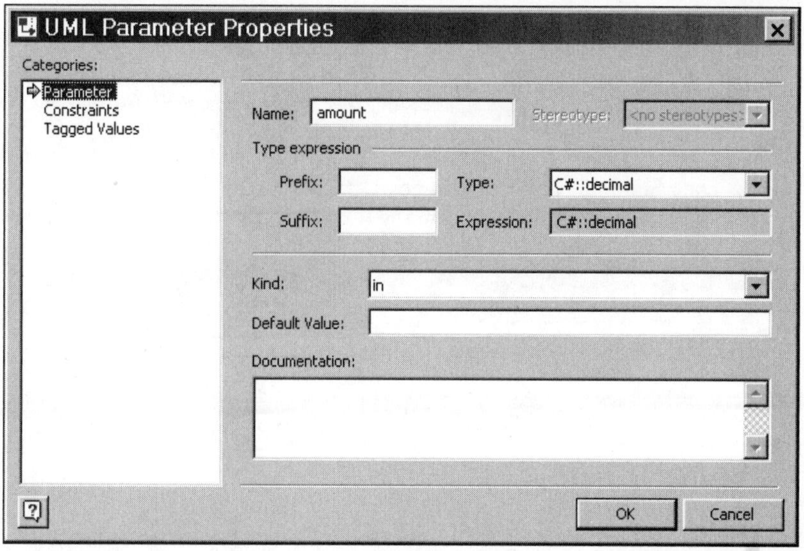

UML Parameter Properties

Categories:
- **Parameter**
- Constraints
- Tagged Values

Name: `amount` Stereotype: `<no stereotypes>`

Type expression

Prefix: `` Type: `C#::decimal`

Suffix: `` Expression: `C#::decimal`

Kind: `in`

Default Value: ``

Documentation:

OK Cancel

Here we can specify the parameter options as described above – the screenshot shows that we've entered **amount** for the **Name** of the parameter and its **Type** is a C# `decimal`. Our **amount** parameter is passed into the method and is not modified, therefore the defined **Kind** is in.

Click **OK** to accept these values and return to the **UML Operation Properties** dialog. From here we can add some code for the method body by selecting the **Method** entry from the list of **Categories**:

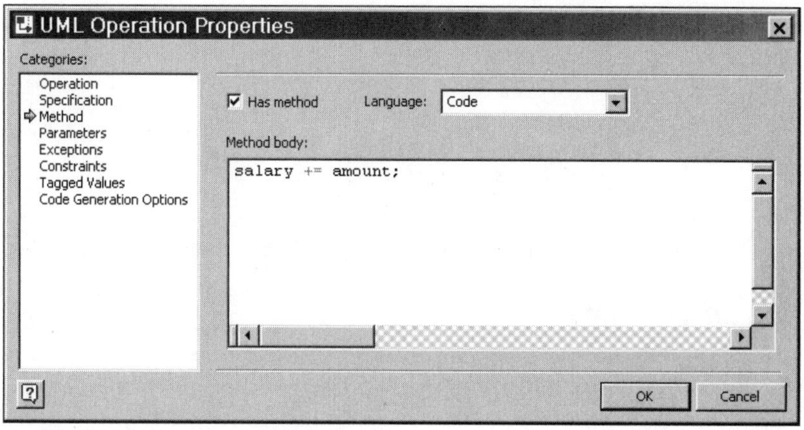

UML Operation Properties

Categories:
- Operation
- Specification
- **Method**
- Parameters
- Exceptions
- Constraints
- Tagged Values
- Code Generation Options

☑ Has method Language: `Code`

Method body:

```
salary += amount;
```

OK Cancel

When first selected, the **Method body** text box will be greyed out. To ungrey the text box and enter your code, the **Has method** checkbox has first to be checked. After this the **Method body** field becomes active and we can define the code for our method as shown above.

In spite of its name, this **Language** drop-down here does not affect code generation, but only the syntax highlighting in the **Method body** text box.

Don't forget that Visio is a modeling tool, and not an integrated development environment, so you don't have any special code editing features such as IntelliSense or any debugging facilities when entering your code here. If you make an error in entering your code here, then you will not be aware of this until your code is generated and you attempt to compile the resulting code. In the future, as Visio is integrated even more tightly with Visual Studio .NET, such a feature may make a welcome appearance.

From the Preview code button in Code Generation Options we can look at the code produced – note the comments before the method produced from the text in the Documentation field:

Now our Employee class should look like the following, with its three attributes and four operations:

Before we actually generate some code from our model, let's look at implementing an interface.

Implementing an Interface

We're going to create a Person interface with properties for the first and last name of a person, and their date of birth.

Begin by dragging the rectangular Interface shape onto the page:

Double-click on the interface to open the UML Interface Properties dialog – here we've changed the name of the interface to Person:

To add properties to our interface, select Operations from the list of Categories, and click New to add a new operation, and then select Properties. Our first property will be called FirstName, and will return a C# string:

Select the **Code Generation Options** entry, and we can determine the nature of this operation. We will set the **Kind** of our operation to **Property**, and check both checkboxes to define get and set accessors.

Let's see what this will generate for us, so click on **Preview Code** to see the following code:

```
// Preview of code that will be generated in the implementation file:

    string FirstName
    {
        get;
        set;
    }
```

Since **Person** is an interface, there is no reason to generate any code for the implementation here. Now click **Close** on the **Code Preview** window, and click **OK** on the **UML Operation Properties** dialog to return to the **UML Interface Properties** dialog. Add two more operations, both properties, and both with get and set accessors:

Operation	Return Type	Visibility	Polymorphic	Scope
FirstName	C#::string	public	✓	instance
LastName	C#::string	public	✓	instance
BirthDate	System::DateTime	public	✓	instance

Now the design of our interface is complete, and so click **OK** to finish the **UML Interface** dialog. Our UML diagram should now look like the following:

Getting the **Employee** class to implement the **Person** interface is trivial – right-click on the **Person** interface and select **Show as Lollipop Interface** – it will change to look like the following:

Now simply drag the Person interface to one of the connection points of the Employee class and the connection point will turn red. When you release the mouse button, the properties of the Person interface will now appear in the Employee class, and if you right-click the Person interface and select Show as Class-like Interface, your diagram should look like the following:

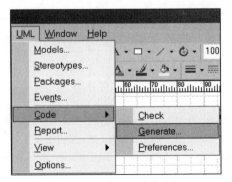

For the sake of completeness, go ahead and add the private fields to the Employee class that will be wrapped by the properties from the Person interface if you like.

OK, we've diagrammed our Employee class, and added some C#-specific code details. Now we're ready to generate some code into files!

Generating Code

Code is generated, and output to files, from the UML | Code | Generate menu:

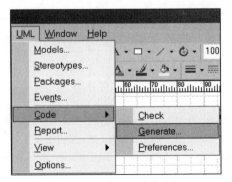

This command opens the Generate dialog window, shown in the screenshot opposite:

In the Target language field the developer can choose the programming language, which becomes the output language for the code – if this disagrees with the choice of language made at any point in the diagramming phase, no error will be reported. We'll look more at this again in a moment.

In the right-hand side of the dialog window you can select namespaces and classes you want to export from your model to the resulting code.

After all the components are chosen – selecting the entire model selects each class in the model – and the programming language to be used is chosen, we can launch the generating process by clicking the OK button. If the directory into which you wish to generate the code does not exist, you will be asked if the directory should be created for you:

Remember the Target Language field that we saw in each of the earlier Code Generation Options dialogs? Well, it turns out that any language choices you made there are irrelevant to the final code generation from the UML | Code | Generate menu.

The choice of language that you make in the Target Language field of the Generate dialog that we saw above determines the language for each class, attribute, and operation involved in the code generation process.

Thus if you choose C# from the Generate dialog but have the target language for some of your methods set as Visual Basic (.NET), then they will still be generated as C#.

The code will be generated and put into the file we specified from the Location field, ready to be added to our projects. Note that the code generating procedure allows us to add the generated code to Visual Studio .NET projects automatically by checking the Add Classes to Visual Studio Project checkbox. With this checkbox checked, the Template drop-down becomes active, and it contains a list of the Visual Studio .NET project types into which the generated code will be added. All possible types of Visual Studio .NET projects are listed. If you want to add your classes to a web project – Empty Web Application, ASP.NET Web Application, or ASP.NET Web Service, then you have to specify a valid URL for the project, rather than a filename, just as you would in Visual Studio .NET.

Code will be generated for each selected class, and will go into a separate file with the name of the class followed by the extension for that language. There are three files created for our example, `Employee.cs`, `Person.cs`, and `DateTime.cs`. `Employee.cs` contains the code for the `Employees` class, the `Person` interface code is in `Person.cs`, and the `System.DateTime` code is in `DateTime.cs` – this file only contains the class definition, since we didn't do anything else to the class.

Here's `Employee.cs`:

```
// Static Model


using System;
public class Employee     : Person
{
```

Here we can see the `using` directive for the `System` namespace – this comes from the `System` package that contained the `DateTime` structure. We can also see that the `Employee` class is indeed implementing the `Person` interface.

```
    private int id;

    private System.DateTime hireDate;

    private decimal salary;
```

Here we have our private fields, and the public members are next – note the read-only properties `ID` and `Salary`:

```
    public string FirstName
    {
        get
        {
        }
        set
        {
        }
    }
    public string LastName
    {
        get
        {
        }
        set
        {
        }
    }
    public DateTime BirthDate
    {
        get
        {
```

```
        }
        set
        {
        }
    }
    public int ID
    {
        get
        {
        }
    }
    public decimal Salary
    {
        get
        {
        }
    }
    public DateTime HireDate
    {
        get
        {
        }
        set
        {
        }
    }
```

Next up is our pre-populated `ChangeSalary()` method, with the information that we specified in the **Documentation** box added as a comment:

```
    // Changes the salary of the employee
    public void ChangeSalary(decimal amount)
    {
        salary += amount;
    }

}// END CLASS DEFINITION Employee
```

You may be wondering why the code has been organized so – we'll see why in a moment.

Here is the code in `Person.cs` for the `Person` interface, with its properties:

```
// Static Model


using System;
public interface Person
{

    string FirstName
```

```
    {
        get;
        set;
    }
    string LastName
    {
        get;
        set;
    }
    DateTime BirthDate
    {
        get;
        set;
    }
}// END INTERFACE DEFINITION Person
```

Regenerating Code

Generating code again will not overwrite an existing file – any existing files that would be overwritten are renamed to <classname>~1 followed by the language extension, and the new code is always of the form <classname> with the language extension.

Thus generating the code again for our example would rename Employee.cs to Employee~1.cs and Person.cs to Person~1.cs, and the new code files would be Employee.cs and Person.cs. Subsequent generations would see Employee~1.cs and Person~1.cs renamed to Employee~2.cs and Person~2.cs, and so on, so that existing code is never overwritten.

Checking Errors

We can investigate any errors that would be produced in the code generation process by first selecting the UML | Check menu item. This command activates the Output window, which is shown below:

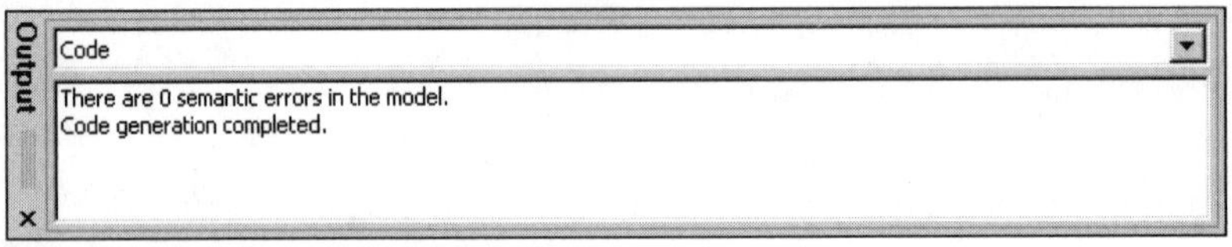

In the drop-down list situated in the top part of the Output window, you can choose the kind of errors to be shown.

If the Errors element is chosen, then the error messages about the semantic errors in UML model will be shown. Semantic errors indicate invalid constructions in UML 1.2. For example, in UML you can't use interfaces as parameter types. The offending classes that contain these errors will be highlighted in red on the diagram.

If the Code element is shown, then the error messages about possible errors in generated code will be shown. Code errors indicate invalid constructions in the target language. For example, in C# and in Visual Basic .NET you cannot have multiple inheritance:

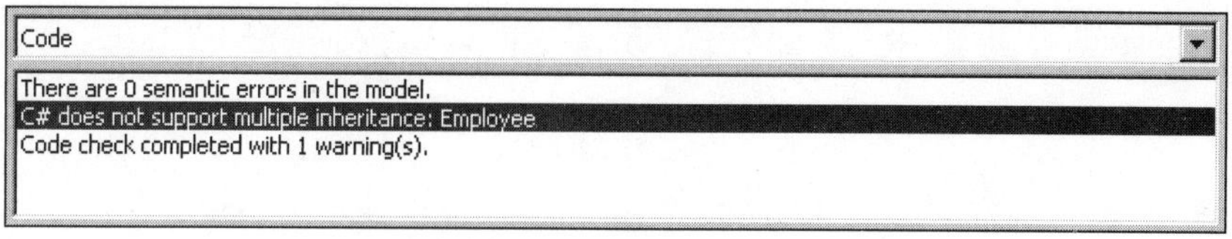

```
Code                                                                    ▼
There are 0 semantic errors in the model.
C# does not support multiple inheritance: Employee
Code check completed with 1 warning(s).
```

Here we've modified the **Employee** class to inherit from more than one class – as you can see, the offending class is named in the **Output** window, and if you the click on the error line then the offending class is highlighted in the diagram.

Code Generation in Different Languages

We have seen how code generation works with C#, but let's take a moment to see compare the code generated for our Employee class in Visual Basic .NET with that in C#. We'll see that although Visio can generate code to other languages, the language-specific choices you make when creating the model have consequences.

Here is the Visual Basic .NET code for the Employee class, as generated by Visio:

```vbnet
' Static Model


Imports TopPackage.System

Public Class Employee
      Implements Person

   Private id As Integer

   Private hireDate As System.DateTime

   Private salary As Decimal

   Public Function FirstName () As String Implements Person.FirstName

   End Function

   Public Function LastName () As String Implements Person.LastName

   End Function

   Public Function BirthDate () As DateTime Implements Person.BirthDate

   End Function

   Public Function ID () As Integer

   End Function

   Public Function Salary () As Decimal
```

153

```
     End Function

     Public Function HireDate () As DateTime

     End Function

     ' Changes the salary of the employee
     Public Sub ChangeSalary (ByVal amount As Decimal)
        salary += amount;
     End Sub

  End Class ' END CLASS DEFINITION Employee
```

Take a look at this code. There are two problems here – the first is the Imports statement:

```
    Imports TopPackage.System
```

This is not the namespace we want imported – we want System imported. This is a peculiar behavior of Visio. When we generated code for the C# project, the **Default Namespace** property was set to **TopPackage** – this property does not affect existing code. It is only used during the creation of new files, when this property is applied to set up a namespace.

In the Visual Basic .NET project the **Root namespace** property is set to **TopPackage**, but this property has a different meaning from the C# **Default Namespace** – in the Visual Basic .NET project any namespace is prefixed with **TopPackage** during compilation. Thus if you have the namespace **System55** in your code, it compiles to **TopPackage.System55**. Therefore, Visio will generate **System.DateTime** to **TopPackage.System.DateTime**. This is a curiosity, and hopefully one that will be corrected in future releases.

The other problem is the code in the ChangeSalary() method body – it's still C#.

```
    Public Sub ChangeSalary (ByVal amount As Decimal)
         salary += amount;
      End Sub
```

Any code that we explicitly add to method bodies will be inserted into generated code files without modification, regardless of the language used for generation. In this situation, our Visual Basic .NET code will not compile.

You should always remember that the closer the you take your model to a particular language by including language-specific code or operations, the more you tie yourself to that particular language.

Code Templates

When Visio generates your code, it goes through classes, interfaces, and associations producing code for you. We remarked earlier that you might be wondering why Visio arranges the fields, methods, and so on as it does. This arrangement is achieved with **code templates**. Visio checks the templates for every entity to be generated, and substitutes entity parameters into the template, such as class name, method name, and the documentation for that entity. In this way, Visio provides you with more control over the structure of your generated code.

We can define particular templates for classes, attributes, operations, and relationships. A default template is used unless we specify otherwise, although we can create our own templates used for the code generation of any particular object based on existing templates.

Using Templates

Visio uses code generation templates to change the structure of the code generated from UML diagrams. This brings several benefits:

❑ Standardization – in-house source code guidelines can be enforced, with a standard arrangement of class members ensuring that the final code is consistent and easy to navigate.

❑ Documentation – documentation added to the model can be realized as code or XML comments, thus the skeleton code is already documented.

❑ Formatting – indenting can be controlled, and parts of code can be marked for special display within Visual Studio .NET.

❑ Extending the UML model – the skeleton classes can be pre-populated with information that is specific to that class that would not otherwise form part of the UML model.

We'll see some examples of these uses as we progress. In Visio, you can use the default templates, create your own, or edit existing ones.

Working with Templates

To work with templates, choose the UML | Code | Preferences menu item – this command activates the Preferences dialog window:

In C# and Visual Basic .NET, code templates can be applied to four entities: classes, attributes, operations, and relationships. The default template for each of these, and other default settings can be selected by selecting the entity from the Default list. Here's the part of the dialog that is displayed when you choose Operations:

The **Operation kind** dropdown allows you to specify the default method type that an operation will be mapped to in code generation. Be careful with changing this setting – you will find that changing this setting will reset all the operations in your model to the new setting, even if they have previously been defined with a different kind of operation.

The **Implementation** dropdown contains the list of current operation templates – these define the layout of the code generated from a UML operation. The list of operation templates (and the other entity templates) can be found from the **Code templates** selection:

The **Categories** dropdown lists the categories of templates, and the entity with which they are associated. We'll select **ClassImpl** – the templates for classes – and the list of all possible templates will be shown in the **Templates** field. Now you can copy existing templates, delete them, edit, or create a new one. First, select **ClassImpl1** and click **Edit**, to see the structure of the default template for a typical class:

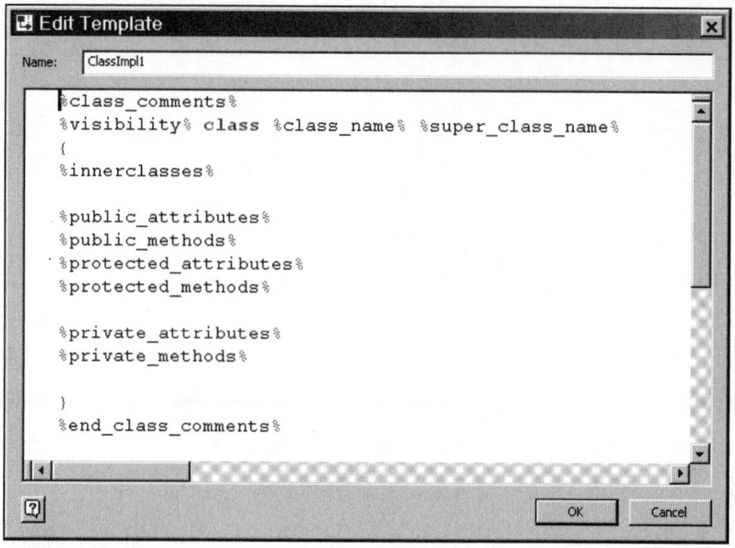

The structure of this template is simple; the keywords enclosed by a % symbol are the names of built-in Visio macros. These keywords act as placeholders, into which Visio will put the requested information. The above template determines the structure of the output code as follows:

First of all, the %class_comments% parameter indicates that Visio will put comments in the resulting file.

The next line specifies the class's visibility, name, and inheritance directives in the class declaration line:

```
%visibility% class %class_name% %super_class_name%
```

The next set of lines indicate the order in which the various members are put into the class definition:

```
%innerclasses%

%public_attributes%
%public_methods%
%protected_attributes%
%protected_methods%

%private_attributes%
%private_methods%
```

The order here is that the inner types will go first, then the public fields, public methods, protected fields, and so on, finishing with the private methods.

This explains how Visio arranged the code generated for our Employees class earlier.

Although we mentioned that these placeholders are actually built-in Visio macros, the Visio documentation states that it is not possible to redefine or extend the existing macros – a limitation as we'll see in a moment.

157

There are other placeholders that can be used in templates:

Placeholder	Description
%comments%	Inserts the text in the Documentation field as comments, prefixed by the language-specific comment symbol, and appends a newline to the text
%package_name%	The name of the package
%attrib_name%	The name of the attribute
%type_name%	Applied to an attribute, it returns the attribute's type, or a operation's return type when applied to an operation
%method_name%	The name of the method
%method_body%	The code for the method body
%parameters%	The parameters for the method
%params_and_comments%	The parameters and their associated comments
%date%	The date the code is generated on
%author_name%	The name of the author of the UML model

Notice that some of these placeholders are "scoped" to a particular UML entity – for example, using %attrib_name% on an operation template will simply produce %attrib_name% in the output code.

Before we get any deeper into looking at these placeholders, let's see how we can apply specialized templates.

Templates for Specific Entities

You can apply a specific template to a particular method. We'll demonstrate this with our ChangeSalary() method. Go to its UML Operation Properties dialog and select the Code Generation Options entry from the Implementation drop-down, and select the existing template MethodImpl1.

The MethodImpl1 template looks like the following:

```
//
// METHOD:
//    %method_name%
// DESCRIPTION:
//    %comments%
```

```
// PARAMETERS:
//    %params_as_comments%
// RETURN:
//    %type_name%
//
%visibility% %type_name% %method_name%(%mark_indent%
%indent%%params%
%indent%)
{
    %method_body%
}
```

When we click **Preview code**, we can see the effect of this template. The diagram below shows the preview code with the relevant parts of the template marked:

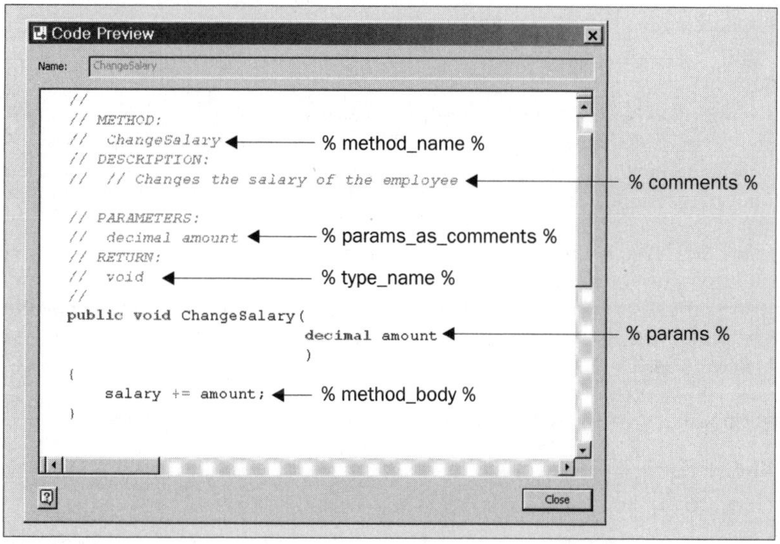

Notice how the %comments% placeholder has insisted on including // with the comments, and a blank line. Rather frustratingly, it does not just display the text from the Documentation field.

The indenting is controlled by the %mark_indent% and %indent% keywords. %mark_indent% specifies the location in the line to indent to (the position of the first % being the location), and %indent% indents the code to this point in the line.

After this, we can generate the code. In the newly-generated code only the ChangeSalary() method has changed since it is the only entity that has a different template specified for it.

With this process, you can combine templates for changing the source code format. Visio usually goes from the bottom up applying templates. This means that when it is generating say, a method, it first checks if there is a specific template for that particular method. If there is, Visio will use that bottom-level template; if there isn't, Visio will use the template specified by the code generation properties for the whole project.

Creating New Templates

Although it may not have been clear initially, with code templates in Visio there is the possibility of doing more than simply arranging the class members in a particular order. We are able to enter any characters into a template, in particular – actual code. It is this, combined with the placeholders that provides Visio's code templates with powerful possibilities as we shall see.

In Visio, there are two ways to create a new, custom template:

❑   Create a new template from scratch

❑   Edit an existing template

Creating a new template is easy – choose the **Code Templates** entry in the **Preferences** dialog window, select the type of template you want to create in the **Categories** drop-down and press the **New** button. After this, a new window with an empty text box will be activated for creating a new template, into which you enter your template code.

It is probably easier to create a template based on an existing one, rather than starting completely from scratch. This is easy too – go to the **Code Templates** entry in the **Preferences** dialog window, select the type of template you want to copy in the **Categories** drop-down and press the **Duplicate** button. This will open a new window with a copy of the selected template, and a new name for the template at the top of the window.

The screenshot below shows the modifications we'll make to the default template:

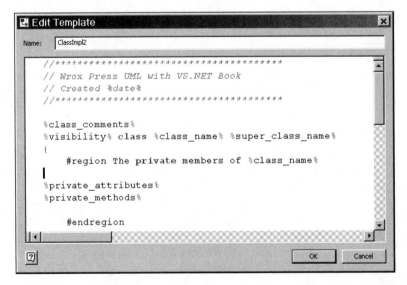

Note the use of %date% to include the current date, and the #region directive before the private members. This illustrates our observation earlier that we are able to include actual code in our templates, not just the placeholders.

Click OK to accept the new template. To edit a particular template, simply select it and click Edit from the Preferences dialog.

You can also Delete templates from here – if you delete a template by mistake, click Cancel and then select UML | Code | Preferences to restore your deleted template.

To test our new template, double-click the Employees class and from Code Generation Options, select ClassImpl2 from the Implementation drop-down in the Class Template section, and then click OK. When this code is generated, and then opened in Visual Studio .NET, the private members are enclosed in a collapsible block thanks to the #region directive, and collapsing that region produces the following:

```
using System;
//*****************************************
// Wrox Press UML with VS.NET Book
// Created 19 October 2002
//*****************************************


public class Employee    : Person
{|
        The private members of Employee
```

In this way of adding code to the code templates we are able to add extra features to our classes, fields, and methods that may not form part of the UML model. For example, if we require that the state of the Employee class be transmitted and later recreated, we would want the Employee class to be serializable – this is done by marking the class with the (.NET) attribute [Serializable]. This is easy to add to a class-level template:

```
%class_comments%
[Serializable]
%visibility% class %class_name% %super_class_name%
{
```

Thus the possibilities offered for fleshing out the skeleton code through code templates become more apparent. However, bear in mind that the code will have to be fleshed out by hand anyway when it is generated, and the more information that you pile into templates the more it ties you to the eventual implementation language, and it is not really contributing to the overall accuracy of your UML model.

The placeholders available for use with code templates are somewhat limited – however, if you wanted to generate properties prepopulated, you could use the following shortcut. Suppose you have a private field called number that you wish to expose by a Number property. You could define a new operation called Number, with its Kind set to Procedure from the Code Generation Options menu. For its method body, you would simply enter number. Apply the following template:

```
%visibility% %type_name% %method_name%
{
   get
   {
      return %method_body%;
   }
   set
   {
      %method_body% = value;
   }
}
```

and you would have a ready-made property, with filled get and set accessors:

```
public int Number
{
   get
   {
      return number;
   }
   set
   {
      number = value;
   }
}
```

This is a sneaky little example, but if you are determined to leverage as much as possible from code templates then it can pay to experiment with them in such a way.

In fact, using templates with properties is somewhat problematic. You'll find that if you want to create a template for properties, you'll have to create one with both get and set accessors, and a separate one if you want only a get accessor, and select the operation kind as procedure and manually choose the required template.

If you are a C# user, there is another interesting use for code templates.

XML Comments and Code Templates

For C# source files, Visual Studio .NET can automatically generate documentation in XML format, through the presence of XML tags in your source code. Text that is to be processed into XML documentation is provided in special comments with three slashes, rather than the usual two. You can create your own code template with such inserted XML tags. Thus there is a chain:

> **UML modeling provides the code, with inserted XML tags providing the documentation.**

Before trying to create such templates, let's have a look at some of the XML tags – a complete list is found in the Visual Studio .NET documentation.

Tag	Description
`<c>`, `<code>`	Each of these tags shows that text inside the element should be marked as code
`<example>`	Marks the text as an example of code for considered component
`<exception>`	Marks the exceptions, which can appear during the working cycle
`<list>`	Used for insertion of the list into the documentation
`<param>`	Describes the parameter
`<paramref>`	Links XML tag with particular parameter
`<permission>`	Provides information about access permissions to some class member
`<remarks>`	Used for defining the descriptions of particular members of the class
`<returns>`	Describes the value returned by method
`<see>`	Makes a hyperlink in a description
`<seealso>`	The tag is used for referencing another element in the documentation/code
`<summary>`	Creates the description of any element of the class
`<value>`	Defines the description of some property

Now that we've seen the tags used for creating internal documentation, let's create some templates to include such tags. We'll begin with a class-level template:

```
%class_comments%
/// <summary>
/// %comments%
/// </summary>
%visibility% class %class_name% %super_class_name%
{
    %private_attributes%
    %private_methods%

    %public_methods%
    %public_attributes%

    %protected_attributes%
    %protected_methods%

    %innerclasses%
}
%end_class_comments%
```

Of course, we also need `MethodImpl` templates for the methods and properties. The example for the method is listed below.

```
///<summary>
///   %comments%
///</summary>
///<param name=%params%></param>
///  <returns>%type_name%</returns>
%visibility% %type_name% %method_name%(%mark_indent%
%indent%%params%
%indent%)
{
    %method_body%
}
```

Finally, we will create new templates for the existing properties – we'll create two, XmlGetSetProperty, with get and set accessors, and XmlGetProperty, with only a get accessor. Here's XmlGetSetProperty:

```
///<summary>
/// %comments%
///</summary>
///  <returns>%type_name%</returns>
%visibility% %type_name% %method_name%
{
    get
    {
    }
    set
    {
    }
}
```

If we apply these templates to the various parts of our Employee example (and add some more documentation), then generate code into a new Visual Studio .NET **Empty Project**, the generated code in Employees.cs will look like the following:

```
/// <summary>
/// // Represents an employee

/// </summary>
    // Represents an employee

public class Employee     : Person
{

...

///<summary>
/// // Returns the employee ID

///</summary>
///  <returns>int</returns>
public int ID
{
```

```
        get
        {
        }
}

///<summary>
/// // Returns the current salary of the employee

///</summary>
/// <returns>decimal</returns>
public decimal Salary
{
    get
    {
    }
}
///<summary>
/// // Returns the current salary of the employee

///</summary>
/// <returns>decimal</returns>
public DateTime HireDate
{
    get
    {
    }
    set
    {
    }
}
///<summary>
/// // Changes the salary of the employee

///</summary>
///<param name=decimal amount></param>
/// <returns>void</returns>

public void ChangeSalary(
                decimal amount
                )
{
    salary += amount;
}
```

The main thing to note here is how awkward the formatting of the comments is – there's a blank line following each comment. With this blank line, the XML documentation process will not produce the desired output. However, this formatting problem is not insurmountable, a simple find and replace in the Employees.cs file in Visual Studio .NET will remove the problem. The screenshot below shows the Replace dialog from Visual Studio .NET with the settings required to remove our extra-line plague:

From Visual Studio .NET we can now generate the XML documentation, by selecting the project in the Solution Explorer and choosing Properties. After that, you need to select Configuration Properties, and enter the name of the file for outputting the XML comments into the XML Documentation file field. When the solution is compiled, the corresponding XML file will be automatically updated.

Alternatively, you can generate comment web pages from Tools | Build Comment Web Pages – this option does not require the project to actually compile, and if all you have is skeleton code, then it is likely that your project will not compile as-is anyway. Here's a look at our quick go at producing comment web pages for our Employee class:

Enhancing the Model

The example we've just looked at illustrated how to generate code from a UML model. However, it is a very simplistic class. We need to work a bit harder to generate code for more sophisticated models.

In this section we'll take a closer look at using Visio to generate the basic constructs that we will use constantly in applications. In particular, we'll look at the following:

❑ Making associations automatically map into what you need in code

❑ Creating an enumeration

❑ Creating a collection and an indexer

❑ Creating events and delegates

In our discussion we will use C# terminology, but most of the things we are talking about can easily be interpreted for Visual Basic .NET.

Let's begin by creating an enumeration, EmployeeType, that will hold information about the employee's role. To create the enumeration, drag a DataType shape onto the page, and select its properties. Set the name to EmployeeType and the stereotype to enumeration. After selecting this stereotype, you can insert the values for the enumeration from the Enumeration entry of the UML Datatype Properties dialog. The literal value for a member of the enumeration can be explicitly specified from here, or the value can be left blank and it will be created by the language compiler when the code is generated and later compiled.

Our enumeration will have three values, and a preview of the generated code will look like this:

```
// Static Model

public enum EmployeeType
{
    Manager,
    Developer,
    CustomerSupport
}
```

Mapping Associations

Let us consider different types of associations that perform the links between objects. In our test model we have utilized the Visio features to show the links between objects.

Every association has two association ends. Double-clicking the association allows you to edit the association properties:

By editing the parameters of these ends, you can change the code generation process. The End Name of each end shows the member name for this association. If you have an association between Class A and Class B say, then setting the parameters for the Class A end will affect the code generation for Class B, and vice versa. The IsNavigable checkbox for each association end defines whether to show the end of the association in code – if the checkbox is checked, then it will be shown. From this dialog you are also able to define the aggregation type, the visibility, and the multiplicity

We'll link the EmployeeType to the Employee class by means of a composite aggregation from the Aggregation drop-down – if you try to connect the datatype with the class by means of any other association, Visio will show a semantic error:

End Name	Aggregation	Visibility	Multiplicity	IsNavigable	
End1	composite	private	1	☐	
employeeRole	none	private	1	☑	

Here End1 is attached to Employee, and End2 (renamed to employeeRole) is attached to EmployeeType. By the rule above, there will be an employeeRole field of type EmployeeType added to the generated code for Employee.

We also add an EmployeeRole property of type EmployeeType to expose the employeeRole field. A preview of the code generated looks like this:

```
private EmployeeType employeeRole;

public EmployeeType EmployeeRole
{
    get
```

```
      {
      }
      set
      {
      }
   }
```

If using the composite association with the **Composition** shape, **employeeRole** will be shown in the **Employee** class with any value of the **IsNavigable** parameter.

Creating a Collection

We'll create a new class called **Employees**. This class will maintain a collection of **Employee** objects, and will have an indexer that returns a particular employee given their ID number. We won't go through the full design of this class, we'll concentrate on the collection and indexer aspects.

Let's begin by creating a class called **Employees**, and create a new attribute called **employees**. Here we come to something really interesting. We will modify the multiplicity of this attribute and Visio will automatically generate a member with a collection type for us.

From the **UML Attributes Properties** dialog of the employees attribute, select 0..* from the **Multiplicity** drop-down. Now if you go to **Code Generation Options** and select **Preview code** you will see how this attribute will coded:

```
private System.Collections.ArrayList phoneNumbers;
```

We also need to add a `System.Collections.ArrayList` type, so that we can specify the type of attribute in the **UML Class Properties** dialog. To do this, right-click on **C# Data Types** in the Model Explorer, and select **New | Datatype**. Enter the name **System.Collections.ArrayList** in the dialog that is launched and click **OK**. After this, you will be able to work with collection type attributes.

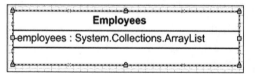

Creating an Indexer

Now for our indexer. Create a new operation, call it **this** – although it can take any name, Visio inserts the word `this` into the output code, and Visio also suggests that indexers should be called **this**. From the **UML Operation Properties** screen, select the return type for this operation as **Employee**, and from the **Parameters** category, add a new in parameter of type **C# ::int** called **index**. From the **Code Generation Options** for this operation, select its **Kind** as **Indexer**. There are two checkboxes for an Indexer, for get and set accessors, but our indexer will only use the get accessor, so check that box. Clicking **Preview Code** shows the following:

```
public Employee this[int index]
{
   get
   {
   }
}
```

In fact, let's also add some code for the get accessor – from the **UML Operation Properties** dialog, select the **Method** category, check the **Has Method** checkbox to indicate code and enter the following:

```
foreach (Employee em in employees)
{
   if (em.ID == index)
      return em;
}

return null;
```

Now the entire read-only indexer will look like the following:

```
public Employee this[int index]
{
   get
   {
     foreach (Employee em in employees)
     {
         if (em.ID == index)
            return em;
     }
     return null;
   }
}
```

This indexer will allow us to access the list of employees with their ID. Of course, we'll need to add some more operations to the class for adding an employee to the **employees** collection, but we don't need to go into that now.

Creating Events and Delegates

Finally, we'll look at creating a delegate and an event. Firstly, we will create the **Task** class, and add an operation called TaskStatusUpdated to this class – we'll come back to its return type in a moment. The **Task** class will inform other object of its status. In a future version of the system managers may want to monitor how their employees are working – this could be easily implemented with the **Task** class and TaskStatusUpdated event

To define our TaskStatusUpdatedDelegate delegate, create a new class, and from the **Class** entry in the UML Class Properties dialog window select **delegate** item in the **stereotype** drop-down list. Create a new operation, and call it TaskStatusUpdated. These actions lead to the following generated code:

```
public delegate void TaskStatusUpdatedDelegate();
```

Now you have to link the delegate with the appropriate operation. This requires the return type of the TaskStatusUpdated operation in the **Task** class to be set to TaskStatusUpdatedDelegate. To define TaskStatusUpdated as an event, go to its **Code generation options** and select **Event** in the **Kind** drop-down list – a checkbox allows us to select add and remove event accessors.

Thus, we have established a link between the delegate and the corresponding event. The generated code for the **Task** class is listed below:

```
// Preview of code that will be generated in the implementation file:
public class Task
{

    public event TaskStatusUpdatedDelegate TaskStatusUpdated;

    public void UpdateTaskStatus()
    {

    }

}// END CLASS DEFINITION Task
```

Overriding Methods

Let's conclude this chapter with some information about abstract classes and virtual methods:

Action	Description
Create an abstract class	Check the IsAbstract checkbox in the Class entry of the UML Class Properties dialog
Create a sealed class	Check the IsLeaf checkbox in the Class entry of the UML Class Properties dialog
Create a virtual method	Check the IsPolymorphic checkbox in the UML Operation Properties dialog of the operation

This looks all very well, but rather disappointingly, if you intend to override some methods in your class, then you have to add the `override` keyword by hand, even if there is a direct connection to the superclass on the diagram, since Visio does not handle override methods.

There are many more examples of UML to C# (and VB.NET) mappings that we could cover – you can find them in the Visio documentation, but the best way to get to grips with Visio and its code generation features is to actually experiment yourself. For starters, open the Visio diagram we created in the previous chapter and look at the code that model produces!

Summary

In this chapter, we have looked at generating code from a UML model in Visio. We began with an overview of code generation, and how it offers the developer skeleton code from the UML model, and how the use of code templates offers fine-grained control over this implementation.

We created a simple `Employee` class, and as we added features to the class we had a look at the code that would be generated, and gained a good understanding of the UML to language mappings that Visio uses to generate your code.

We then went on to configure code-generation options and look at code templates. We saw how to create new and custom templates, some of the drawbacks of code templates, and looked at the possibility of using code templates to simplify the documentation process for our code, including the use of XML comments and comment web pages.

Code generation is a simple process and the material in this chapter can help you to simplify your work with Visio and use its simple, but powerful features.

In the next chapter we'll look at the reverse of this process – taking existing code and producing a UML model from that structure.

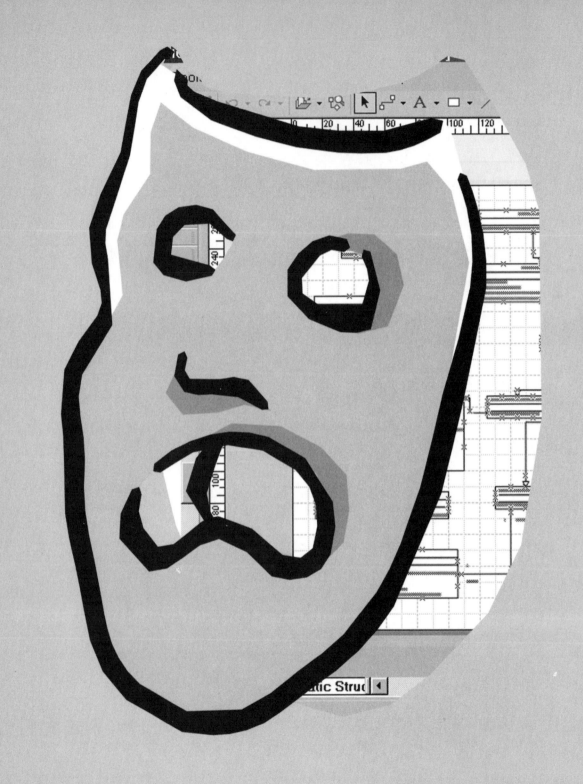

Reverse Engineering

The Visual Studio .NET Enterprise Architect and Visio for Enterprise Architects combination provides a facility for reverse engineering existing C#, VB.NET, or C++.NET source code into a Visio UML Static Structure model. In this chapter we'll look at the reverse engineering feature and you will discover the following:

❑   Why reverse engineering is useful

❑   How to reverse engineer .NET source code from within the Visual Studio .NET IDE

❑   The structure of a typical reverse-engineered Visio UML model

❑   The code-to-UML mappings for important constructs such as generalization (inheritance) and association

❑   How to use reflection to reverse engineer any compiled assembly written in any .NET language, with no source code required

Why Reverse Engineer?

We all know that you should design an application before coding, right? – if not all in one go then at least a bit at a time in some incremental fashion. The problem is, sometimes we're a bit lazy or – with the best of intentions – we like to prototype an idea in code before designing it formally. Furthermore, we might be interfacing with another team or a third party supplier that is not as disciplined as we are when it comes to up-front design, or we might simply have inherited a load of source code from the guy who has now left the company.

Regardless of the circumstances, we're likely to have a body of existing code that we'd like to somehow incorporate into our model.

Reverse Engineering from Source Code

In this section we'll look at how you can reverse engineer the source code of any .NET solution or project into a Visio UML model. Specifically, this section provides:

❑   A quick-start guide to invoking the reverse engineering feature

❑   A summary of the key features and limitations of reverse engineering

❑   A sample reverse engineered project, as a vehicle for discussing the resulting model structure

Later you will see a technique for reverse engineering an application for which you no longer have – or never did have – access to the source code.

Reverse Engineering QuickStart

Just select a project or an entire solution in the Visual Studio .NET Solution Explorer and then choose Project|Visio|UML, Reverse Engineer menu option as shown here.

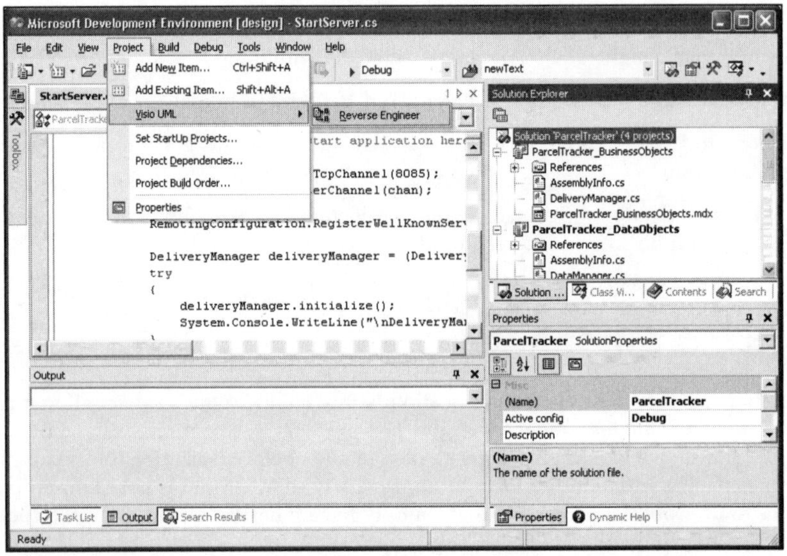

You'll be asked to give a name for the destination Visio (.vsd) file, before seeing the progress via a series of dialogs and a sequence of messages in the Visual Studio .NET Output window like this:

```
Performing pass number: 1.
Reverse engineering: ParcelTracker_DataObjects
Extracting information from...
     ParcelTracker_DataObjects
      DataManager
       ParcelTracker_DataObjects
        DeliveryDataSet
         DeliveryRowChangeEventHandler
         CustomerRowChangeEventHandler
          ...
Reverse engineering: ParcelTracker_BusinessObjects
Extracting information from...
     ParcelTracker_BusinessObjects
      DeliveryManager
Reverse engineering: ParcelTracker_Server
Extracting information from...
     ParcelTracker_Server
      StartServer
Reverse engineering: ParcelTracker_WindowsInterface
Extracting information from...
     ParcelTracker_WindowsInterface
      DeliveryDataForm

Performing pass number: 2.
Reverse engineering: ParcelTracker_DataObjects
Extracting information from...
     ParcelTracker_DataObjects
      ...
Reverse engineering: ParcelTracker_BusinessObjects
Extracting information from...
     ParcelTracker_BusinessObjects
      ...
Reverse engineering: ParcelTracker_Server
Extracting information from...
     ParcelTracker_Server
      ...
Reverse engineering: ParcelTracker_WindowsInterface
Extracting information from...
     ParcelTracker_WindowsInterface
      ...

Number of warnings: 0.

Exporting UML model to Visio...

Reverse engineering succeeded.
```

Visio will be launched automatically and as the information is imported, another series of dialogs will report the progress. The end result will be a new set of classes – in the Visio Model Explorer – which you can drag onto any Static Structure Diagram. For illustration, in the following figure I have dragged a `DeliveryManager` class from the Model Explorer onto a Static Structure Diagram.

That was your quick-start guide, which will get you up and running in the shortest possible time. Of course there's more to it than that, and we'll dig deeper as you read on. Let's start by looking at some of the key features and limitations of this toolset, which set it apart from the other reverse engineering tools that you may have used before.

Key Features and Limitations of Reverse Engineering

The reverse engineering facility is very useful, but not perfect, so now I'll state up-front some of the key features and limitations.

Reverse Engineering Granularity

Although you initiate the reverse engineering process from within Visual Studio .NET, the help documentation for reverse engineering is accessed via the Help menu in Visio. According to that documentation you can choose the reverse engineering granularity such that:

> *"The selections you make in the Visual Studio **Solution Explorer** determine what is reverse engineered to the Visio UML."*

Taking that to its logical conclusion you might expect to be able to select an individual source file for reverse engineering, or an individual class from the Class View. From Visual Studio .NET you can select a source file or a single class in the Solution Explorer, then invoke the reverse engineer, but you will still end up with the entire project (not the entire solution) in Visio.

> **The division into projects within a Solution will determine the granularity for reverse engineering.**

Semantic Errors

If you have semantic error checking turned on in Visio you may see a series of error messages in the Visio Output Window of this kind:

An interface cannot be used as the type of a parameter.

or:

No behavioral feature of the same kind may have the same signature in a classifier.

According to the Visio UML documentation such errors occur when the resulting model breaks certain rules of the UML 1.2 specification. All you need to provoke that kind of error is a method definition like this:

```
public System.Collections.IEnumerator GetEnumerator()
{
    return this.Rows.GetEnumerator();
}
```

It doesn't look too bad, does it? What's more it wasn't written by a human, rather it was generated automatically by Visual Studio .NET in the process of converting an XML schema into a .NET `DataSet`.

Unless we're reverse engineering an application with a view to re-engineering it we can't really attempt to fix such problems. If we did, our UML model would not be a representation of the original code. As the .NET Framework itself contains such method definitions those errors could appear more frequently than you think.

So if we ought not to fix these problems, and if they'll appear more frequently than we would like, what can we do? Well, we can hide the messages by un-checking the **Check semantic errors on UML model element** option of the UML | Options dialog.

Of course, when designing a new application we have an opportunity to avoid such problems from the outset.

Static Structure Diagrams

When the reverse engineering has completed you will notice that the Model Explorer is populated with the reverse engineered classes, as we saw in a previous screenshot, but they do not appear automatically on any static structure diagrams. In fact, the only reason the `DeliveryManager` class appears on a diagram in the previous figure is because I dragged it from the Model Explorer onto that diagram.

If you're new to reverse engineering, that might be a little disappointing but it's pretty much the same story for most UML modeling tools. The fact is that static structure (namely class) diagrams represent **views** onto the underlying static model. You might want a view that represents the classes of a particular package, or those classes that participate in a particular package, or a super-view of every class in the model. The tool has no way of knowing what you want to appear on the diagrams, so it doesn't draw them for you.

That has an important implication – Visio EA is a little peculiar in that an association exists between two classes **only if that association is drawn on at least one diagram**. No diagrams means no associations in the reverse-engineered model, so when reverse engineering from code that you have previously generated you will not necessarily finish up with a replica of your original model – this is one reason why round-trip engineering is not really feasible.

> *You won't have lost any information as such because the associations will still be represented by member variables within the associated classes. All inheritance (generalization) relationships will have been preserved and will be drawn automatically on static structure diagrams.*

Round-trip Engineering

Many tools claim to offer round-trip engineering – the ability to generate code from a UML model, modify the code in your IDE, and then reverse engineer the changes back into your original model. In a very loose sense you can round-trip engineer with this toolset. That is to say that you can generate a Visual Studio .NET solution from a Visio UML model, and then reverse engineer that solution back into a Visio UML model.

The problem is that you can reverse engineer into a new model, but crucially not back into the **same** model, which defeats the objective. Furthermore, if you go on to do a new round of code generation from your model you will find that you'll get new skeleton code with none of your original method implementations included.

Although I find code generation and reverse engineering both to be very useful individually, in my experience round-trip engineering is somewhat overrated by tools vendors. It's quite a difficult trick to pull off, requiring sophisticated synchronization techniques, often with the extra step of marking up of the code with special tags. Also, the process is not helped by the fact that an arbitrary number of changes may be made in the model or in the code before the user next chooses to generate code or reverse engineer.

> *More recently a different approach has been taken, in which the UML modeling tool and the code IDE are combined into a single environment. The UML model and the code are kept synchronized at all times, with no separate code generation and reverse engineering phases as such. This is true of Together Control Center (for Java) and Rational XDE (for .NET).*

Projects that Don't Compile

Because the reverse engineering works directly from source code (see below) it's not necessary that your project fully compiles before attempting to reverse engineer. This could be very useful in those situations where you want a UML representation of a partial project or solution. Of course, there is a Garbage-In-Garbage-Out factor to consider here – there may be good reasons why your project does not compile and the resulting UML model will only be as good as the code you feed in.

> *Towards the end of this chapter you will see an example of what happens if your solution does not reference all of the required assemblies.*

Source Code Required

Some other UML visual modeling tools allow you to reverse engineer from source code (for example Java `.java` files) or from compiled code (such as Java `.class` or `.jar` files). Visual Studio .NET is limited to reverse engineering from source code and there is no obvious way to reverse engineer an already-compiled .NET **assembly**. I do have a solution to that problem, which I'll share with you towards the end of this chapter.

One effect of that restriction is that it's not easy to get the .NET Framework classes themselves into a UML model in Visio; again this contrasts with other tools that often incorporate, for example, the Java runtime classes. This can be quite a limitation, because it means the attribute types, parameter types, and associations in a new Visio UML model are restricted to the C#, Visual Basic.NET, or C++ .NET fundamental language types – remember in Chapter 3 when we had to add the `System.Data.DataSet` class to our Visio diagram by hand? Once more, there's a solution to this problem later in this chapter.

I used the phrase "new Visio UML model" in the previous paragraph to mean one that you've constructed up-front without reverse engineering. That's because my claim about the lack of .NET Framework classes is not entirely true for a reverse-engineered model. Any .NET Framework classes that are referenced in your code – for example via inheritance – will be reverse engineered into the model. This is limited to those classes that are explicitly referenced in code, and the resulting UML classes will be included by name only. We'll look more at this topic later in this chapter.

Reverse Engineering Example

In the download code for this chapter there is a Visual Studio .NET solution that we'll use as a test case for reverse engineering. The solution name is `ParcelTracker`, and from that name you'll have guessed that the application was originally intended as a simulation of the kind of system that might be used by UPS, TNT, ParcelForce (in the UK), or any other national or international package delivery company.

For our purposes here it matters very little what this application actually does, because we won't be looking in detail at how it works or even running it. What is most important is that the application is sufficiently complex to be a credible test case for reverse engineering.

From a design point of view the application is divided into three layers, each layer corresponding with a separate project within the `ParcelTracker` solution. The layers are:

❑   Windows Interface Layer (in project `ParcelTracker_WindowsInterface`)

❑   Business Objects Layer (in project `ParcelTracker_BusinessObjects`)

❑   Data Objects Layer (in project `ParcelTracker_DataObjects`)

There is an additional project called `ParcelTracker_Server` that contains an executable program that would start up the server aspect of the application.

In terms of .NET coverage this application was designed to make use of Windows Forms, Remoting, and a `DataSet` that uses XML for persistent storage.

Reverse Engineering the ParcelTracker Application

The steps for reverse engineering the sample application are as described in the *Reverse Engineering from Source Code* section earlier in this chapter. To recap:

❑   Open the solution `ParcelTracker.sln` in Visual Studio .NET.

❑   Choose the menu option Project | Visio UML | Reverse Engineer.

As mentioned in the earlier *Semantic Errors* section, reverse engineering may result in the output window containing error messages of the form:

An interface cannot be used as the type of a parameter.

That's true for this application and it's also true when the .NET Framework class libraries themselves are reverse engineered, as described later. Since we're reverse engineering an existing application, we don't have the option of fixing the model to meet the UML 1.2 criteria as we would if we were designing from scratch; which leaves little alternative but to simply switch off the UML semantic checking.

Reverse-Engineered Model Structure

The `ParcelTracker` application is packaged as a solution containing multiple projects, as can be seen on the left-hand side of the following figure. The right-hand side of the figure shows the resulting UML model structure in Visio, as you would see in the Model Explorer.

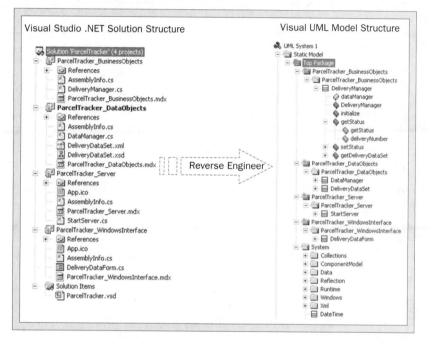

You can see that the **Top Package** (the default top-level package in Visio) contains four UML Subsystems (represented in the Model Explorer with pink-colored package icons). These subsystems are ParcelTracker_BusinessObjects, ParcelTracker_DataObjects, ParcelTracker_Server, and ParcelTracker_WindowsInterface corresponding with the four projects contained within the original solution.

> **Each project within a Visual Studio .NET solution is reverse engineered into a UML subsystem in the Visio model.**

You may wonder why a package with the same name appears within each subsystem. That's because this application has a package structure that reflects the project structure. Let's take the `DeliveryManager` class as an example – it is defined within the `ParcelTracker_BusinessObjects` package (thus falls within the subsystem of that name), and in addition, its definition specifies the class as being contained in the `ParcelTracker_BusinessObjects` namespace as you can see from looking at the code:

```
namespace ParcelTracker_BusinessObjects
{
    public class DeliveryManager : MarshalByRefObject
    {
```

Nested Classes

The `ParcelTracker` application contains some nested classes that are not apparent in the model structure shown in the previous figure. Consider the following code from the `DeliveryDataSet` class, which shows at least two classes – `DeliveryDataTable` and `DeliveryRow` – as having their definitions nested within the definition of the `DeliveryDataSet`.

```
namespace ParcelTracker_DataObjects
{
    ...
    public class DeliveryDataSet : DataSet
    {
        ...
        public class DeliveryDataTable : DataTable ...
        {
            ...
        }
        public class DeliveryRow : DataRow
        {
            ...
        }
```

To see those nested classes in the Visio Model Explorer you can simply expand the containing classes to expose their constituents, like this:

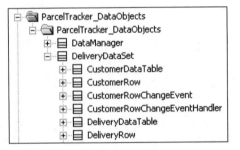

Referenced .NET Classes

Another interesting feature of the reverse engineered model structure is that a `System` package has been generated, with contained packages that reflect the namespace structure of the .NET Framework itself. We'll see later that Visio for Enterprise Architects does not provide a base .NET Framework model, and nor does it allow such a model to be reverse engineered without additional work, but the presence of these packages is explained by the fact that any .NET Framework classes that you refer to in your application – for example by inheriting from them – will be included in the reverse engineered model.

> However, the .NET Framework classes you refer to in your code are not populated with operations and attributes – only the class name is provided.

The sample application refers to certain classes from the `System.Data` namespace, and as you can see from the following figure those classes – and only those classes – have been included by name in the UML model structure.

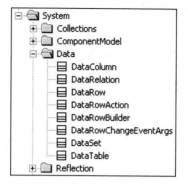

Code-to-UML Mapping Examples

In this section we'll look at the mapping between common code constructs and the corresponding UML notation. Each example will be in the context of the ParcelTracker sample application, so you'll be able to look for yourselves at the original code in Visual Studio .NET and the resulting UML in Visio.

All of the examples originate in C# code, which is not to imply that you must use this language. Unlike **code generation**, which results in a single UML concept being mapped to a slightly different code construct in each language, **reverse engineering** maps code constructs of the supported language – C#, Visual Basic .NET or C++.NET in our case – back to a single UML representation. In other words, although member variable declarations look different in C# and Visual Basic .NET the resulting UML **attribute** looks the same when reverse engineered.

The information presented here is intended to whet your appetite for looking deeper into the mapping between various code constructs and their UML representations; which you can do simply by coding a few classes in a Visual Studio .NET and looking and the reverse engineered results in Visio.

Generalization (or Inheritance)

The ParcelTracker_DataObjects project includes a class called DeliveryDataSet (in the namespace ParcelTracker_DataObjects) that inherits from the .NET System.Data.DataSet class. In code, the class definition is the following:

```
namespace ParcelTracker_DataObjects
{
    ...
    public class DeliveryDataSet : DataSet
    {
```

The reverse engineered model contains a DeliveryDataSet class (in the package ParcelTracker_DataObjects) and a DataSet class (in the package System | Data). Simply dragging those two classes onto a static structure diagram produces the following result:

Data::**DataSet**	**DeliveryDataSet**
	-tableDelivery : DeliveryDataTable
	-tableCustomer : CustomerDataTable
	-tableInvoiceAddress : InvoiceAddressDataTable
	-tableFromAddress : FromAddressDataTable
	-tableToAddress : ToAddressDataTable
	-tableStatusHistory : StatusHistoryDataTable
	-relationCustomer_InvoiceAddress : DataRelation
	-relationDelivery_Customer : DataRelation
	-relationDelivery_FromAddress : DataRelation
	-relationDelivery_ToAddress : DataRelation
	-relationDelivery_StatusHistory : DataRelation

+DeliveryDataSet()
#DeliveryDataSet(in info : SerializationInfo, in context : StreamingContext)
+Delivery() : DeliveryDataTable
+Customer() : CustomerDataTable
+InvoiceAddress() : InvoiceAddressDataTable
+FromAddress() : FromAddressDataTable
+ToAddress() : ToAddressDataTable
+StatusHistory() : StatusHistoryDataTable
+Clone() : DataSet
#ShouldSerializeTables() : bool
#ShouldSerializeRelations() : bool
#ReadXmlSerializable(in reader : XmlReader)
#GetSchemaSerializable() : XmlSchema
+InitVars()
-InitClass()
-ShouldSerializeDelivery() : boolShouldSerializeCustomer() : bool
ShouldSerializeInvoiceAddress() : bool
ShouldSerializeFromAddress() : bool
ShouldSerializeToAddress() : bool
ShouldSerializeStatusHistory() : bool
-SchemaChanged(in sender : object, in e : CollectionChangeEventArgs)

First you'll notice that a **generalization** (or inheritance) relationship has been drawn automatically between the two classes to show that DeliveryDataSet inherits from DataSet. I did not draw that in myself, it was already present in the reverse engineered model as a result of the inheritance between the two classes in code.

The second thing you'll notice is that the DeliveryDataSet is fully populated with attributes and operations whereas the DataSet is not. That's because the first class is defined in the solution that we've reverse engineered, whereas the second class is simply **referenced** via the inheritance in code. This is yet another illustration of the fact that the .NET Framework classes that are only referenced and not defined in the application will be reverse engineered into the resulting UML model by name only.

If you want to look into the code of the DeliveryDataSet class in Visual Studio .NET, you'll find that at first glance there is no source code file for it. That's because this class was not hand-coded but was auto-generated from an XML schema during the application design. To investigate the code, you can switch to the Class View in the IDE and click the DeliveryDataSet class as shown here:

Associations and Attributes

The following figure once again shows the `DeliveryDataSet` class from the previous example, this time combined on a static structure diagram with the `DataManager` class.

ParcelTracker_DataObjects::**DataManager**	ParcelTracker_DataObjects::**DeliveryDataSet**
-deliveryData : DeliveryDataSet	-tableDelivery : DeliveryDataTable -tableCustomer : CustomerDataTable -tableInvoiceAddress : InvoiceAddressDataTable -tableFromAddress : FromAddressDataTable -tableToAddress : ToAddressDataTable -tableStatusHistory : StatusHistoryDataTable -relationCustomer_InvoiceAddress : DataRelation -relationDelivery_Customer : DataRelation -relationDelivery_FromAddress : DataRelation -relationDelivery_ToAddress : DataRelation -relationDelivery_StatusHistory : DataRelation
+DataManager() +Initialize() +persist() +DeliveryDataSet() : DeliveryDataSet	+DeliveryDataSet() #DeliveryDataSet(in info : SerializationInfo, in context : StreamingContext) +Delivery() : DeliveryDataTable +Customer() : CustomerDataTable +InvoiceAddress() : InvoiceAddressDataTable +FromAddress() : FromAddressDataTable +ToAddress() : ToAddressDataTable +StatusHistory() : StatusHistoryDataTable +Clone() : DataSet #ShouldSerializeTables() : bool #ShouldSerializeRelations() : bool #ReadXmlSerializable(in reader : XmlReader) #GetSchemaSerializable() : XmlSchema +InitVars() -InitClass() -ShouldSerializeDelivery() : boolShouldSerializeCustomer() : bool ShouldSerializeInvoiceAddress() : bool ShouldSerializeFromAddress() : bool ShouldSerializeToAddress() : bool ShouldSerializeStatusHistory() : bool -SchemaChanged(in sender : object, in e : CollectionChangeEventArgs)

I can tell you that when I designed this application originally – using Visio for Enterprise Architects – I had an association drawn between the DataManager and DeliveryDataSet classes, yet in my figure (above) no association is shown between the reverse engineered classes. To see what I mean take a look at my original static structure diagram below, which was used to generate the application code initially according to the process described in Chapter 4.

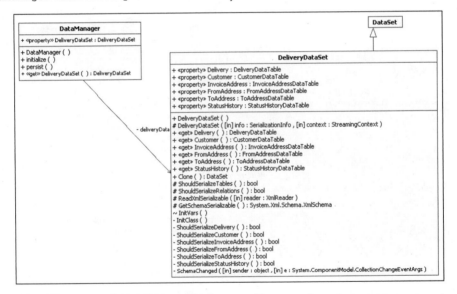

This reinforces the point we made earlier that a reverse-engineered model in Visio has no static structure diagrams initially, and in Visio **no diagrams means no associations**.

In contrast, a Rational XDE reverse engineered model would show an association between the DataManager and DeliveryDataSet classes as you can see here:

For the Visual Studio .NET and Visio combination we have seen here that reverse engineering is not an exact reversal of code generation. But no information has been lost in the sense that during code generation the association was mapped in code to a member variable of the DataManager class (-deliveryData : DeliveryDataSet), which is shown in the UML diagram and which corresponds with this code:

```
public class DeliveryManager : MarshalByRefObject
{
    private DataManager dataManager;
```

UML attributes are used therefore as an indication of associations between two classes, in the case that the type of an attribute is that of another class in the model. I can see why it makes sense to retain attribute representations of member variables, but not assume them to be associations, because otherwise it's difficult to see where the line should be drawn.

Given the following reverse engineered class definition in Visio, should the attribute -deliveryDataGrid : DataGrid be drawn automatically as an association between our DeliveryDataForm class and the .NET Framework DataGrid class?

```
ParcelTracker_WindowsInterface::DeliveryDataForm

-deliveryDataGrid : DeliveryDataGrid
+components : Container = null

+DeliveryDataForm()
#Dispose(in disposing : bool)
-InitializeComponent()
-Main()
```

Maybe not, because I'd like to treat .NET Framework classes – particularly classes like String – as fundamental types just as if the attribute type was a true fundamental type like int or bool, or even string (with no initial capital).

> *In my C# Today article "C# to UML Reverse Engineering"*
> *(http://www.csharptoday.com/content.asp?id=1837) I described a technique for reverse*
> *engineering a .NET assembly into a Rational Rose model. I chose to model a source code member*
> *variable as a simple attribute if the type was a fundamental C# type or a .NET Framework class,*
> *otherwise as an association to another class in the model. This was a halfway house between Visual*
> *Studio .NET and Visio (which maps all member variables to simple attributes) and Rational XDE*
> *(which forms associations for all member variables not of fundamental types).*

Regardless of whether the attribute represents a fundamental data element or an association, the Visio rendering will show the attribute preceded by -, +, or # according to whether the member variable was **private**, **public**, or **protected**.

Operations and Properties

In simple terms, operations – or methods – in code map to the operations of a class in UML, modified with a -, +, or # for the visibility and underlined if they are **static**, like this:

```
StartServer

-Main(in args : string[])
```

which corresponds to the code:

```
class StartServer
{
    [STAThread]
    static void Main(string[] args)
    {
```

But not all operations are the same; in Visio Enterprise Architect, an object **property** is also modeled as an operation. Looking back at the representation of the DataManager class (reproduced below) you may be surprised to learn that the DeliveryDataSet() operation actually represents a **property**. Surprised because there's nothing in that representation that explicitly marks it out as such.

```
ParcelTracker_DataObjects::DataManager

-deliveryData : DeliveryDataSet

+DataManager()
+Initialize()
+persist()
+DeliveryDataSet() : DeliveryDataSet
```

So how do I know that it's a property? Firstly, I know because I wrote the code and it looks like this!

```
public class DataManager
{
    private DeliveryDataSet deliveryData;
    ...

    public DeliveryDataSet DeliveryDataSet
    {
        get { return deliveryData; }
    }

}
```

Secondly I know because I can double-click the class in Visio, select the Operations category, click the DeliveryDataSet operation and press the Properties button, and then select the Code Generation Options category to give this dialog:

As you can see here, the operation has Kind set to **Property** and the **Create Get Method** option is checked. Looking back at the code above confirms that this operation does indeed have a `get()` method but no `set()` method.

Operations will normally have their Kind marked as **Procedure**. They may also be marked as **Property** (as you have seen), **Constructor**, **Destructor**, **Event**, **Indexer**, or **Operator** depending on what kind of code construct has been reverse engineered to yield the operation.

> *It's interesting to compare the Visio representation of properties with the Rational XDE representation shown earlier. In XDE the property is rendered as a combination of an attribute with <<property>> stereotype and an operation with <<get>> stereotype.*

Method Bodies

As we saw in the last chapter on the **UML Operation Properties** dialog you can click the **Method** entry and actually insert prototype code as the implementation for the operation.

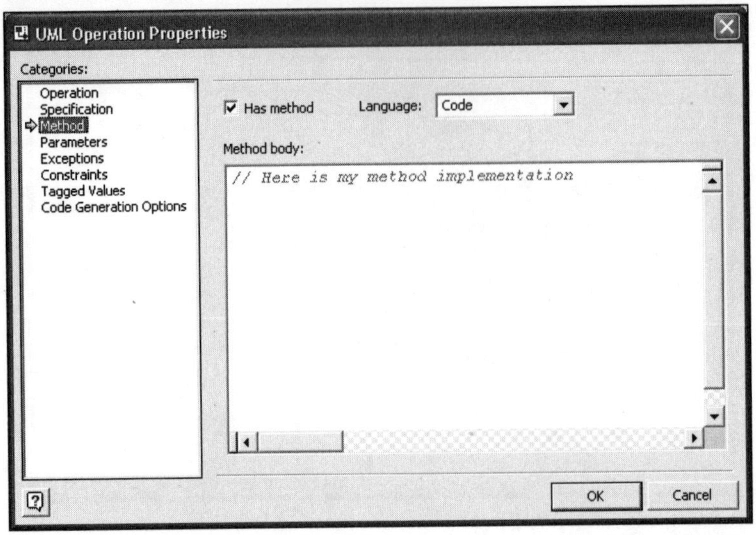

By pressing the Preview Code button in the UML Operation Properties (Code Generation Options) dialog you can then see that during code generation your prototype code – in this case just a comment – will be inserted into the body of the operation.

```
// Preview of code that will be generated in the implementation file:

public string getStatus(string deliveryNumber)
{
    // Here is my method implementation
}
```

As we're not dealing with code generation here, why am I telling you this? Well, I was hoping that this would work in reverse so that each reverse engineered operation would be populated with the implementing code. Sadly, no, so maybe that's one for the wish list.

Primitive and Value Types

For each of the primitive or value types for the Visual Studio .NET languages, there is a corresponding Visio UML type, pre-built into any Visio UML model as shown here:

```
Model Explorer                          □ ×
⊟ 🗀 C# Data Types                         ▲
    ├─ 目 bool
    ├─ 目 byte
    ├─ 目 char
    ├─ 目 decimal
    ├─ 目 double
    ├─ 目 float
    ├─ 目 int
    ├─ 目 long
    ├─ 目 object
    ├─ 目 sbyte
    ├─ 目 short
    ├─ 目 string
    ├─ 目 uint
    ├─ 目 ulong
    ├─ 目 ushort
    └─ 目 void
⊞ 🗀 C++ Data Types
⊞ 🗀 IDL Data Types
⊟ 🗀 VB Data Types
    ├─ 目 Boolean
    ├─ 目 Byte
    ├─ 目 Char
    ├─ 目 Date
    ├─ 目 Decimal
    ├─ 目 Double
    ├─ 目 Integer
    ├─ 目 Long
    ├─ 目 Object
    ├─ 目 Short
    ├─ 目 Single
    └─ 目 String                          ▼
◄                                    ►
```

Those pre-populated types are useful, but not sufficient in themselves; which is why it is necessary for the reverse engineer to incorporate referenced classes in a model, at least by name, and also why a base .NET Framework model (discussed later) would be so valuable.

Reverse Engineering, No Source Code Required

Visual Studio .NET allows you to reverse-engineer the source code for any project into a Visio for Enterprise Architects UML model. That's great if you have the source code available, but what if you don't? – and what if you're using a third-party library assembly and you'd like a representation of those third-party classes in your model? Taking this to its logical conclusion, wouldn't you like a UML representation of the .NET Framework classes themselves; simply to learn more about the framework or as the basis of your design models?

In this section we'll discuss the idea of reverse engineering from a compiled .NET assembly, with no source code required. In doing so we'll bring the functionality of the Visual Studio .NET and Visio for Enterprise Architects combination closer to that provided by other modeling tools.

> *For some time, Rational Rose has allowed Java programs to be reverse-engineered for compiled byte-code – in* `.class` *and* `.jar` *files – as well as from source code in* `.java` *files.*

Reverse engineering from a compiled assembly will be a two-stage process:

❑ Run the **RE.NET Lite** utility described below, which uses reflection to extract class definitions from the assembly and writes these out as C# source code.

❑ Use the Visual Studio .NET to Visio reverse engineering feature, described above, to transfer the C# source code class definitions into a Visio UML model.

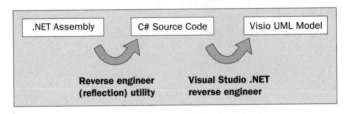

Running the RE.NET Lite Reverse Engineer

In the next section I'll take you through the source code for the RE.NET Lite software and I'll explain how it works. In this section I'll show you how to use it so that you can find out what it does before looking at the internals, or you may even skip the source code discussion altogether.

> This utility is a cut-down version of the RE.NET assembly-to-UML reverse engineering utility described at **http://www.lotontech.com/visualmodeling**.

The software we look at here is a command-line utility, ReverseEngineer.exe, whose complete source can be found in the download code. To run it you first need to launch a Visual Studio .NET command window by choosing the Windows option Start | All Programs | Microsoft Visual Studio .NET | Visual Studio .NET Tools | Visual Studio .NET Command Prompt.

At the command prompt type the command ReverseEngineer followed by the name of an assembly DLL (without the DLL extension), and redirect the output to a file with a .cs extension.

As an example we'll reverse engineer one of the assemblies from the ParcelTracker solution. With the DLL – ParcelTracker_DataObjects.dll – copied into the same directory as the ReverseEngineer program, we would enter the following from the command line:

```
ReverseEngineer ParcelTracker_DataObjects > ParcelTracker_DataObjects.cs
```

This command takes the assembly ParcelTracker_DataObjects.dll as input for reverse engineering, and redirects the results to a C# source file called ParcelTracker_DataObjects.cs.

> You can reverse engineer any assembly located in the global assembly cache or the application directory. In other words, this might be a DLL in directory C:\WINDOWS\Microsoft.NET\Framework\v1.0.3705 or a DLL that you have copied into the directory from which you launch the **ReverseEngineer** program.

The resulting C# source file contains definitions for the DataManager and DeliveryDataSet classes that are located in that assembly. Here we've formatted the output for easier reading:

```
namespace ParcelTracker_DataObjects
{
    public class DataManager : System.Object {}

}

namespace ParcelTracker_DataObjects
{
    public class DeliveryDataSet : System.Data.DataSet ,
                                   System.ComponentModel.IComponent,
                                   System.IDisposable,
                                   System.IServiceProvider,
                                   System.ComponentModel.IListSource,
                                   System.Xml.Serialization.IXmlSerializable,
                                   System.ComponentModel.ISupportInitialize,
                                   System.Runtime.Serialization.ISerializable {}
}
```

You might be intrigued by the multiple definitions of the same namespace in the code, one for each separate class. That does not adversely affect the next stage of the process, and it made the utility much easier to write.

The next stage is to load the source file into a Visual Studio .NET project and reverse engineer it as you would any other C# source code. The steps are:

❑   Launch Visual Studio .NET.

❑   Choose File | New | Project.

❑   On the New Project dialog select C# Projects | Empty Project.

❑   In the Solution Explorer, right-click the empty project and choose Add | Add Existing Item.

❑   Choose the reverse-engineered source code file.

At this point the contents of the Solution Explorer will look something like this:

Now choose Project | Visio UML | Reverse Engineer as described earlier in this chapter and you will be rewarded with a Visio model containing classes and interfaces from the assembly DLL plus any referenced classes from other namespaces.

You were probably expecting to see more of the .NET Framework classes in the Model Explorer, weren't you? The `System.Object` is there, but what about the `System.Data.DataSet` class from which the `DeliveryDataSet` inherits in our reverse-engineered source code?

Including the Required Assembly References

The earlier statement "...you will be rewarded with a Visio model containing classes and interfaces from the assembly DLL plus any **referenced classes from other namespaces**" deserves a closer look here. The fact is that when we included the reverse engineered source file in a new C# project we did not take the extra step of actually referencing the required assemblies, which means that the resulting model in Visio is incomplete and – in fact – the project compilation will fail with messages of the form:

> The type or namespace name 'Data' does not exist in the class or namespace 'System' (are you missing an assembly reference?)

By referencing the required assemblies in the project (see below) we can compile the solution in Visual Studio .NET and build a fully populated UML model in Visio.

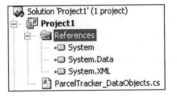

> **You must include references to the required assemblies in Visual Studio .NET if you want the project to compile and if you want a fully-populated model in Visio.**

Here is the final model structure comprising the two classes from the `ParcelTracker_DataObjects` project and the referenced classes from the other assemblies:

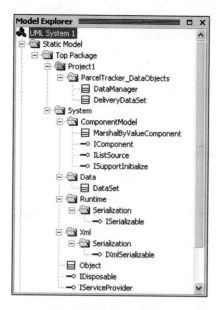

Dragging some of those classes onto a Static Structure Diagram serves to prove that the model contains the appropriate inheritance relationships.

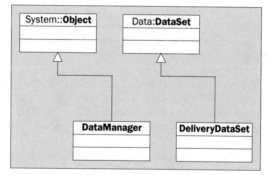

Creating a .NET Framework Base Model

You can reverse engineer any .NET assembly regardless of the origin, whether home grown or supplied by a third party. Although C# is used as an intermediate source code, this technique is not limited to assemblies that were implemented originally in the C# language. It works just as well for assemblies that were authored using any of the .NET languages.

With that in mind, you could easily use this technique to reverse engineer the .NET library assemblies themselves. But why is that so valuable?

Well, if you've ever used another UML modeling tool you'll know that these often come provided with base framework models for each of the languages that they support. Rational Rose comes supplied with UML representations of the Java API classes, and now Rational XDE includes UML representations of the .NET framework classes.

Visio for Enterprise Architects includes no such model of the .NET Framework classes, which to me seems something of an oversight. After all, many of the classes that compose your design model will inherit from the framework classes.

> **Using the RE.NET Lite utility you could create a base Visio UML model pre-populated with a subset of the .NET Framework classes.**

RE.NET Lite Internals

Now that we've seen the RE.NET Lite utility in action let's look at how it actually works. Well, it wouldn't work at all without a .NET feature called **Reflection**.

Reflection allows you to write programs that can load .NET assemblies dynamically and investigate the contents of those assemblies at run time. Investigating the contents means discovering what types (classes and interfaces) are included in the assembly, what other types they are related to (such as through inheritance), and what attributes, operations, and properties are defined for those types.

> *The RE.NET Lite utility uses refection to obtain information about the class structure of an assembly, and then reconstructs a class definition from this information. The definition produced can then be reverse engineered from Visual Studio .NET to obtain the Visio UML model.*

The source code for the RE.NET Lite assembly reverse engineering utility, listed next, has been kept as simple as possible to get you started with reflection purely in the context of reverse engineering into UML. If you'd like to dig deeper into reflection after reviewing this code you can refer to an article *Introducing .NET Regular Expressions with C#* at http://www.csharptoday.com/content.asp?id=1812, or take a look in *Professional C# 2nd Edition*, Wrox Press (ISBN 1-86100-704-3).

All of the code for this utility can be found within the file `ReverseEngineer.cs`, which is included in the download. In this first part we're referencing the `System.Reflection` namespace, which provides access to the .NET **reflection** features, and we're defining a class – named `ClassDefinition` – that will hold the details of each type that we encounter in an assembly.

```
// ************************************************
// ** RE.NET Lite Assembly Reverse Engineering **
// ** Produce by Tony Loton / LOTONtech Ltd.    **
// ** for Wrox Press, September 2002.           **
// ************************************************

using System;
using System.Reflection;

namespace reverse
{
    // ** This structure represents a Class or Interface
    // ** defined within the target assembly.
    public class ClassDefinition
    {
        public String name="";
```

```
        public bool interfaceFlag=false;
        public String visibility="";
        public bool abstractFlag=false;
        public String superClass="";
        public String interfaces="";
    }

    public class ReverseEngineer
    {
```

The `Main()` method is the entry point for this utility and is where we make use of reflection.

```
        // ** The main method is invoked from the Visual Studio .NET
        // ** command prompt with a command like:
        // ** C:> ReverseEngineer System.Data > System.Data.cs

        public static void Main(String[] args)
        {
            // ** We can specify more than one assembly in the command,
            // ** So step through each of them.

            foreach (String assemblyName in args)
            {
```

The next line of code loads an assembly from the Global Assembly Cache or the local directory thanks to a call to the static method `Assembly.LoadWithPartialName()`. As an alternative to this method you can load any assembly DLL by passing its full path, rather than the actual assembly name, to the `Assembly.LoadFrom()` method.

```
        Assembly sourceAssembly = Assembly.LoadWithPartialName(
                                                    assemblyName);
        if (sourceAssembly==null) return;

        // ** Get the Types (classes and interfaces) from the assembly
        // ** and step through them.
```

Next, we get a collection of the types contained within the assembly and step through them one by one, ignoring some of the .NET internal types that we won't be interested in.

```
        Type[] types=sourceAssembly.GetTypes();

        foreach (Type thisType in types)
        {
            ClassDefinition classDefinition=new ClassDefinition();

            // ** Ignore Types with the following names.

            if (thisType.Name.Equals("AssemblyRef")
              || thisType.Name.Equals("ExternDll")
              || thisType.Name.Equals("ThisAssembly")) continue;
```

If this type is an interface we discover the interface name and its visibility, both of which are stored in a `ClassDefinition` instance:

```
if (thisType.IsInterface)
{
    // ** We have found an Interface type.

    classDefinition.name=""+thisType;
    classDefinition.interfaceFlag=true;

    // ** Is it public visibility?

    if (thisType.IsPublic)
        classDefinition.visibility="public";
    else
        classDefinition.visibility="";
}
```

If this type is a class we discover the class name, the name of any super-class, and any `abstract` modifier for the class. We also use the `GetInterfaces()` method to return the interfaces implemented by the class. All of the information we discover is stored in a `ClassDefinition` instance.

```
else if (thisType.IsClass)
{
    // ** We have found a Class type.

        classDefinition.name=""+thisType;
        classDefinition.superClass=""+thisType.BaseType;

    // ** Is it abstract?

    if (thisType.IsAbstract)
        classDefinition.abstractFlag=true;
    else
        classDefinition.abstractFlag=false;

    // ** Is it public visibility?

    if (thisType.IsPublic)
        classDefinition.visibility="public";
    else
        classDefinition.visibility="";

    // ** Find out which interfaces this class implements.

    Type[] interfaces = thisType.GetInterfaces();
    int interfaceCount=0;
    foreach (Type thisInterface in interfaces)
    {
        if (interfaceCount!=0) classDefinition.interfaces
            =classDefinition.interfaces+", ";
        classDefinition.interfaces
            =classDefinition.interfaces+thisInterface;
```

```
                              interfaceCount++;
                }
        }
}
```

Regardless of what type we've just investigated – interface or class – we'll have the details of that type within a `ClassDefintion`. To print out that class (or interface) definition as C# source code we'll call a separate method called `printSource()`.

```
                // ** Print the C# source code for this class definition.
                printSource(classDefinition);
        }
    }
}
```

We're using the C# language as a bridge between the assembly contents and the Visual Studio .NET reverse engineering feature. The following method will print out any class or interface definition as C# source code.

```
        // ** This method writes out a class or interface definition
        // ** as C# source code.

        public static void printSource(ClassDefinition classDefinition)
        {
            // ** If the class name contains any unwanted characters or
            // ** is of zero length then return.

            int nameLength=classDefinition.name.Length;
            if (nameLength<=0) return;
            if (classDefinition.name.IndexOf("+")>=0) return;
            if (classDefinition.name.IndexOf(">")>=0) return;
            if (classDefinition.name.IndexOf("<")>=0) return;
```

At this point we're sure we have a class or interface with a valid name that will compile. We need to separate the namespace from the fully qualified class name and write it out as code:

```
            // ** Extract the namespace from the full class name.

            int lastDotPos=classDefinition.name.LastIndexOf(".");
            String nameSpace="";
            if (lastDotPos>0)
            {
                nameSpace = classDefinition.name.Substring(0,lastDotPos);

                classDefinition.name=classDefinition.name.Substring(
                                lastDotPos+1, nameLength-lastDotPos-1);
            }

            // ** Write out the namespace source code.

            if (nameSpace.Length>0)
            {
                System.Console.WriteLine("namespace "+nameSpace);
                System.Console.WriteLine("{");
            }
```

Next, we begin the reconstruction of the class definition – we first write out its visibility, whether it's an interface or a class, and then the class name:

```
// ** Write out the class visibility.

System.Console.Write("     "+classDefinition.visibility+" ");

// ** Write out the "class" or "interface" keyword.

if (classDefinition.interfaceFlag)
    System.Console.Write("interface ");
else
    System.Console.Write("class ");

// ** Write out the class name.

System.Console.Write(classDefinition.name+" ");
```

Next we add the name of the class that our class inherits from (if any), followed by the list of interfaces it implements:

```
bool firstInheritance=true;

// ** Write out the superclass name if there is one,
// ** and set the firstInheritance flag.

if (classDefinition.superClass.Length>0)
{
    System.Console.Write(": "+classDefinition.superClass+" ");
    firstInheritance=false;
}

// ** Write out the names of any implemented interfaces.

if (classDefinition.interfaces.Length>0)
{
    if (firstInheritance) System.Console.Write(": ");
    else System.Console.Write(", ");

    System.Console.Write(classDefinition.interfaces+" ");
}
```

Finally, we write out a blank class body, and finish off the display of the namespace with a closing curly brace.

```
// ** Write out a blank class body.
System.Console.WriteLine("{}");
if (nameSpace.Length>0) System.Console.WriteLine("\n}");

        }
    }
}
```

If you decide to adapt the code above for your own purposes you can recompile it by issuing the following command from the Visual Studio .NET Command Prompt.

```
>csc ReverseEngineer.cs
```

As a reminder, you can run the utility against the DLL you wish to reverse engineer, say the supplied ParcelTracker_DataObjects.dll assembly, by issuing the following command:

```
>ReverseEngineer ParcelTracker_DataObjects > ParcelTracker_DataObjects.cs
```

RE.NET Lite Limitations

The output from this version of the utility is useful as it stands, as a way to get basic representations of assembly classes – including the .NET Framework classes – into a Visio model; simply to visualize the assembly contents, or to inherit from those classes and interfaces.

Using the supplied source code as a basis you could devise an even better reverse engineering utility that makes use of reflection down to the level of **methods**, **fields** and **properties**. In addition to inheriting from the reverse engineered classes, you could call the methods on those classes as part of your design-level use case realizations as shown here:

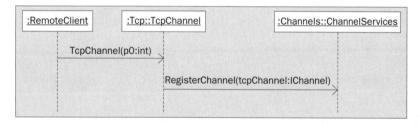

If you don't want to do the hard work yourself, you can find an enhanced version of the RE.NET utility – which addresses these limitations – at http://www.lotontech.com/visualmodeling.

Summary

This chapter began by noting why a reverse engineering feature is useful at all – for whatever reason, it's likely that we'll have some existing code that we'd like to incorporate into our Visio UML model.

Next we looked at how the source code of any Visual Studio .NET solution could be reverse engineered into a Visio UML model, and discussed some of the key features and limitations of this reverse engineering facility. In particular, the location of the relevant help documentation, the reverse engineering granularity, the fact that static structure diagrams are not drawn automatically, and the limited extent to which round-trip engineering is possible.

We looked at an example VS.NET solution, and used it to investigate the following:

❑   The reverse-engineered model structure

❑   Some of the important mappings between code constructs and UML notation

In the second half of the chapter we discussed a technique for reverse engineering any compiled .NET assembly – **no source code required**. This technique helps to bring Visual Studio .NET and the Visio EA reverse engineering feature closer to the standard set by other UML modeling tools, like Rational Rose, which provides for reverse engineering of compiled Java byte-code (`.class` files) as well as source code (`.java` files).

The technique is even more valuable when you consider that it allows any third-party library to be reverse engineered, so that you can show your usage of those third-party classes in your UML design model. Taking this to its logical conclusion, it opens up the possibility of starting any UML project with a base model containing representations of the .NET Framework classes themselves.

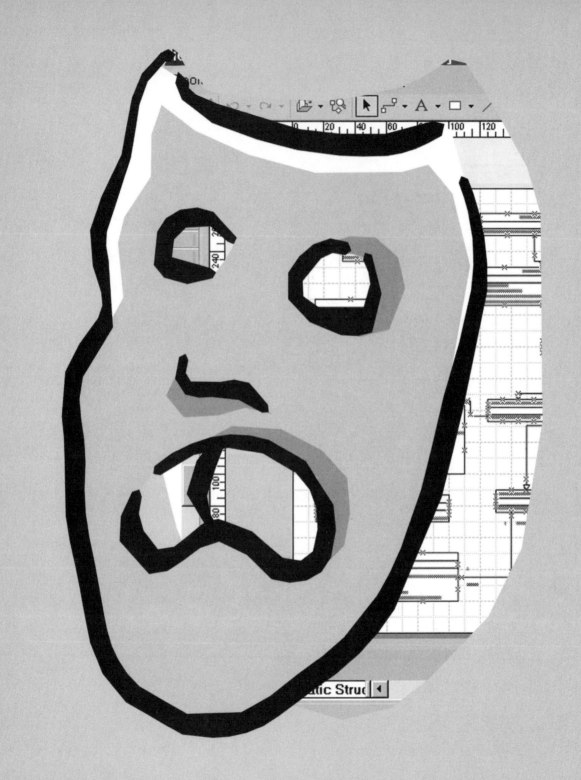

Documenting the Project

Throughout this book, we've seen detailed examples of using Visio and UML in various development scenarios. The purpose of this chapter is to take a step back and look at the role of Visio and UML in the entire software development lifecycle. In effect, we'll be discussing how we document our work at different stages of a typical development project using Visio and UML. Most developers know from first hand experience that participating in a development project or even managing that project requires us to play different roles as a project progresses from requirements through design and coding and into production. As many readers already understand, the role and types of UML artifacts we produce also change as a project matures. Hopefully, at the end of this chapter you'll take away some additional insights into using Visio and UML in the course of working on your own projects.

Here are the goals for this chapter:

❏   Define typical project stages in the software development lifecycle and the role of UML artifacts at each stage.

❏   Illustrate the creation and use of UML diagrams and provide some insights regarding their use at each project stage.

❏   Illustrate the interaction of early project stage documentation with users and needs in later stages.

❏   Provide a set of sample Visio UML documents that can be adapted for future development work.

So here's how the discussion will unfold. We'll review the major stages of a typical development project, their basic purpose, and their outcomes and how those outcomes flow into subsequent steps. Then we'll jump right into discussing each project stage in some detail including the needs of each stage, the needs of the users in each stage and how Visio and the UML fulfill those needs. Along the way, we cover the most common UML diagrams, their construction, and some Visio-specific details.

In terms of the UML, here are the diagrams we will encounter again:

❑   Use Cases

❑   Class Diagrams

❑   Activity Diagrams

❑   Sequence Diagrams

❑   State Diagrams

❑   Component Diagrams

❑   Deployment Diagrams

We'll review the purpose of each diagram when we first encounter it in our discussion and point out relevant project-stage-specific uses or other details where appropriate.

The Typical Software Development Lifecycle

Regardless of what kind of software you are building or what industry you may be working in, there exists a common set of steps or stages that most development projects follow. Of course project size and scope, the style of project leaders and developers, and other environmental and cultural factors have a significant impact on the structure of a development project. In quite a few software development organizations, proprietary methodologies exist, but you'll probably find that the UML still applies to those methodologies as well. At some level of detail, your experiences will certainly vary in some way from the basic steps we'll discuss here. For the most part, however, software development projects do indeed share the same general progression of figuring out what the software has to do, how it will do it, how the software will be tested and rolled out, and some kind of post-rollout production support phase. We'll get into more details of each these general stages as we discuss the role of UML and Visio throughout the project.

The diagram opposite contains the order and general process flow of common, major software development stages. We'll organize our discussion of the UML and Visio around these major steps as the rest of the chapter unfolds.

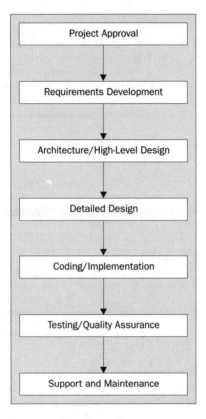

The diagram illustrates the following nature of most common development methodologies. That is, one major project step depends on the output from an immediately preceding stage. In practice, however, it is possible and not uncommon to see project stages repeat, particularly early requirements, and architecture stages. Projects are also organized to repeat groups of stages in order to design, develop, and test portions of the entire project. That approach generally minimizes risk and helps get applications into users' hands faster.

Requirements Development

After an initial approval process that varies by organization, one of the most difficult stages of any development project begins – determining what exactly is to be developed, how it will be used and why. More times than not the stage is called **requirements analysis** or **requirements development**. At this stage, the project team has to decide what the software will do. Most of the input for requirements is from application users and others directly familiar with the problem or task the software will address. The output of this stage is some kind of description, a requirements document of how the software should work, who the users are, and some characteristics of each user group.

Architecture or High-Level Design

At this stage, requirements are translated into high-level designs – designs without much constraining technical detail, designs that work out high-level issues including integration with other applications, supported computing platforms, and so on. Many decisions made at this stage of a development project are critical to the success of an application and the issues that must be addresses are numerous. At this stage we are beginning to define how the software will deliver on requirements we've already developed. Input into this stage comes mainly from gathered requirements and other details from sources that include applications with which the new software will interface, environmental constraints, etc.

Detailed Design

Once a broad architecture is developed, the task of detailing much of the application's design begins. Often a difficult process, fundamental requirements and architecture issues haven't been entirely worked out; this stage is where we first see flaws with a technical approach to our applications. The final 'how' of a software project is worked out in this stage. 'How' in terms of how we will meet the technical and business requirements we've already identified. Inputs into this stage are requirements documents and architecture documents and the individuals who prepared them. Expected output from this project stage is typically documents and diagrams detailed enough to hand to a developer familiar with the project to produce code.

Coding/Implementation

This stage is where the rubber meets the road, so to speak. All of the work of defining requirements and architecting designs has to come together into database structures, code and components, and other physical stuff. The first true test of a design comes here. Developers will begin implementing a design and its ability to ultimately deliver will be proven. We often see hurriedly organized staff meetings to figure out code workarounds or solve problems that weren't anticipated in earlier architecture or detail design stages. I know because I've organizing those meetings many times! Coders will be working directly from design documents produced in earlier stages of the project. Of course initial requirements and architecture documents play a role by providing background and high-level descriptions of the application being developed.

Testing/Quality Assurance

The testing stages of a software development project shouldn't have a formally defined start and a defined end. Testing and other QA activities should permeate the entire project. That's not always the case, of course, but it's a good habit to start from the beginning of any new project. One theme you'll see explored in more detail later on in this chapter is the idea that early technical documentation (UML or something else), if done well and shared, has a direct impact on the effectiveness of any subsequent testing work. The biggest input into a testing stage is code, of course, but we also find testing and QA groups relying heavily on requirements documents and other design documents, particular for complicated processes. It's here where we first encounter the issue of ensuring a software process behaves exactly as designed and also testing that the design behaves exactly as the requirements state. More than once a developer has coded a piece of the application beautifully, then finds that the details they were using to build their code were faulty when testing against initial requirements.

Rollout

If you've ever written an installation script for a moderately complicated application, you'll understand the importance of good rollout planning and documentation. The success of a software rollout is often proportional to the amount of effort expended early in the architecture and design stages.

Support/Maintenance

Software designed and built with the "end in mind" generally has a better chance at succeeding in the marketplace than designs that didn't consider support and maintenance issues. These issues can include ease of updates, extensibility, and adaptation to new environmental conditions, customization by users, etc.

Interestingly these same steps are generally present in the smallest and the largest of development projects. Whether you're building a small utility for which the requirements are in the head of one developer and the testing and rollout stages are performed by that same person or you're working as one of dozens of developers on a larger application that might take years to implement, the basic process is similar. What we need to do know is identify how Visio and the UML can play a role in the development of software regardless of scope or project size. That's what the rest of this chapter will focus on.

Role of UML and Visio in the Project

So, having seen the common, major steps of a typical development project, let's start looking at each step in terms of how and where the UML and Visio play a role. Of course, not all Visio features revolve around UML, but in this chapter, we'll focus on UML produced by Visio.

UML as Documentation

Often, we see UML applied as a design tool, helping developers work out and express their ideas and designs in a consistent syntax that other developers will understand. One of the primary benefits of the UML is its ability to be read and understand by most developers, either because of their exposure to the UML directly or to similar notations, or just because the notation fundamentally makes sense even when read for the first time. Even in many trade journals and books, we see UML as a device that helps prepare for coding.

> In other words, the UML is used to help craft designs and express ideas before code is written.

The impression is sometimes given, however subtly, that UML's benefit decreases once code is written and an application is deployed. That couldn't be further from the truth. Early stage application of the UML is certainly important, but it is also important to realize the long-term benefits of using UML as a device to capture the details of how and why a piece of software was built. The persistence of details about the design and implementation of a project is a concept we're going to explore in depth in this chapter. How will we use the UML to document our projects? That's a question we'll answer as the rest of this chapter unfolds.

What does the UML give us in terms of documentation capabilities? Many readers will be familiar with UML diagrams and understand how each of the common diagrams can add to the overall documentation of a project. For instance, a class diagram can describe classes, their attributes, and their relationships to other classes. That class diagram will most likely have been created during the design and construction phases of the project, but, it can serve several roles after code is written. First of all, the details in that class diagram should be made available to other developers within the organization in some kind of internal, technical documentation. The class diagram in some simplified form should also be available to support, implementation, and other groups who may need to understand, at least at a high level, how a particular application is constructed. Of course, the key is to ensure development team members take the time to keep documentation updated. Using a tool such as Visio certainly helps, but it is important to instill the expectation that documentation produced early in the project will most certainly be used in later stages.

So let's have a look at the application of UML throughout the software development lifecycle, stage by stage, and see how the concept of building UML diagrams with documentation in mind actually plays out. For our discussion let's create a simple application scenario: the development of an order entry application for our fictional client, the ACME company. Although we won't necessarily dig into the details of how this application works, it is useful to have a simulated project to refer to in the course of our discussion.

ACME has asked us to build an order entry application to help it take orders faster and with higher accuracy levels. It also expects some of the standard features of an order entry app to increase its levels of customer service – tracking inventory levels, estimating delivery time, reviewing order status online, etc. The basic features required in the application are the ability to create new orders, some kind of online order review mechanism for internal users, and an interface to ACME's manufacturing system. Of course, we have some schedule and budget constraints and we have a limited number of development and other technical staff – we do need to make this realistic.

Let's work our way through the major project steps starting with requirements development and review the following items at each stage:

❑ How can UML or other Visio produced documentation be used during the current stage?

❑ What types of users will consume this information?

❑ How can documentation produced at this stage benefit users and needs in subsequent stages?

❑ What changes can be made in our procedures and habits in early project stages to help support later project work?

Requirements Development Documentation

As we've already mentioned, the primary goal of requirements development is figuring out what the software product should do. How the goal of this stage is stated is rather simply, but the distinction between 'what' software should do and 'how' it actually does it is an important one. The 'how', the implementation, is saved for later stages – architecture and design. The larger or more complex an application is the more important it is to concentrate on requirements of the product instead of jumping into design and implementation details. It's a warning we hear all the time and it's a warning that most of ignore to some degree. The fun part of building software is actually designing and building, not sitting in long boring meetings discussing detailed aspects of software requirements.

Most project management and other software development lifecycle experts will tell you, however, that getting your project's requirements right from the beginning of the project is critical to ensuring success.

> **If requirements aren't done right your designs will suffer, your users could be left without key pieces of functionality, and you may have to answer some hard questions.**

Have you ever seen or heard of an application that got into production but was never used because the users said that it didn't meet their needs? That was probably a project that didn't gather requirements properly.

Requirements development itself is more of an art than a scientific process. Moreover, gathering requirements for one application and group of users can be an entirely different experience when gather requirements for a different application with different users. Often times, finding and developing requirements is lengthy, tedious and, frankly, so much work with so little immediate, obvious benefit that it rarely gets done well, if at all. Hopefully, you'll see the benefits of doing requirements at all and, in the next few pages, how Visio and UML offer some tools to make requirements gathering easier.

The goal of developing requirements, the test to determine if we as designers and developers have captured what the application has to do, is a collection of necessary actions and behaviors of the application in the course of doing its work and a description of the interactions of various users and the application. A good requirements collection consists of at least two primary components – a requirements document and use cases. The requirements document is some kind of statement of various business, technical, and other requirements organized in a logical fashion around features of the product. Although there is no formal method for expressing requirements, it's common to find a requirements document full of direct statements about how the product should work or how results are generated in various situations. When written well, those statements are generally direct, unambiguous, and leave little room for interpretation by the reader. For instance, if our order entry application requires that web users have the ability to review their order history online we might see the requirement written as follows:

❑   The product will allow external users to access their order history via a web browser.

A more detailed requirement for our order entry application might relate to how we calculate shipping and tax expenses:

❑   The product will calculate shipping expenses using standard overnight carrier shipping expense tables.

❑   The product will calculate sales and/or value-added taxes by country or regional government regulations.

The best requirements tend to have some characteristics in common. First of all they are correct and succinctly stated. They also have to be verifiable. A good requirement is traceable. That means that we should be able to identify a requirement early in the project lifecycle and trace its inclusion and implementation throughout design and coding. Finally, a requirement has to be testable. Testing a requirement includes verifying that the final product has at least addressed the requirement and that it has implemented an appropriate solution. In other words, did the application deliver a feature or capability that meets the need, stated as a requirement, of some user of the application?

Clearly there are many methods of developing requirements and each has its own merits. Since most requirements come from application and business users, the best tend to focus on some method of capturing the information obtained from users and restating that information in some logical, consistent form. Once captured and restated, the information is conveyed back to the people from whom the information was gathered for review. The UML has a very useful tool for doing this called **Use Cases**.

Use Cases

Use Cases are the definition of a process. The process is generally a user or business process, but is always a series of logically grouped steps necessary to complete some task in a system. System in this case can be an application or manual process completed without the aid of software. Generally, use cases are written in either a text or graphical form. The text format is generally more narrative oriented, that is, more oriented toward telling a story about how a particular process is completed from beginning to end.

> *The Use Case Diagram is good at showing the major steps of a process and how those steps may be shared among other major processes.*

At the requirements development stage of a project it is important to understand how a processes should work and what users are involved in that process. UML use cases are great at expressing that information. Let's start with the use case diagram then discuss the textual implementation of a use case.

As you have seen in other parts of this book and in other books and articles, business process and the users involved in these processes are represented in a use case by small ovals and little stick figures. An oval can represent a single discrete task or a more complicated but self-contained process consisting of many simple tasks. In fact, the oval shape in the diagram represents the use case itself. The scope of the use case itself generally determines how detailed the individual processes are. For example, a simple use case diagram representing the creation of a new order in our order entry application would contain this shape:

Obviously, creating an order consists of multiple steps, both by the user and by an application. The user would have to indicate that they want to create an order and give some details about products, quantities, etc. The application would also have to do some work that isn't immediately obvious in the single **Create Order** use case. If the detail of how an order is created is important to deciding what an application does, then you'll want to express the **Create Order** use case in more detail. Be careful, though, of falling into the trap of determining how an order should be created by the application during the requirements stage. At this point we are entirely interested in the business and user implications of creating an order and any requirements imposed on the application from their perspective.

If we wanted to illustrate the fact that internal and external users can use the **Create Order** use case, we'd add stick figures to the drawing to represent both user types. Although it's still a bit simplistic, here's what the drawing fragment would look like with an Internal **Order Entry User** and an **External Customer** role added to the **Use Case**.

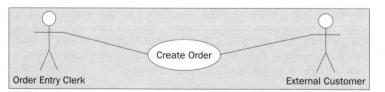

As we know, the stick figures are called **Actors** in UML-speak. An actor can be a person or another application that executes the **Use** case. In this example we have to actors – **Order Entry Clerk** and **External Customer** who can execute the use case – create an order. Even if a diagram reader didn't know the details of creating an order, it is immediately obvious that there are at least two user groups.

The real benefit of the use case diagram is when you bring many uses cases together to illustrate an entire process. For instance, choosing a product from a catalog and buying it might constitute a common process that we'd like to document. A use case diagram representing that process and the actors involved might look like this:

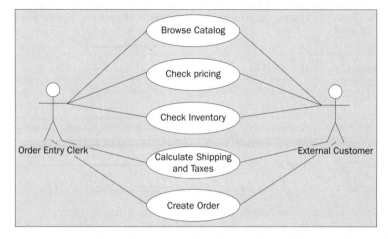

These diagrams illustrates that our **Order Entry Clerk** and an external customer should have the ability to browse products, get pricing and inventory information, calculate shipping and taxes, and place an order. For the purpose of this use case, both an internal and an external user seem to need access to the same processes. In this example, that's entirely possible. In many cases though, we'd probably have one actor performing a set of use cases and another actor performing other uses cases within the same drawing. For instance, if our client's organization offered some kind of customer service or call center for customers to call to place orders, we might want those call center reps, still playing the role of an **Order Entry Clerk**, to have the ability to check customer credit. That's not something an external customer should be able to do. In the drawing, we'd express that as follows:

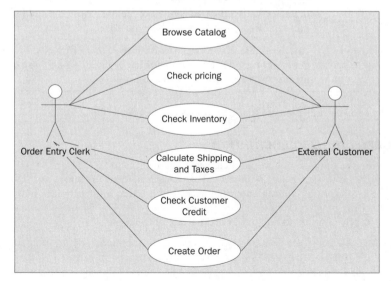

Notice the additional Check Customer Credit use case near the bottom of the drawing; only the Order Entry Clerk communicates with that use case in this process.

The other method for communicating use case information is in some textual format. Most requirements gathering processes rely on a textual format of some sort. Although the format and contents of use cases vary from organization to organization, the basic components of a written use case probably contain the following elements:

Use Case Element	Description
Number	A number or lettering scheme used to organize use cases and serve as an easy reference when use cases are included in other documents.
Title	A short description of the purpose of the use case. In our example above, we had "Check Inventory", "Create Order", etc.
Primary Actor	The main actor who executes the use case.
Secondary Actor	Any other user or application that can execute the use case.
Starting Point	A description of where the use case begins. This is typically a sentence or two describing the starting state of the use case, what the user is doing or sees, etc.
Ending Point	A description of where the use case ends. This is typically a short description of what the user sees or what state an application is in when the use case is completed.
Measurable Result	A description of what the use case accomplished. Sometimes the ending point and result described in this section are the same thing.
Flow of Events	A narrative of everything that occurs in the use case from Starting Point to Ending Point including a description of the Measurable Result. This element of the use case is the real content of the use case and should include as much information as possible about how the use case is executed.
Alternative Flow of Events	Anything that doesn't occur within the Flow of Events. This section generally includes exception and error handling and any other flow of events that isn't typical for this use case.

As an example, consider this use case for "Creating a New Order".

Using Use Cases for Documentation

As time-consuming as they may be to produce, use cases are one of the most powerful tools we have in software development to gather user requirements and capture them for future use. The first, immediate use of use cases is to capture requirements from users and use that information to help create some shared understanding of what exactly an application is being asked to do and what features and capabilities the application has to contain to make it useful to users.

Use cases also play an important role in helping project leaders develop initial scope and schedule estimates. After completing an initial round of use case development, developers and project managers should have a body of information to use as input for determining the complexity, and hence, cost in terms of budget and schedule for a development project. Of course use cases are not the sole input into the budgeting and scheduling process, but they offer the best source of "what do we need to do?" type information at this point in a development project.

Some of the overlooked value of use cases is their far-reaching implication for later-stage project tasks like testing, training, and post rollout support. Although testing shouldn't really have a defined start and a defined stop, it commonly occurs toward the end of a development cycle. Use cases can be tremendously useful for testing groups trying to write good test plans. Testing and Quality Assurance groups are charged with a double-edged task. First, they have to test the software as written. That includes installing the software and mimicking users in the field as we expect them to interact with the application. It also includes acting exceptionally – doing things a normal user really shouldn't do, but happen anyway. The second aspect to testing is determining if the software that gets delivered will actually meet the needs of users. If requirements are done well and use cases are written, the testing group can access that information and write accurate, real-world test scripts that help determine if our delivered software not only works as intended, but also meets the originally stated needs our of users. It's a common trap to test what the developers wrote and not what the users actually need.

Another use for the information contained in use cases is post rollout support. In most software development groups there's development done by a relatively small group of people. Then there are other, usually larger, groups of people responsible for rolling out the product and supporting customers when they have problems. Since the demands of time and other issues (like unsocial developers) often preclude a good flow of information about an application to customer-facing groups like support, use cases can be used to describe what an application should be able to do. The narrative portions of a use case give a lot of details in a, hopefully, easy-to-read format that support and other groups can use as a starting point in their understanding of the product.

Using Use Cases

Hopefully, I've made the point about trying to use use cases or a similar device in your requirements development. Whether you use them or not, the requirements development process is not something you can avoid. One way or the other you'll have to gather requirements if your applications are to succeed. Doing requirements deliberately, at the beginning of a project, is the best way to get a project started properly.

Just a few comments about building and using use cases before we move to architecture:

❑ When building use cases, focus on the user and other entities like external applications that interact with a process. That seems obvious, but the whole point of writing them is to capture a narrative description of what the user does, sees, etc. with an application or process. Many times developers write use cases themselves and it is very easy to change perspective from seeing the application as a user to looking out at the user from the application's perspective. If that happens you'll fall into the trap of building the application instead of figuring out what it should do first.

❑ Don't go overboard writing use cases. The phrase "analysis paralysis" applies here. Remember that we're paid to build software and not use cases. Pick the processes that are critical to the success of the application and write use cases for those processes. Another way to look at the issue of when to write use cases is by risk. Figure out what processes present the greatest risk and focus on writing use cases there first. Risk in this case could be the risk of a very complicated user process or even the risk of being able to pull off some process technically given stringent application integration requirements or something like that.

❑   Always review use cases with users. Always get them to buy in. For these statements about basing your understanding of an application's requirements on your use cases to have any merit, the data you collect in your use cases has to be absolutely correct. Test your use cases with users. Use cases are an effective technique for describing to your users what you understand of their processes.

Architecture Documentation

Architecting an application is probably one of the more interesting stages of building an application. In many cases, you're starting with a clean whiteboard with a bunch of ideas about how best to pull off the requirements you've identified earlier in the project. This stage is also one of the riskiest. The decisions made at this stage of a project are very costly to reverse once coding has started. Obviously, good requirements and a good understanding of those requirements are crucial to architecting a good application.

In this section of the chapter, we'll review the most common UML diagrams used in the Architecture stage and how they get used. We'll also review the longer-term implications of building good diagrams from a documentation standpoint since that's one of the themes of the entire chapter.

Although every designer and developer has a different style, there are a few common diagrams that we can predict to be used at this stage. These include the class diagram and activity diagram. In addition, even though they are more oriented toward implementation, we find some developers working with component diagrams at this stage of a project in an attempt to visualize how the application will be deployed eventually. Let's start with Class Diagrams.

Using Class Diagrams

The most commonly used (or at least most commonly demonstrated) UML diagram is probable the Class Diagram. The Visio UML template calls it the **Static Structure Diagram**. Class diagrams illustrate the objects that compose a system and the relationships between those objects. Class diagrams can be written from one of two different perspectives – a logical approach to objects in a system and their relationships or a detailed, implementation-specific approach that includes methods, attributes, data types, etc. During early stages of a development project, it's common to use class diagrams to illustrate and communicate relationships between large conceptual objects in a system. We call these types of diagrams Conceptual Class Diagrams.

For instance, in our order entry application, we would spend some time working out the relationships between Customers, Orders, Products, etc. The existence and relationships of these objects is important as we transition out of requirements development and into more application-oriented thinking. Here's an example of a simple conceptual class diagram:

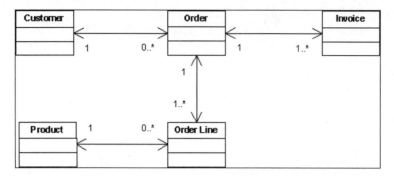

From this diagram, we can see the larger conceptual relationships of key objects in the application. For instance, we know from this diagram that every Order has to belong to one Customer. That's probably a logical arrangement and typical of most order entry applications. The diagram expresses that relationship using the association line end multiplicities 1 and 0..*. We also know that each Order object can somehow navigate back to its Customer and vice versa, a Customer object can identify its Order objects. The arrows on the lines indicate that to us. A similar amount of information is expressed in every other relationship in this diagram. For instance, every Order Line object has to have an Order and each Order Line has to navigate back to a Product.

Working out relationships between key objects in an application is vital at this point in a development project. Once the details of attributes and methods of each object are added, the job of working out these relationships becomes harder, if, for no other reason than that there is a lot more information expressed about each class. You can also see how requirements are already playing a direct role in our architecture, and are expressed almost immediately in our UML diagrams. Consider the relationship between Customer and Order. If our users give us a requirement that any Order can be assigned to more than one Customer then we have a significant architecture issue to deal with. For one thing, it's not a common requirement of these types of applications. We easily could have assumed that Orders belonged to one Customer and that was it. After the first beta install or demo someone in the room would have asked to see the multiple Customer feature and one of our developers would have said "what's that?" and the room would get quiet for a few moments. Not a good scenario, is it?

Once the conceptual relationships between objects are worked out, we'd hand off this class diagram to the detailed design stage of the project where methods and attributes of each class would be worked out in as much detail as possible.

Using Activity Diagrams

Activity Diagrams illustrate a sequence of tasks or actions taken by a user or external process. They tend to be detailed and are often found as supporting diagrams that help explain a particularly detailed portion of an application. They are also very useful when used at a high level to illustrate the flow of information or control through an application. Activity diagrams have the ability to nicely display branching for exception handling and other logical changes in the course of a process.

For architecture purposes, it is sometimes nice to be able to express a series of major steps in an application and work through issues with other designers and developers. Although the term is ambiguous sometimes, most developers call the order of execution or process flow through an application its **workflow**. To illustrate workflow in our order-entry application we might create a diagram like this:

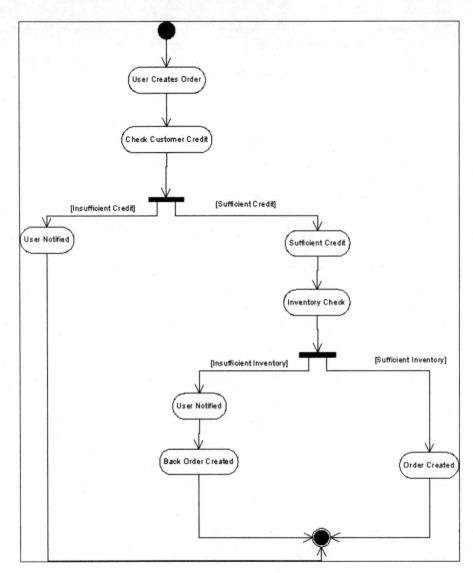

Notice how the two simple decision points help illustrate the workflow of this particular application or group of applications. From an architectural standpoint, consider that each activity step is a separate application or something like a web service. The implications of working out workflow at this stage are very important.

From a documentation standpoint, a diagram such as the simple one we've just seen would be valuable for several reasons:

❑　Other developers who are responsible for writing smaller pieces of the entire application will understand the environment in which their code runs. This kind of diagram will illustrate at what point their code is actually involved and what happens immediately before and after their code is executed.

❑ Testing groups will have a clear understanding of the major processes in an application, particularly exception processing. Since some of our most complicated work when writing applications is dealing with and protecting against exceptions, getting the testing people a good illustration of how processes flow will only serve to make our applications better.

❑ After a product is in production, it will ultimately go through change of some sort. They all do. If we can give developers responsible for those future changes an illustration of the basic flow of an application, they will not only be forever in our gratitude, but the applications we build will be better and stronger for a longer period of time.

> In my experience, the more architectural design information I presented to other developers, the better my designs became. Activity diagrams are a great mechanism for illustrating and communicating designs to others, particularly if the application is managing a process or workflow.

Using Component Diagrams

The last diagram we'll cover in the Architecture section is the **component** diagram. Although these diagrams are typically used to illustrate the physical implementation of binary files like an EXE or DLL, you might find them useful during the early stages of a project. For one thing, start thinking early about how you'll roll out your product. From experience, I've dealt with messy implementations that could have been averted had we dealt with installation and rollout issues from the beginning. Often, it's an easy process to sit down with a design and look ahead to predict issues that may arise when it comes time to deploy. It also helps to instill the thinking in the development team that the only real goal of a development project is to ship software. If you start sketching components and deployments early in a project, you'll get people thinking about shipping software instead of thinking in conceptual terms. That's an easy trap at this stage of the project – abstract designs always work on the whiteboard. Start with the end in mind and your chances of delivering a successful product increase. For those more pessimistic types, we can restate that last point: if you start with the end in mind your chances of failing decrease.

So, what does a component diagram look like at this stage? Well, it's not too different from component diagrams anywhere else in a project. They aren't very complicated diagrams. In fact, at this point in the project, a component diagram is really more of a conversation starter used to illustrate some assumptions about how best to package your code. Let's have a look:

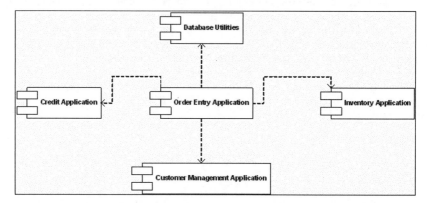

It's immediately obvious that our Order Entry Application has quite a few dependencies – a Credit Application, an Inventory Application, and a Customer Management Application. From an architecture standpoint, the benefits of expressing the relationships between several applications and our new Order Entry application are obvious.

Detailed Design Documentation

After a project has progressed through requirements development and architecture, project members are hopefully ready to begin working on the details of the application design. As we saw in our introductory discussion of detailed design, we expect to use documentation produced during the previous two project stages to help craft design documents in enough detail to hand to coders.

Even well run projects incur some risk as this point. For one thing, the detailed design of an application is the first time any substantial test of basic architecture is done. The test isn't necessarily a formal test and review of architecture decisions; rather, it's a casual, incremental review done by all of the developers and designers associated with the project. Designers and developers responsible for portions of the application will be testing the design for soundness and adapting the basic design into their own detail designs. The effect is a continual review of the application architecture until everyone responsible for different portions of a detailed design is comfortable with their own pieces. By exposing architecture and high-level decisions to a variety of other developers, the project runs the risk of losing any core design principles that application architects were motivated by.

Regardless of how a project's architecture and requirements are received by other members of the project team, there are some commonly used UML diagrams to express detailed design. In this section, we'll review the use of class diagrams, sequence diagrams, and state diagrams. In the case of class diagrams, we'll note differences between their usage at this stage of a project and the usage we saw during earlier, architecture stages. Sequence diagrams are one of my personal favorites for expressing the flow of messages between detailed components or objects within an application. Let's start with Class Diagrams.

Using Detailed Class Diagrams

The biggest difference between the usage of class diagrams during detailed design and class diagrams during architecture is the level of detail we'll build into the diagrams. Previously we've been more interested in expressing relationships between major application objects and acknowledging the presence of application objects. At this point in a project, we are concerned with filling in the details of what interface each class will support. Although we won't be coding yet, at this point our class diagrams are being written with the intention of using them to generate code using a tool like Visio or having a developer write code that mirrors exactly what is contained in the class diagram.

Like most things, it's best to see an example then discuss it. Here's our conceptual class diagram from earlier in the chapter reworked to contain implementation details.

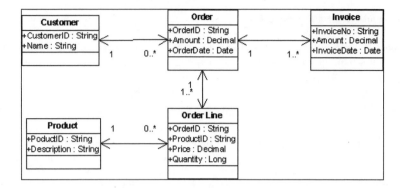

The first thing we notice is the addition of details about each one of our original conceptual classes. In this simple example, it's reasonable to expect that each conceptual class will map to one detailed design class. That isn't always the case, though. Complicated objects and complicated relationships between objects often get broken into small groups of detailed design objects. It's similar to a logical many-to-many relationship between two database tables. Showing the logical relationship is easy; just draw a line with 1...* at each endpoint. Actually implementing that relationship in a SQL database, however, requires an additional table that lives between the two main data tables.

Although we might be missing a lot of detail in our simple example, the differences between a conceptual class diagram and a detailed design version of the same diagram should be evident. As we said earlier, you should expect to be able to give a detailed class diagram to a developer to start building an application. In this case, the attributes of our classes are relatively terse – there aren't too many of them. However, we could easily take the class diagram above and build five classes just from the information we've been given.

There are details within the class diagram that may not immediately be obvious to a casual observer. Notice the lines between the classes. They obviously contain multiplicity information – an Invoice can exist for only one Order, etc. We covered this briefly during the architecture discussion. The line ends themselves also have meaning – navigability. It's a fancy term for the idea that an object should be able to navigate from itself to the other classes it references. The easiest example to understand is Order and Order Line. An Order consists of one or more Order Line objects. That makes sense because Order Lines are just the products and quantities that make up the order, one Order Line for each Product (do you see that Order Line-Product relationship in the class diagram?). According to the class diagram each Order should know how to find its Order Lines and each Order Line should know to which Order it belongs. The arrows on each end of the line tell us this.

This is a great example of the information that we need to include at the detailed design stage of our projects. The difference between including navigability information and omitting it until later can result in wasted time and effort on the part of our developers. It can also result in some sloppy code, as in this case. If our developers didn't logically understand that an Order needed some mechanism for managing its constituent Order Line objects, how would we have coded most of our order management components? Database lookups every time we accessed an Order and needed to generate a total order amount? Granted, this is a simple example, but the point should be clear – carefully consider what you document in your diagrams during detailed design. Even the simplest of omissions can have far-reaching consequences.

Using Sequence Diagrams

One of the best illustrations of how objects and the components that contain those objects communicate with one another is a **Sequence Diagram**. From a documentation standpoint, they are very useful to describing the order of messages from one object to another. By tracing messages from the top of the diagram to the bottom, it's easy to represent even complex messaging between several objects.

Sequence diagrams, and their cousins the collaboration diagram, serve another purpose at this stage of a project. They help designers and developers work through final issues regarding what methods objects expose and what parameters are passed around between objects. A sequence diagram, in effect, allows developers to role-play by diagramming request and response messages from one object to another. By watching messages and their payloads (input and output parameters) flow from one object to another, we can see how objects should interact with each other once they are built. To illustrate let's add a new object to the group we've already been working with. It's only responsibility it to manage the order creation process. Since the object will be full of business rules, it could reside in a middle tier. Let's call it the OrderManager

Front-end application will use the OrderManager to request new Order objects. Via the Order object that is created, applications can create Order Lines, save Orders, etc. Using the sequence diagram we can work through all kinds of issues including how and when object instances get created, the order of method calls from one object to another, what kinds of input and output parameters are necessary to perform some work. Sequence diagrams are really useful once you've worked about a fundamental detailed class diagram. Here are our Order and Order Line objects at work with the new Order Manager:

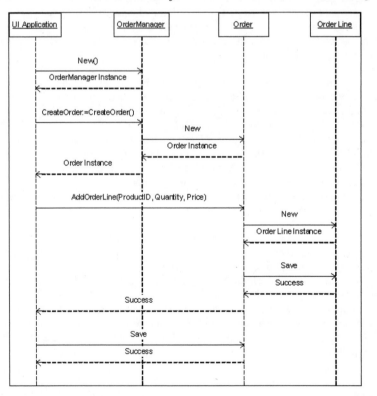

Some of the issues this diagram might bring up during the course of design discussions could include the creation and destruction of child object instances, methods of passing input parameters and methods of passing output parameters. Other issues might include management of errors that occur in the **Order Line** class and any behavior that's required by the **OrderManager** to report those errors back to the UI Application. Using a sequence diagram helps focus on these kinds of issues.

The sequence diagram we just created also helps team members working further down the project lifecycle. For one thing, it's a clear definition of the order in which our main working objects are created and which object is responsible from creating others. Testing and support team members might get involved in difficult troubleshooting scenarios where the order of object creation might help shed light on particularly difficult errors (or particularly difficult-to-translate error messages!). Another huge benefit of a sequence diagram from a documentation standpoint is the head start it gives developers who are asked to modify code a year after the product is released. How many times have you picked up code for a maintenance assignment and not had any idea where to start. Wouldn't a sequence diagram have helped to get you started in the right direction?

At this point, we are ready to talk about the **Coding** and **Implementation** stages of a software project. This point marks the transition from being a producer of documentation to more or less a consumer of documentation. Of course coding and testing and related activities produce their own documents, but we are focusing on using UML as a documentation tool and not on other forms of documentation. A theme throughout this chapter has been producing documents for future use in addition the immediate need of requirements, architecture, and detailed design. Now is when we discuss how that need manifests itself and how we will see some of the benefits.

Coding and Implementation Documentation

It seems that we've talked a bunch about writing software, but we haven't written any software yet. Does that seem odd? Well, not if you've spent much time on large, new software projects that properly focused on gathering requirements and other early stage activities before anyone opened Visual Studio to start coding. As important as coding is, the several stages of a project that lead to coding are every bit as important. As we've seen up to this point, doing a good job in requirements development, architecture and detailed design increases your chance of delivering a successful product. From a cost standpoint, studies have shown (and common sense tells us) that fixing problems before coding starts is significantly cheaper than fixing problems after code is written. The later in a project a defect is discovered the more expensive it is to change, test, and make up lost time.

That having been said, what documentation role does UML and Visio play at this stage of the game? Well, several, and all of them are important.

Requirements Documentation for Coding

Some of the best sources of information on how an application should behave and why are found in the data we gather during requirements development. Coders should always have access to use cases and other documentation. Not only will it give a developer perspective from the user that they may not be able to get otherwise, but it will give the developer a chance to see some of the raw input the designers and architects of the application used in making their decisions. I'm a big believer in exposing the people who are responsible for making designs work have access to as much background information as possible to help them do their job. Of course, you don't want every junior developer on the team reading use cases every day, but if you give talented people access to information that helps them do their job it can only result in a better product in the end.

Architecture Documents for Coding

High-level design documents help developers understand where their particular "piece of the pie" fits into the "big picture". Seeing conceptual class diagrams of activity diagrams illustrating work flow of a large system pinned up on cubicle wall is a good sign that developers are working on understanding more than just their potentially small slice of the world. Similar to the points made regarding requirements documentation during coding stages, the more information you can give to the folks responsible for turning designs into reality, the better the product will be and the smoother the entire project will run.

In addition, it is altogether possible that developers working out issues at some detail level will uncover unseen flaws in product designs.

Testing and Quality Assurance Documentation

Testing may be the single most under valued stage of a development project. To be done correctly, testers must be included early in the project and invited to as many requirements and high-level design meetings as possible. In many ways, lead testers should be treated the same way lead developers and designers are treated. Keep them on the inside of the core project team, not the outside as so often happens, and make sure they have access to as much information as any developer. In fact, the one group that probably cannot be given too much background information, particular use cases and other user requirements, are testing and quality assurance team members.

Here's how a testing group might use all of the UML diagrams likely to be built during the course of a typical software project:

Use Cases (Requirements) – if testers don't have a fundamental understanding of the needs of users then they shouldn't be testing the software. If they are testing without understanding how and why users will use the software, then the project is headed for trouble. The use cases and other documents produced during requirements development are ideal for testing. From those requirements, a test group can write scripts and implement other testing devices to increase the overall quality of the software we produce.

The testing group also helps ensure that the software that's been developed actually addresses and solves the true issues of end users, and not the issues development team members think need to be addressed. This is a point I made earlier in the chapter and it bears repeating: give your test people access to the requirements that came straight from end users and give those testers the ability to double-check even the most basic of assumptions regarding what it is that the software is attempting to do. The tester will be role-playing as the user, so the more insight we can give testers, the better our software will be in the end.

Class Diagrams (Architecture and Detailed Design) – there is some benefit in exposing class diagram information to testing groups, although it's probably limited only to conceptual class diagrams in most cases. Illustrating relationships between major application objects to help testers understand how the software is constructed is certainly useful.

In some projects with particularly adept testers, detailed class diagrams can be useful to help explain some complex procedures or to help troubleshoot difficult situations where more powerful background information can help. Detailed class diagrams often accompany sequence diagrams in those situations.

Sequence Diagrams (Architecture and Detailed Design) – if it wasn't clear during our previous discussion of sequence diagrams, I'll say it again: I really like them. I think they have a great deal of benefit for system architects and developers throughout detailed design and coding. They also serve a role during the testing stages of a project. Similar to detailed class diagrams, sequence diagrams help illustrate particularly complex portions of the code, but they add an important extra dimension that class diagrams don't have – time. Sequence diagrams show an order of operations that could be very useful for testing. First of all, the order an application does things may not be the order users always want those tasks done. Secondly, the order of tasks within an application might result in serious errors or failures if one of the operations fails and other subsequent operations don't detect that failure. A good test group will see the sequenced nature of key operations and arrange testing scripts to expose any potential flaws.

Activity Diagrams – whenever some process occurs and the order of events is important and the conditional routing of process flow is important, then we'd expect to see activity diagrams, right? Of course we would. One of the nicest diagrams I have personally given to a test group was an activity diagram that showed the process flow of a complicated transactional process, including all of the exceptions I accounted for in my design and code, with a clear illustration of what the application was supposed to do with each exception. Without an activity diagram, I could have gotten the testers to understand how the code worked, but not as quickly nor as well. That test group found several flaws in the code, which ultimately made the product very stable and very useful once it made it to production.

Using Visio Reports throughout the Project

One feature of the UML diagram in Visio is the ability to create professional reports of the detail contained in your drawings. These reports can be shared with the development team and added to any change control policy your organization or project may have in place. Visio UML ships with support for creating reports for static structure (class diagrams), activity, statechart, component, and deployment diagrams. In this section, we'll review the creation of Visio UML reports and discuss the reports you may commonly want to include in your own project work.

Each of the reports contains a listing of the contents of the report and quite a bit of detail about each of the components within whichever diagram the report is run for. For instance, an activity diagram report will include each action state and each transition from one state to another. It will also include most of the important UML-related information included in the Visio shape properties.

To get started, let's use the sample UML diagram that ships with Visio Enterprise Architect – Championzone UML. This is a fictional application design for referee certification. To open the sample UML model, start Visio and select File | New | Browse Sample Drawings. You'll see an Open File dialog like the screenshot overleaf. Select Champtionzone UML.vsd and press the Open button.

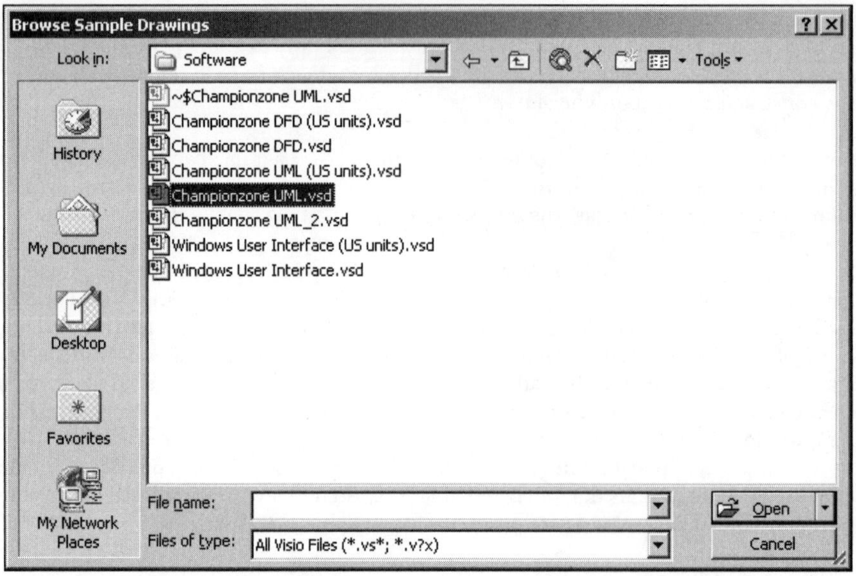

Browse Sample Drawings

Look in: Software

~$Championzone UML.vsd
Championzone DFD (US units).vsd
Championzone DFD.vsd
Championzone UML (US units).vsd
Championzone UML.vsd
Championzone UML_2.vsd
Windows User Interface (US units).vsd
Windows User Interface.vsd

History
My Documents
Desktop
Favorites
My Network Places

File name:

Files of type: All Visio Files (*.vs*; *.v?x)

Open
Cancel

This is actually a great sample UML model to review. It contains most of the common UML diagrams that you are likely to encounter. I personally wouldn't have spent the time to format colors and shading, but otherwise, this is a good UML example to use as guidance for your own diagrams.

Notice the **tab** bar at the bottom of the drawing page. If you scroll through the available drawings, you'll find **Static Structure, Collaboration, Sequence, Component, Statechart, Deployment, Activity,** and **Use Case** Diagrams.

Let's create a report and discuss its contents. We'll start with the **Static Structure Report**. From the Visio **Main** menu, find the **UML** menu and select **Reports**, and you'll see this dialog:

Notice the list of available reports. We are going to run the Static Structure Report, but let's take a moment to review what options are available in this dialog first. Toward the bottom of the dialog, we see buttons to Print, Preview, and Export the report. Printing and previewing reports have obvious benefit, but if we are using our UML reports as a part of a development project, we probably want the information contained in these reports for some historical or change control purpose. For that reason, exporting the reports is a good thing to review. Visio will export our report to Rich Text Format, (RTF). RTF can be read by just about any word processor. The main benefit of exporting your reports is the creation of a file that you can save, include in a change control package, or even add to your source code version-control application like SourceSafe.

We'll get to exporting a report shortly; let's finish with the other tabs in this dialog. Click on the Title tab and you see a form that lets you modify the default Title and Subtitle of the report.

In the Report title textbox you can add text to be printed at the top of your reports. Changes will be displayed in the Sample Report textbox near the middle of the form. You can also insert common fields like Document Title, Current Date, File Name, and Author. Put your cursor somewhere in the Report title box and press the Insert button. From the list that appears, select Current Date. Depending on where you had the cursor in the Report title box, your display will look something like the following:

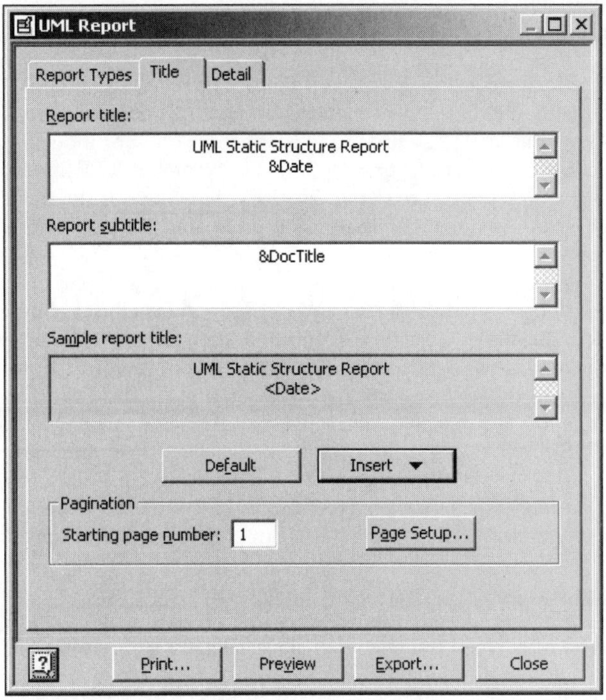

UML Report

Report Types | **Title** | Detail

Report title:

UML Static Structure Report
&Date

Report subtitle:

&DocTitle

Sample report title:

UML Static Structure Report
<Date>

[Default] [Insert ▼]

Pagination

Starting page number: [1]   [Page Setup...]

[Print...] [Preview] [Export...] [Close]

The **Default** button will reset whatever changes you made to the report title and subtitle to the original settings. Another option that is convenient is the ability to assign the starting page number of the report. If our report is to be included with other documentation, a project wrap-up document for instance, then we might to start our page numbering well after page one. The **Page Setup** button opens the standard **Page Setup** dialog you'd expect to find in any Windows application.

The **Detail** page lets you select what items are to be included in the report itself. These include:

❑   **Code Generation** – the target language and code template you've selected in the diagram.

❑   **Constraints** – any constraints you've identified within the drawing shapes.

❑   **Documentation** – a standard tagged value that most Visio drawing shapes and all UML shapes contain.

❑   **Tagged Values** – predefined and user-defined values contained in each shape's properties within the Visio diagram.

If your diagrams contain a lot of detail stored within the shapes themselves, then turning on all of these options is probably a good idea. If you are not generating code from your diagrams, that option obviously isn't necessary. It will just clutter up the report.

Static Structure Diagram Report

OK, let's generate a Static Structure diagram. Still in the `Championzone UML` file, from the menu select UML | Reports…. In the dialog that appears select UMLStaticStructure Report, and press the Export button. You'll see a Save File dialog so browse to a directory on your machine and name the report file Static Structure Report. Notice that our only option is to create an RTF file. Press the Save button. The report is generated very quickly. Browse to the directory that contains the new file and open it with a word-processing application. In our case, we're using Microsoft Word. WordPerfect or even WordPad that ships with Windows will work too.

The report itself is very long – over 40 pages in Word. It contains all of the detail that is available from the Visio diagram about the Static Structure diagram. Although we won't run through each of the sections of the report in too much detail, let's review a couple of major sections.

The first section of the report is a summary of the diagram. It contains the name of the diagram, the model type (in this case Static Structure), it's visibility, and the packages it contains, among other things. The next section is a statistical review of the contents of the diagram. It counts interfaces, classes, the total number of attributes, parameters, etc. It's a lengthy list and I wonder how useful it really is. Other than curiosity, do we care how many methods we have in our entire diagram? In most cases, probably not.

The balance of the report is a lot of detail about the packages and classes contained within the diagram. In this sample Static Structure diagram there is only the standard Top Package and it contains all of the classes in the diagram. In Word the header of the Package section looks like this:

Each class within the diagram has its own section as well. The details in these class detail sections are probably the most useful in terms of documentation. Here's what the `Applicant` class looks like in the report:

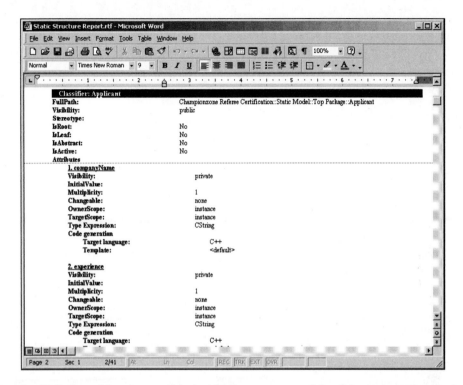

Notice the **Attributes** of the class are listed with a large amount of detail for each attribute including Visibility, scope, and instancing information. Also, notice the **Code generation** section of the **Attributes** detail. In this diagram the diagram author chose C++ and the default code template. The **Operations** of the class follow its **Attributes**. That section if formatted similarly, as the following screenshot illustrates:

Each operation is listed with a tremendous amount of detail about the operation, its scope, and all of the input and output parameters. You can see why these reports can get so long – there's a lot of information included for even the most simple of attributes and operations. One nice feature about the **Operations** section if you've included **Code Generation** detail in the report is information about the code that was generated. Specifically, where the code file is and what language was used to generate the code.

The last portion of the class detail in this report is information that describes the associations our class has with other classes. This information is probably the second most useful data contained within the report, behind details about attributes and operations. We won't review the meaning of generalizations and associations in a UML context, but here's what the report tells use about the **Applicant** class in this particular **Static Structure** diagram:

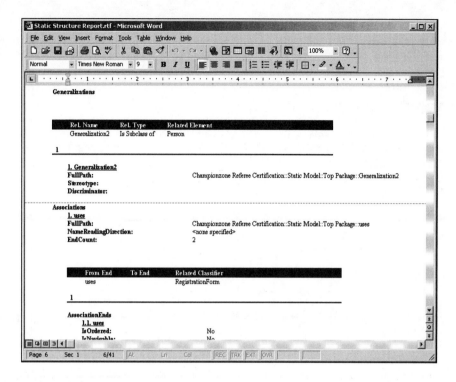

Deployment Diagram Report

After a Static Structure diagram report, another useful report is the Deployment diagram report. It includes a detailed listing of Nodes and Components contained within the Deployment diagram. In the case of our Championzone UML example, the diagram is rather simple so the report is much smaller than our previous example. It's only three pages. The diagram itself contains two Nodes and each Node contains one Component.

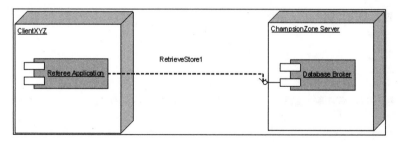

The report itself is nicely compact (I wonder about the pages and pages of detail in the Static Structure report and how much it will get used). The report contains details about the Top Package just like our Static Structure report. Then, each node (ClientXYZ and ChampionZone Server) has its own sections of the report.

The deployment report can easily be created and distributed to development, support, and implementation groups. Given the lack of overwhelming detail that we found in the Static Structure report, we can expect team members in these other groups to use and understand the contents of this report, making it much more valuable throughout the entire project lifecycle.

Component Report

The last report we'll look at in this section is the **Component Report**. It is very closely related to the Deployment report, but provides us with a bit more information about our components and their relationships to one another.

In the Championzone UML example the Component diagram looks like this:

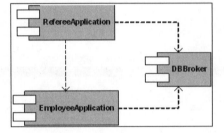

Like the Deployment diagram, it is simple and easy to understand. We can therefore expect the report to be simple and easy to understand. The information that a Component diagram, and hence its report, contains that we don't find in a Deployment diagram is dependency or relationships with other components. The diagram shows those dependencies as dashed lines. In the report, we see those dependencies as sub sections, as the following screenshot illustrates:

In this report, we see that the component named EmployeeApplication is dependent upon the component named DBBroker. If the diagram included Node information for the DBBroker component, that detail would also be displayed. It is probably reasonable to expect Component and Deployment diagrams and their reports to be used together.

Summary

In this chapter, we discussed the role of Visio and the UML as a documentation tool throughout the software development lifecycle. Although every project might be managed differently on a day-to-day basis, most projects follow the same major stages through development. We highlighted the most common UML diagrams at each of those stages and discussed their usage and role in subsequent stages of building a software application. We also briefly reviewed the features and benefits of UML Reports in Visio and how they can be used in a software development project.

After reading this chapter, you should have come away with a better understanding of the application of Visio and the UML diagrams it produces, as well as the interaction of documentation produced in one project stage with the needs of other project stages. More importantly, you'll have some ideas and tools to work into your own development projects no matter what your role is.

In the next chapter, we'll look at designing a distributed system, so keep on reading!

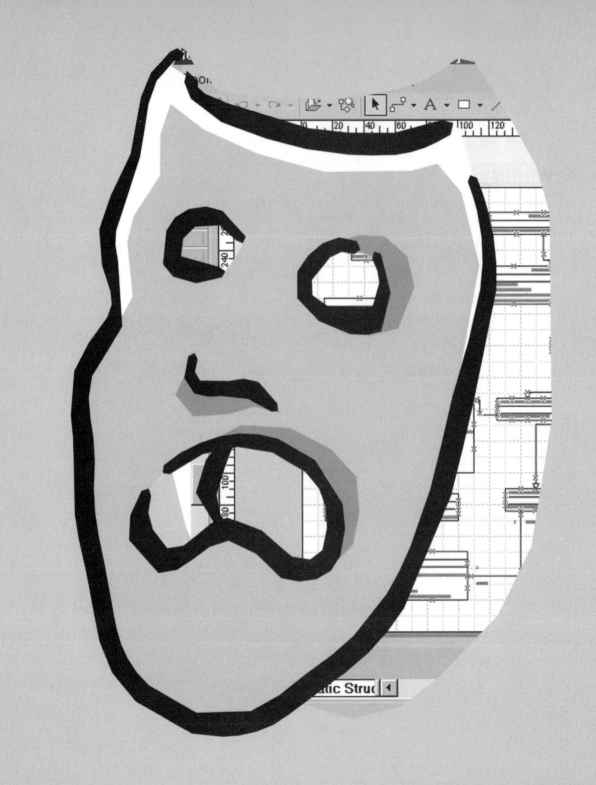

7

Distributed System Design

Designing a distributed system is an iterative process starting from **requirements analysis** to **modular breakdown** and to **packaging and deployment strategies**. The process is largely the same as the process for designing a non-distributed system, a system whose objects are all running in the same process. However, there are inherent differences between a distributed systems and a non-distributed one as pointed out in a seminal paper, "*A Note on Distributed Computing*" by Jim Waldo, Geoff Wyant, Ann Wollrath, and Sam Kendall. (This paper can be found at: http://research.sun.com/features/tenyears/volcd/papers/intros/I5Waldo.pdf as well as at other sites.)

The main differences are latency, different memory access model, concurrency, and partial failure. We'll have more detailed explanations of those differences later in the chapter. For now, the point is that designing a distributed system is different from designing a non-distributed one and those differences cannot be completely papered over by framework modules. Designers of distributed systems therefore have to take extra precautions and take into account those factors specific to distributed systems.

Fortunately, most knowledge we gained from designing non-distributed systems can be carried over. UML would be of little value if it required us to use a very different set of tools for different tasks. All the materials covered in previous chapters of this book are still valid no matter if we are designing a distributed system or a non-distributed system. With the help of good infrastructures, distributed systems require only some extra treatments and those extra treatments are mainly in the component packaging and distribution stages. Here our infrastructure of interest is of course the .NET Framework.

In this chapter, we will use a common Bank application built upon the .NET Framework as an example to demonstrate the various design decisions a designer will face in the process of designing a distributed system. However, because the initial stages like preparing use cases, class diagrams, and activity diagrams are the same no matter what system we're designing, we are not going to cover the whole design process from head to toe. Instead, we will put emphasis on the parts that are pertinent to distributed systems.

The structure of this chapter is like this: We'll first deal with terminology issues and explain what we mean by distributed system. Then we'll have some discussions on .NET's distributed infrastructure, namely .NET Remoting, that will be used in the later parts of the chapter.

After that, we look at the Bank example application. Through the example, we'll see how to decide which classes should be .NET Remoting types, how to decide the activation mode of each .NET remoting type, what code elements should be grouped in a component, how to prepare a component diagram, the technical details of compiling a component, and how to prepare a deployment diagram.

We'll cover the technical details of compiling and distributing .NET assemblies, NET's mapping of UML components.

Object-Based Distributed Systems in .NET

In this section, we'll lay the groundwork for discussion by answering the following two questions:

❑   What do we mean by distributed systems?

❑   What are the major issues that challenge designers of robust and reliable distributed systems?

Distributed Systems and Local Systems

So, what exactly is a **distributed system** and what is a **local system**? Simply put, a distributed system consists of components that run in different processes possibly (but not necessarily) on different machines. In other words, it consists of components that access different address spaces. In contrast, all components of a local system only run in one process, and are confined to a single address space. Therefore, to tell if a system is local or distributed a simple rule of thumb is to ask whether a pointer to a memory address will be valid if it's passed to another component of the system. Here, a component is a part of a system. It can be an executable, an exposed function or object in a dynamic linking library (DLL), an HTML page in a browser, etc. Take HTML pages for example. Say you have an HTML page on your machine's hard drive. You open it up with IE (Microsoft Internet Explorer) browser. When opened, the HTML page will load a COM component and invoke a method on one of the component's COM objects. Together the HTML page, the IE browser, and the COM component form an application system.

The system can be local or distributed depending on IE and the COM component. In our example, the system is distributed if the COM component is in an EXE file (we call this type of COM components out-of-process components); local if the COM component is in a DLL file (we call this type of COM components in-process components). However, if IE were implemented in a way that it would load the HTML page in one process and the COM component in another, then the system would be distributed no matter what COM component is loaded.

There is more than a single way to categorize distributed systems. For example, we can have a category for 'locally distributed systems' (sometimes referred to as logical distributed systems) that have components running in different processes on the same machine and another category for 'generally distributed systems' (sometimes referred to as physical distributed systems) that have components running in different processes on different machines.

ORPC (Object Remote Procedure Call) Protocols

Another way to categorize distributed systems is to categorize them according to the ways remote components are consumed. For example, some distributed systems make a remote function call look like a function call in the same address space. Remote procedure call (RPC)-based systems fall into this category. Other distributed systems make remote objects (instances of types) look like local objects. Components that make up this type of system communicate at an object-oriented level. Systems based on object RPC (ORPC) protocols such as DCOM and CORBA's IIOP/GIOP (Internet Inter-ORB Protocol/General Inter-ORB Protocol) are examples of this category. Readers interested in knowing more details about these protocols, their similarities, and their differences can refer to a MSDN article by Don Box, "*A Young Person's Guide to the Simple Object Access Protocol*", MSDN Magazine, March 2000 issue: http://msdn.microsoft.com/msdnmag/issues/0300/soap/soap.asp.

Another example of ORPC protocols is SOAP (Simple Object Access Protocol), the standard at the heart of Web Services. What makes SOAP different from the other ORPC protocols is its transport-neutral nature and the way it uses XML as the data format for recording payload information. For example, you have a `HelloWorld` Web Service that accepts requests from clients and returns a greeting message. The message in a request the `HelloWorld` service receives will be something that looks like the following.

```
<SOAP-ENV:Envelope xmlns:xsi='http://www.w3.org/1999/XMLSchema-instance'
xmlns:xsd='http://www.w3.org/1999/XMLSchema'
   xmlns:SOAP-ENC='http://schemas.xmlsoap.org/soap/encoding/'
  xmlns:SOAP-ENV='http://schemas.xmlsoap.org/soap/envelope/'
  SOAP-ENV:encodingStyle='http://schemas.xmlsoap.org/soap/encoding/'>
<SOAP-ENV:Body>
    <Hello xmlns="http://tempuri.org/">
        <Name>UML</Name>
    </Hello>
</SOAP-ENV:Body>
</SOAP-ENV:Envelope>
```

We can easily decrypt the request XML message and tell something about the interface of the `HelloWorld` service – the interface has a `Hello` method that accepts a `Name` parameter. The payload that the `HelloWorld` service will put in the XML message it returns to the client in response to the above request message will be something that looks like the following. The result of the `Hello` method call on the `HelloWorld` object is a greeting that says "Hello UML!"

```
<soap:Envelope xmlns:soap="http://schemas.xmlsoap.org/soap/envelope/"
xmlns:soapenc="http://schemas.xmlsoap.org/soap/encoding/"
xmlns:xsi="http://www.w3.org/1999/XMLSchema-instance"
xmlns:xsd="http://www.w3.org/1999/XMLSchema">
  <soap:Body>
    <HelloResult xmlns="http://tempuri.org/">
      <result>Hello UML!</result>
    </HelloResult>
  </soap:Body>
</soap:Envelope>
```

In contrast, other ORPC protocols do not use XML as the data format for recording payload information. DCOM uses a format called Network Data Representation (NDR) for its payload and IIOP/GIOP uses a format called Common Data Representation (CDR). Later, in the next section, we'll see that .NET Remoting as an infrastructure for object-based distributed systems supports SOAP among other protocols as the ORPC protocol for remote object communication. Interested readers can find the SOAP protocol specification at the W3C web site. (http://www.w3.org)

As we know, UML is an object-oriented analysis and design method. Applying UML to our design of a distributed system is most appropriate if the components of the distributed system we are designing communicatesat an object-oriented level. Therefore, in this chapter when we say distributed systems, we obviously mean object-based distributed systems.

Major Issues that Challenge Designers of Robust and Reliable Distributed Systems

The next question we want to answer relates to the major issues that challenge designers of robust and reliable distributed systems. We've mentioned the four major differences between local and distributed systems at the beginning of this chapter. Those differences are **latency**, **different memory access model**, **concurrency**, and **partial failure**. In addition to those four differences, one also needs to be careful about aspects such as **security** and **transaction** in a distributed environment if the system in question requires those features.

Below is a list with brief explanations of the major issues that will often concern us when we design a distributed system. We'll also see what issues on the list are taken care of at the system level by the .NET infrastructure. This is very important to know because if the infrastructure you rely on does not help with a certain issue on the following list, you as a designer have to solve that at the application level.

❑   **Performance**, including latency, network traffic, load balancing, and object pooling. **Latency** is the time-period of inactivity a user experiences from sending a request until receiving the response to the request. **Load balancing** is a performance boosting technique that dispatches client requests to the least busy service. **Object pooling** is also a performance boosting technique that eliminates the cost of object construction and destruction by keeping a pool of reusable object instances in memory. Features like load balancing and object pooling are usually provided by system-level infrastructures. To reduce the latency of a remote method invocation, you have to spend money on expensive network equipment. Latency of a remote method invocation has to do with network speed, while latency of a local method invocation has to do with the local machine's processing power. Network traffic flowing among components of a distributed system depends greatly on the system's design. A well-designed system will boost the system's performance by reducing the network traffic flowing among components. During the proof-of-concept stage, it's a good idea to prototype the system, deploy the system's components in a representative network, and see if the quality of service meets requirements.

❑   **Memory Access Model**. Remote components run in different processes and each process has its own address space. A pointer to a memory address is not valid in another process's address space. In .NET, things are a bit more complicated because of the introduction of AppDomain and Context. In .NET, a process can be divided into one or more AppDomains. Each AppDomain can be divided into one or more Contexts. Method invocations on objects in other AppDomains are remote calls. Method invocations across Contexts are remote calls as well. Those remote method calls have to go through the same marshaling and unmarshaling steps as all cross-process remote method calls do. Readers interested in knowing more about AppDomains and Context can refer to the .NET Documentation for more details.

❑ **Concurrency**. Parts of a distributed system are running in different processes possibly on different machines concurrently. At implementation time or detailed technical design phase, concurrency issues that need to be addressed are threading, execution synchronization, race conditions, deadlocks, etc. However, when working with UML in Visio, we approach problems at a more abstract level where concurrency doesn't necessarily map to programming threads. Sometimes it is sufficient to set to check the IsActive checkbox of the class shape in a Class diagram to mark classes whose instances might be accessed concurrently.

❑ **Partial failure**. Distributed systems introduce new types of failures that are not present in local systems. For example, a network link that connects two remote objects might go down. A remote machine might be powered off or crash. For a client of an object on a remote machine, it's very difficult to tell whether the problem is the network link, the remote or something else when the remote object is dead.

❑ **Distributed security and distributed transaction**. These two features are usually provided by system-level infrastructure.

UML is not tailored for the design of a particular type of application systems. One can use it to design a local system as well as a distributed system. Its generalization allows us to apply it to various kinds of system designs. It's a great bonus that UML is flexible and extensible. It allows the addition of new elements into design artifacts when necessary. Later in this chapter, we'll show how to document our design decisions on the issues listed above in UML diagrams when we come to the Bank example.

.NET Infrastructure for Distributed Systems

Now is time to ask ourselves what support we have from .NET for distributed system development and what issues concerning the design of a distributed system it takes care of. The infrastructure .NET provides for developing distributed programming comprises .NET Remoting and ASP.NET Web services. .NET Remoting is an ORPC implementation similar to DCOM and IIOP/GIOP we mentioned in previous sections. ASP.NET's ancestor ASP (Active Server Pages) was Microsoft's web server-side script engine run by Microsoft IIS (Microsoft Internet Information Service) web server. One of the major improvements ASP.NET has over ASP is its support for Web Services. It is because of this support for Web Services that clients can send SOAP messages to ASP.NET web services to invoke methods on server-side objects in an object-oriented fashion. Below we'll have a whirlwind coverage of .NET Remoting as it is less familiar to most developers and some basic knowledge of it is necessary for later discussion in this chapter. Following the whirlwind coverage of .NET Remoting is a comparison between .NET Remoting and ASP.NET and some guidelines on when to use which.

> *For more information on ASP.NET, we recommend readers towards 'Professional ASP .NET 1.0', Wrox Press (ISBN 1-86100-703-5).*

.NET Remoting

Let's start with a quick tour of some basics of .NET Remoting. We'll briefly go through some concepts and terms in .NET Remoting in this section and set the background for later discussion. For a good introduction to .NET Remoting, see *Visual Basic .NET Remoting Handbook*, Wrox Press, (ISBN 1-86100-740-X) or Chapter 21 in *Professional C# 2nd Edition*, Wrox Press (ISBN 1-86100-704-3) for a C# view.

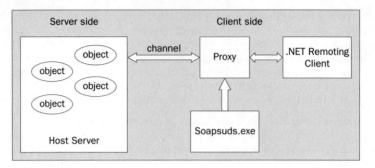

The objective of .NET Remoting is to help develop objects that can be consumed remotely in an object-oriented way. The figure above shows the relationship between a .NET Remoting server and client and how they fit in the big picture. In the above figure, we see that Remoting objects reside in a host server. Depending on how objects are activated, and their states maintained, they can be categorized into three types – Singleton, SingleCall, or ClientActivated.

- ❑ **SingleCall** objects: A SingleCall object is an object that is created for each method call and destroyed when the call is completed. A SingleCall object holds no state information between method calls.

- ❑ **Singleton** objects: A Singleton object is an object that services multiple clients. There can be only one object instance of a Singleton class. The state of a Singleton object is shared among clients. By **state** we mean values kept by member variables of a class. This type of object is called a Singleton object precisely because it follows the Singleton pattern discussed in *Professional Design Patterns in VB.NET: Building Adaptable Applications, Wrox Press (ISBN 1-86100-698-5)*.

- ❑ **Client-activated** objects: A Client-activated object is quite simply an object that is activated on the client's request. A Client-activated object can hold state information between method calls triggered by the same client. However, you cannot easily share state information among several clients with a Client-activated object.

Objects can reside in an executable host (an EXE file) of their own, or they can have IIS or the .NET Component Service as their host. Communication channels between client and server can be HTTP, SMTP, TCP, etc. When using an HTTP channel, request and response messages are SOAP messages by default. An HTTP channel can use other types of message formatters as well.

The figure above also shows one of the several ways a client can use to generate a proxy of a remote server object. A proxy is a local representation of a remote object. The main purpose of having a proxy at the client side is to make the remote object's location transparent to the client so that a method call on a remote object looks like a method call on a local object. Without proxies, clients of a remote object will have to serialize calls to and deserialize results from remote objects. For a proxy to represent a remote server object on the client side, it needs to have some knowledge about the server object in order to represent it. The knowledge is the server object's type information. .NET provides a utility, soapsuds.exe, which developers can use to get the service description of a Remoting object remotely. The service description contains the server object's type information. If the client has a local copy of the .NET Remoting server assembly, soapsuds.exe can generate a proxy from that too. .NET Remoting is all about exposing remote objects for clients to consume.

.NET Remoting allows you to extract some attributes of server objects and put them into a separate configuration file. In the configuration file, you specify what port and protocol the server object will use to communicate with clients, whether the server object is `Singleton`, `SingleCall`, or `ClientActivated`, and sometimes what formatter to use to serialize objects into streams.

The advantage of this approach is that you can change any of the settings in the object's configuration file without any code change in the object itself, and therefore without recompiling the object source files. This is very helpful at the deployment phase. Usually, (and hopefully!) your software will be sold to several customers. Each customer might have a different deployment scenario. If you put configuration settings such as a remote object's transport protocol plus port number, activation mode (`Singleton`, `SingleCall`, or `ClientActivated`), and serialization formatter in a configuration file, your field engineers can fine tune those parameters according to the customer's production environment with ease.

Remember that we said earlier that Remoting objects can be hosted in IIS, .NET Component Service, or an EXE? Here we'll write a host program, compile it into an EXE file and demonstrate how the host program reads configuration settings from a file at run time. The code for the host program is listed below. Notice the **emboldened** line in the code list. By calling `RemotingConfiguration.Configure()`, the host program reads the `server.config` configuration file, and registers channels and Remoting objects with the .NET Remoting service according to the settings you put in the configuration file. `server.config` should be in the same folder as the host EXE file.

```
using System;
using System.IO;
using System.Runtime.Remoting;

class Host
{
    static void Main(string[] args)
    {
        RemotingConfiguration.Configure("server.config");
        Console.WriteLine("Host is ready.");
        Console.WriteLine("Press ENTER to exit.");
        Console.ReadLine();
        Console.WriteLine("Exit.");
    }
}
```

A typical configuration file would be something that looks like the following.

```
<configuration>
  <system.runtime.remoting>
    <application name="HelloService">

    <service>
      <wellknown mode="SingleCall" type="Bank.Account, Bank"
                 objectUri="Account.soap" />
    </service>

    <channels>
      <channel ref="http" port="888" />
    </channels>
```

```
      </application>
   </system.runtime.remoting>
</configuration>
```

ASP.NET Versus .NET Remoting

While both .NET Remoting and ASP.NET help with object-oriented remote method invocations, they differ in a number of aspects such as allowed data types, the way the service schema is presented and stored, security support, performance, interoperability, host process, and transport protocol.

❑ **Service schema**: ASP.NET describes schemas of web services it exposes in WSDL (Web Service Description Language), a W3C standard for describing web services. Remember that in previous sections, we said that for a proxy to represent a remote server object, the proxy needs to have knowledge of the server object's type information. The service schema here is what we called type information at that time. At the .NET Remoting side, as we already said in the .NET Remoting section, type information of remote objects is stored in assemblies. .NET provides a utility, soapsuds.exe, for you to retrieve that information from assemblies.

❑ **Host process**: In the .NET Remoting section, we said that .NET Remoting objects can be hosted in an executable, in IIS or in .NET Component Service. ASP.NET Web services on the other hand run only in the aspnet_wp.exe execution process started by IIS.

❑ **Transport protocol**: .NET Remoting objects and clients can communicate over a wide range of protocols such as HTTP, TCP, SMTP, etc. ASP.NET web services and clients can communicate over only HTTP because ASP.NET relies on IIS web server for receiving and sending requests and responses.

❑ **Security**: Because ASP.NET relies on IIS for receiving requests and sending responses, it can benefit from all the transport-level security features IIS provides, including Basic Authentication, Digest Authentication, Certificate Authentication, and Windows NT Challenge/Response. ASP.NET also supports authentication based on .NET Passport. As to .NET Remoting, if remote objects are hosted in IIS with ASP.NET, they will benefit from the same security features IIS has; otherwise, they are on their own and designers and developers of the remote objects have to concern themselves with security issues from ground up.

❑ **Performance**: .NET Remoting objects communicating in a binary stream with clients over TCP has the best performance. .NET Remoting objects communicating in a binary stream with clients over transport protocols other than TCP, and .NET Remoting objects communicating in a SOAP stream with clients over any transport protocol, have no performance advantage, or even prove mediocre, when compared to ASP.NET.

❑ **Data types**: You can use only a limit set of data types, specifically data types supported by the XML Schema standard, when building ASP.NET Web services. If you use data types outside the scope of XML Schema in your ASP.NET Web services, those types cannot be expressed in the WSDL schema. With .NET Remoting, all data types supported by the CLR (Common Language Runtime) can be used.

❑ **SOAP Interoperability**: .NET Remoting objects have poor SOAP interoperability with clients on platforms other than .NET. The SOAP messages to and from .NET Remoting objects contain many .NET-specific tags for the rich features (object activation mode, object leasing, callbacks, etc.) that .NET Remoting provides. Clients must understand those tags in order to communicate with .NET Remoting. ASP.NET has a much better interoperability because it's comparably simple and it limits the allowed data types to those portable ones supported by XML Schema.

We have two .NET infrastructures for building distributed components. When should we favor one over the other? From the above list of differences between the two infrastructures, the assessment and final judgment is easier to make. If interoperability is necessary, and you cannot control client environments, then ASP.NET is the favored choice. If some security mechanism like certificate authentication is required and for some reason you can't host .NET Remoting objects in IIS and building the required security feature is the last thing you would like to do, then ASP.NET is the favored choice.

Preparation Work in Visio

We'll look at how to create new stereotypes specific to .NET Remoting in Visio. However, before creating the stereotypes, we have some preparation work to do in Visio. The preparation work includes creating a UML solution and adding an Implementation Model (see the box below for detailed explanation) to the solution. The Implementation Model folder will serve as the place for storing UML artifacts we'll create in the remaining parts of this chapter.

> **Visio organizes UML artifacts into models of a system. You can think of a model in this context as a design phase of a system. In the Visio Model Explorer, a model is merely a folder under the root node. The folder helps designers to group UML artifacts that belong to a certain design phase in a single place. For example, you can have a model that corresponds to the use case analysis phase of the system design process. The model will be a store for use case diagrams, use case shapes, actor shapes, etc. You can have another model that corresponds to the implementation model phase of the system design process. The model will be a store for component diagrams, deployment diagrams, component shapes, node shapes, etc.**

When Visio starts, you have the option of choosing the drawing type for your new drawing. In our case, we'll choose the Software category and UML Model Diagram as the drawing type for our new drawing. Alternatively, you can choose a drawing type by clicking on the menu item File | New | Choose Drawing Type…. After making the choice of a drawing type, you'll see the shape stencils specific to that drawing type. In our case, we'll see stencils for various kinds of UML diagrams. In addition, we'll also see the Model Explorer that organizes your UML artifacts in tree structures. If you don't see the Model Explorer on the screen, you can bring it up by clicking on the menu item UML | View | Model Explorer.

The Model Explorer on your screen should look like the one shown overleaf.

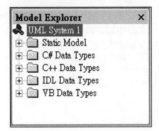

The root of the tree in the Model Explorer represents the system we're modeling. We'll change its name from **UML System 1** to **Bank System**. To make the name change, right-click on the root node, choose **Rename** in the pop-up menu, and then type in the new name. Under the root node are folders that represent models or that contain data types of the system. In our screen snapshot above, we see a **Static Model** folder that represents one model of the **Bank System**. We also see four data type folders that contain different kinds of data types. Here we'll add a new model to the Bank system. To add a model folder, right-click on the **Bank System** root node, choose **Models** in the pop-up menu, and you'll see that the **UML Models** window pops up. In the **UML Models** window, there is already an entry for **Static Model**. To add an entry for our new model, click on the **New** button, or the blank row below the entry for **Static Model** and type in **Implementation Model** in the **Model** column as the name of our new model. Click the **OK** button to confirm the changes you've made. Now you should see the **Implementation Model** folder in the **Model Explorer**. This folder will be the place where we store the component diagrams, deployment diagrams, component shapes, node shapes, etc, of the **Bank System**. By now, your **Model Explorer** should look like the one shown below. Visio will automatically create a **Top Package** under the **Implementation Model** folder for you.

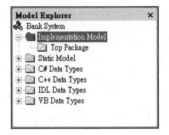

Custom UML Stereotypes for .NET Distributed Systems

In previous sections, we saw that the .NET infrastructure for distributed systems introduces many programming constructs. Some of those constructs like a Remoting type's `Activation` mode have no direct mappings in UML. In this section, we'll show you how to extend UML in Visio when the need arises by using .NET Remoting activation mode as an example. We will extend the UML model elements by defining a stereotype called `RemotingType` for modeling .NET Remoting types.

UML Model Elements for Extension

Extending UML is a very common and necessary practice because of UML's nature of being a general modeling language. In fact, it is so common and necessary that UML is specified with extensibility at its heart. The key model elements in UML for extensibility are: **Stereotype**, **TagDefinition**, **TaggedValue**, and **Constraint**. If you package a custom set of these model elements defined for a special purpose, that package is called a UML *profile*. Although we'll briefly cover the basics of those model elements momentarily, we are not going to give detailed and rigorous explanations of the terms like Stereotype, TagDefinition, profile, etc. Readers can refer to the UML Specification (version 1.4, section 2.6 Extension Mechanisms) for strict definitions of those terms. Here is a quick list of some facts about Stereotype, TagDefinition, TaggedValue, and Constraint.

- ❏ A stereotype (an instance of Stereotype) is used to add additional properties and constraints to other model elements.

- ❏ A stereotype can have multiple TagDefinition instances and multiple Constraint instances.

- ❏ A TagDefinition instance (a tag) has a tag name and some tag values.

- ❏ Tag values are instances of the TaggedValue model element.

- ❏ A tag depending on its multiplicity attribute may have multiple tag values.

- ❏ A tag has a tagType attribute and a multiplicity attribute.

- ❏ The tagType attribute of a tag specifies the data type of the tag's value.

Overleaf is a figure that shows the declaration of the stereotype we'll create in Visio. The figure gives us a lot of information about the stereotype. First, the name of the stereotype is RemotingType. The stereotype is used to brand the Class model element. In plain words, the stereotype is to used to brand C# classes that are modeled as instances of the UML Class model element. The Class model element in this context is also called the **base class** of the stereotype. From the figure, we can also tell that the stereotype has a tag (an instance of TagDefinition) called ActivationMode in the Tags compartment. Information about the ActivationMode tag is not fully shown in the figure. The figure shows that the tagType attribute, that is, the data type of the tag's value, of ActivationMode is String. What's not shown here in the figure is the ActivationMode's multiplicity attribute, which should be set to 1 in this case since a .NET Remoting type can have only one activation mode. The stereotype has a constraint as seen in the Constraints compartment. The constraint says that the value of the ActivationMode tag can only be one of the three values: Singleton, SingleCall, or Client-Activated.

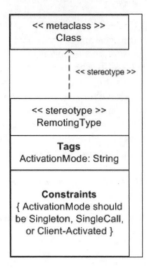

Create Custom Stereotype in Visio

Now it is time to see how to create a custom stereotype specific to .NET Remoting in Visio. Open the UML solution we created earlier if it hasn't been opened. To create a custom stereotype, select the UML menu, and then click on Stereotypes…. In the pop-up UML Stereotypes window, click the New button and you'll see a new row is added to the table of existing stereotypes. Click on the new row to make it the active row and then click the Properties… button. The UML Stereotype Properties window pops up. This window is the place where we tell Visio everything about our RemotingType stereotype. A screenshot of the UML Stereotype Properties window is shown below.

To change the name of the Stereotype to RemotingType, select Stereotype in the Categories column and type RemotingType in the Name field. In the Base Class field, click on the drop-down button and select Class. Don't worry about the value in the Full path field if it does not reflect the changes you make to the Name field. The next time you open up the UML Stereotype Properties windows for the RemotingType stereotype, it will show the correct value.

To specify the tags of the RemotingType, select Required Tagged Values if the tag is mandatory or Tagged Values if the tag is optional in the Categories column. Because we want users of the RemotingType stereotype to specify the activation modes of their .NET Remoting types every time they use the stereotype, we made the decision that the ActivationMode tag is mandatory. So select Required Tagged Values in the Categories column and then click on the New button on the right-hand side to add a new mandatory tag. The UML Tagged Value Properties window pops up. Type ActivationMode in the Tag field. In the Value field, type Singleton, SingleCall or Client-Activated. After completing the above settings, click the OK button to confirm the change. After making the changes, you should see the equivalent of the following screenshot on your computer. Notice that the string we type in the value field is not necessary. You can actually leave the field blank. We chose to type in the string because as we'll see later when branding a type with the RemotingType stereotype, the string in this case serves as a reminder of what values are valid. Notice also that there's no field for us to specify the two attributes, multiplicity and tagType, of the ActivationMode tag in Visio.

To specify the constraints of the RemotingType stereotype, select Constraints in the Categories column and then click the New button on the right-hand side to add a new constraint. A row is added to the Constraints table after you click the New button. Make the row the active row by clicking on it. Then click on the Properties... button. The UML Constraint Properties window pops up. A screenshot of the window is shown overleaf. Fill in the Name field with ActivationMode Value Constraint. Fill in the Body field with ActivationMode should be Singleton, SingleCall, or Client-Activated. Leave the Stereotype field blank as none of the stereotypes listed in the drop-down list is relevant to our constraint. Leave the Documentation fields blank or type whatever you want to say about the constraint for documentation purposes. For the Language field, click the drop-down button and select Text since we are using plain text to express our constraint in the Body field.

The RemotingType stereotype is all set. Click the OK buttons to dismiss the pop-up windows. At this point, you can test the stereotype by dragging the Class shape from the UML Static Structure stencil and dropping it in the drawing area. Double-click on the shape to bring up the UML Class Properties window. Select Class in the Categories column. Then click on the drop-down list button of the Stereotype field. There you'll see our newly created RemotingType appear on the list. If you select RemotingType as the stereotype for the Class shape and then select Tagged Values in the Categories column, you'll see the ActivationMode tag appear in the Tags list box. (If you don't see the ActivationMode tag, you might have to close the window and reopen it again.) Select the ActivationMode tag in the Tags list box and set its value in the Tag ActivationMode value text box below.

After branding the Class shape with the RemotingType stereotype, the Class shape will look like the one shown below if you set the value of ActivationMode to Singleton. If you don't see the tag value, {ActivationMode = Singleton}, appear in the Name compartment of the Class shape, you have to make it visible by right-clicking on the Class shape, select Shape Display Options… in the pop-up menu, and in the UML Shape Display Options window that pops up, check the Properties checkbox under the General options group.

```
              <<RemotingType>>
                  Class1
          {ActivationMode = Singleton}



```

Package and Deploy the Bank Application

In this part of the chapter, we'll use a Bank application as an example to demonstrate the design process starting from class diagrams to the completion of component and deployment diagrams. Although the design process is in several places tailored for distributed systems built on the .NET platform, it's general in essence and can be easily applied to systems built on other platform.

Through the various steps in the process, we'll make the following design decisions:

- What classes should be .NET remoting types and what their activation modes should be
- How to identify the elements that should go into one component
- How to share components
- How to map components to physical deployment nodes

Unlike design-level diagrams such as use case diagrams, class diagrams and other types of UML diagrams, component diagrams and deployment diagrams are implementation-level. It is therefore very helpful having a basic understanding of how things are done technically. Unlike working at the design level, working at the implementation level can be platform specific. Here the platform of interest is of course .NET. We'll show in later sections the technical details of compiling and distributing .NET assemblies, and NET's mapping of UML components.

System Requirements

For background information, we'll first make a brief system requirements list of the Bank application and give a partial class diagram of the system. Instead of formal use cases, we'll only briefly list out the parts of systems requirements pertinent to our discussion and demonstration. The Bank system we are going to build must fulfill the following requirements:

- Bank customers can manage their accounts via web browsers. They can do things like checking account balance and transferring funds.
- Bank staff can manage customer and account data. They can do things like creating or removing a customer or an account, setting an account's balance or credit line, get details of a customer or an account, etc.
- Staff records are stored in a LDAP server. Administrators of the Bank application will add or remove a staff member, get details of a staff member, set a staff member's privileges, etc., through a central management console. Our application should read staff data from the LDAP server and allow a staff member to make changes to the business data according to their privilege settings. It is also known that our client's HR system uses the LDAP server for staff authentication and authorization.
- The system must be able to conduct business with peer banks electronically using industry standards.
- Our client has two data stores. One is for customer records. The other is for account records.

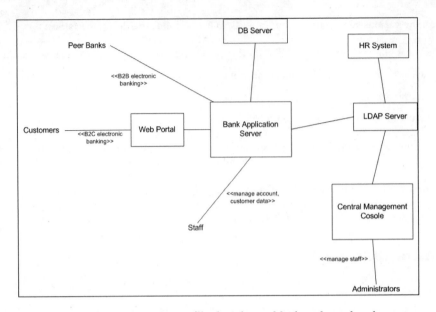

From the very primitive requirements list, we'll take a leap of faith and say that the system comprises the following types: AccountController, Account, CheckingAccount, SavingsAccount, CDAccount, Tx, TxLog, and others. Below is a class diagram showing part of the system's classes.

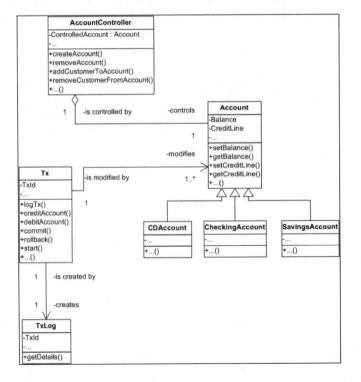

We'll use the types listed as the starting point of our discussion. Based on the types, our goal is to come up with a design for packaging and deploying our distributed **Bank** application. In other words, our goal is to start from the class diagram and end with component and deployment diagrams.

.NET Remoting Type and Activation Mode

At this point of the design process, we would like to examine the class diagram and identify the classes that should be made .NET remoting types. If a type in the class diagram will be invoked remotely by some code in a different process, then the type has to be a .NET remoting type. In other words, it has to inherit `System.Runtime.Remoting.MarshalByRefObject` either directly or indirectly. Deciding whether a type should be a .NET remoting type is straightforward.

In our Bank example, we have the following account-related types: `AccountController`, `Account`, `CheckingAccount`, `SavingsAccount`, `CDAccount`. The job of `AccountController` is to control/manage bank accounts. It has methods for creating accounts, removing accounts, adding customers to an account, removing customers from an account, etc. The `Account` class and its derived types are to represent the various kinds of bank accounts. Which one of them should be accessible to programs running on remote machines? None. The account-related types should be used internally in our application. We don't want clients of our application to access those types directly. We don't want clients to gain unnecessary insights into our system, so that we have the flexibility to change the internals of our system without breaking client programs. Clients of our application don't want to access those types directly either. They are not interested in such detailed knowledge of our system, and would like to interact with an interface that can hide the systems details.

To that end, we add a new type, `AccountFacade`, to our system. The purpose of adding `AccountFacade` to our system is to consolidate and simplify the account-related interface our system exposes to clients. By adding `AccountFacade` to our system, we also eliminate the need to make the other account-related types .NET remoting types. `AccountFacade` will be a .NET remoting type itself. All account-related requests from remote clients will go through `AccountFacade` and `AccountFacade` will work together with the internal account types to fulfill those requests.

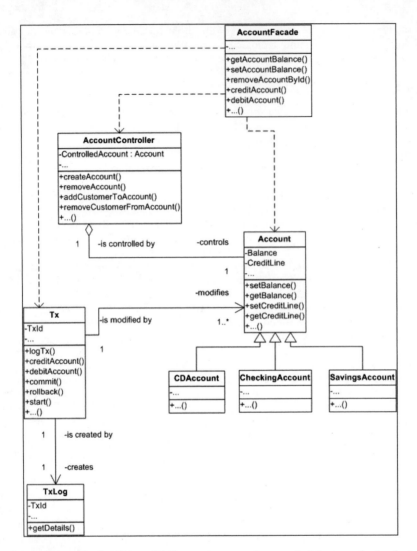

Once you decide that a type should be a .NET remoting type, the next decision to make for the type is its activation mode. Deciding the activation mode of a remote type is based mainly on whether the type is stateless. Remember that in the *.NET Remoting* primer section, we mentioned that there are three possible activation modes for remote objects: `Singleton`, `SingleCall`, and `ClientActivated`. If the type is stateless, then it should be `SingleCall`. If the type is `stateful` and has only class level states, then it should be `Singleton`. If the type is `stateful` and has only instance-level states, then it should be `ClientActivated`. The activation mode of a remote type should be decided as we prepare the class diagram.

In our Bank example, we know that `AccountFacade`, `CustomerFacade` and `TxFacade` are .NET remoting types. Although we didn't show it in a class diagram, those types are all `stateful`. They have member variables to maintain their states. Therefore, they cannot be `SingleCall`. They cannot be `Singleton` either because the states they maintain are instance-level states.

Identify the Elements that Should Go into One Component.

A component is a collection of elements that form a cohesive and logical unit of functionality. The question is: how do we identify the elements that should go into one component and how do we compose the component from those elements?

Identifying the elements that should go into one component is a harder decision to make than the previous ones. The basic rules for grouping are:

- ❑ **Functionality**: package elements that work together and that form a logical unit of functionality into a component. This is the essence of assemblies.

- ❑ **Deployment**: Package elements that form a fundamental unit of deployment.

- ❑ **Reuse**: Package elements for reuse. Elements that work together to provide a cohesive set of functionalities should be packaged for reuse.

- ❑ **Security**: Packaging for security is sometimes necessary in not only distributed systems but also local systems. However, for distributed systems, security is an area that needs particular attention. For example, a local system might have some parts that run under the system account and other parts that run under a less privileged user account. A distributed system might have some parts such as web components that run outside the protection of firewalls and some parts such as business components that run under the protection of firewalls.

- ❑ **Performance**: Many performance boosters such as load balancing and object pooling are implemented in system-level infrastructure. For application-level designers, the main focus for improving system performance should be on packaging components so that network traffic flowing among components can be minimized.

When designing a system, one can take a bottom-up or a top-down approach. Using a bottom-up approach, the designer recognizes types from use cases first and then groups those types into larger piece components. Using a top-down approach, the designer recognizes the larger pieces first and then breaks down each piece into smaller parts. The designer can verify their top-down design by checking if the design covers all types that one can derive from use cases via a bottom-up approach.

From the naming of the types listed above, you can see that we took a mix of both the top-down and bottom-up approaches when designing the system. When we were designing the system, we had an idea that the system would consist of components such as account, customer, and transaction. Therefore, we gave the types in each potential component descriptive names. Here we'll start from the packaging rules listed above and verify if our grouping of the account-related classes into the Account component is adequate.

Adding a Detailed Component Diagram

After identifying components of the Bank system and the elements each component contains, we are now ready to use Visio to model that information and prepare component diagrams of the Bank system. We'll add to the Implementation Model folder the UML shapes and diagrams that belong to the implementation model phase of the system design process. Therefore, we'll add a component diagram and several component shapes to the Implementation Model folder. The component diagram will give a detailed view of the components the Account subsystem of the Bank.

Remember that in the *.NET Remoting* section we said that remote objects (instances of .NET remote types) need a host process to house them. In our `Account` component, we have a .NET remote type, the `AccountFacade` class, and we need a host program for it. Assume that the host program is the `Host.cs` file listed in the *.NET Remoting* section. We use the following command to compile `Host.cs` and generate `Host.exe`.

```
csc /r:System.Runtime.Remoting.dll Host.cs
```

Also, remember that in the .NET Remoting section we said that an `EXE` host program usually reads run-time configurations of remoting objects from a configuration file. A sample configuration file was shown in that section. Putting all those pieces together, the `Account` assembly, the host program, the configuration file, and the underlying .NET remoting infrastructure, we can draw up the component below:

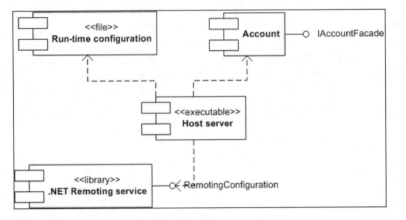

The component diagram above shows four components: the `Account` assembly, the host server, the run-time configuration file, and the .NET remoting infrastructure. We'll now walk through the steps of creating the above diagram in Visio.

1. Add a Component diagram

First, we'll add a component diagram to the Implementation Model under the Top Package and name it `AccountComponent`. Right-click on the Top Package subfolder of the Implementation Model folder and select New | Component Diagram in the pop-up menu. Rename the newly created component to AccountComponent by right-clicking on the component, selecting Rename in the pop-up menu and then typing in AccountComponent.

2. Add Component shapes

In the AccountComponent diagram, we'll add four component shapes for each of the four components shown in the above diagram. To add a component shape to the drawing space of a diagram, locate the Component shape in the UML Component stencil, drag it and drop it onto the drawing area. To add the Account component to the AccountComponent diagram, drag and drop the Component shape and rename it Account.

Notice that as you add the Account Component shape in the drawing area, an element appears in the Model Explorer under the Top Package folder. This is handy because from the Model Explorer, you can quickly see the elements in a package and the packages in a model. What's more, the elements shown in the Model Explorer and their dependencies can be reused in other UML artifacts as we'll see later in the chapter when we prepare Deployment diagrams. Repeat the steps for adding the Account component and add the other three Component shapes to the AccountComponent diagram. You should see the three corresponding elements under the Top Package folder.

3. Add Interface shapes

After the Component shapes are in place, the next thing we'll do is model the public interfaces of components in our Component diagram. We do so by attaching interface lollipop shapes to Component shapes so that users of our diagram can tell the public interfaces of a component. We'll attach an interface lollipop shape to the Account component shape and name it IAccountFacade. By doing so, we model into the AccountComponent diagram the fact that the Account component exposes to the public the IAccountFacade interface. To attach the IAccountFacade interface lollipop shape to the Account component shape, locate the Interface lollipop shape in the UML Component stencil, drag and drop it to the drawing area. Attach the Interface lollipop shape to the Account component shape. Rename the Interface lollipop shape to IAccountFacade. Repeat the same steps for adding the RemotingConfiguration interface to the .NET Remoting service component. Notice that like Component shapes, the Interface lollipop shapes we just added to the drawing appeared in the Model Explorer.

4. Add Dependency shapes

Besides components and interfaces, we also need to model dependencies among components in the AccountComponent diagram. This is done by dragging the Dependency shapes in the UML Component stencil and dropping them in the drawing area. In the AccountComponent diagram, we modeled three dependencies, one between the Account and the Host server component, one between Run-time configuration and Host server, and the other between Host server and .NET Remoting service. Notice that Dependency shapes are not elements under the Top Package folder in the Model Explorer.

After completing the above steps for preparing the AccountComponent diagram, the Model Explorer should look like the one shown overleaf.

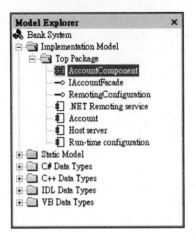

Adding a Bird's-Eye-View Component Diagram

A component diagram can show the components that make up a system in great detail. It can also give a bird's eye view of components that make up a system and their dependencies. The diagram below is also a component diagram of our Bank application. However, unlike the diagram in the previous section, it shows only the larger pieces. If you break down the Account component in the diagram below, you get the more detailed diagram like the one shown in the previous section.

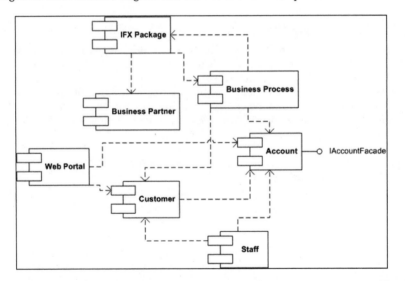

The component diagram above shows that our Bank application consists of seven large components. The four components at the top are for conducting B2B electronic banking with business partners. The four components at the bottom are for customers to do online banking and for staff to manage accounts and customers.

You can follow the procedures and steps we used in the previous section to draw the above diagram. The name of the Component diagram we created in this section is BankComponent. Notice that when drawing the BankComponent diagram, we should not drag and drop a Component shape from the UML Component stencil for the Account component. The Component shape for the Account component was drawn in the previous section when we prepared the AccountComponent diagram and it appears in the Model Explorer as an element. To draw the Account component in the BankComponent diagram, we should drag and drop the Account element in the Model Explorer instead. After completing the drawing, the Model Explorer should look like the one shown below.

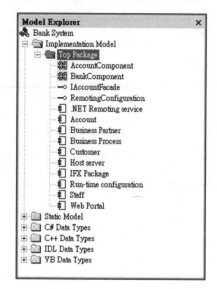

Component Packaging

In the previous sections, we prepared Component diagrams of the Bank application. The designing and drawing of Component diagrams is platform independent. Exactly how code pieces belonging to the same component are compiled and grouped together depends on the platform you build your application upon. Here, we'll look at the technical, implementation-level details of how to compile types into modules and modules into assemblies for packaging related, cohesive types into components on the .NET platform.

First, we want to ask what the mapping of a UML component is in .NET. Let's refresh our notion of a UML component a little. A UML component is, as described in the UML Specification (version 1.4, section 2.5.2.12), "a modular, deployable, and replaceable part of a system that encapsulates implementation and exposes a set of interfaces." The description is very general and gives us only the traits a component should possess. From that description, a UML component can be a broad range of things. Typically, a UML component will be an executable (EXE), a dynamic-link library (DLL), and a bunch of source code files or binary code files. In .NET, there is a specific name for UML components. We call them assemblies.

A .NET assembly is, as described in the .NET documentation, "a collection of types and resources that are built to work together and form a logical unit of functionality." Furthermore, the .NET documentation says an assembly is "a fundamental unit of deployment, version control, reuse, activation scoping, and security permissions." It is apparent that this description of an assembly matches the traits of an UML component.

If you have an assembly to package and share, you have to consider the following two questions:

❑ How do you want to share the assembly? That is, do you want to share the assembly privately or publicly?

❑ What do you need to do to share the assembly the way you want?

In .NET, an assembly can be shared with other assemblies locally or globally. Sharing an assembly locally means only a certain set of assemblies can locate and access the shared assembly. Sharing an assembly globally means all assemblies can locate and access the shared assembly. You have to decide how you want to share an assembly, locally or globally. Usually, when an assembly is intended to be used by not only your application but also unknown applications developed by others, the assembly should be shared globally. An example for this type of assemblies is a third-party .NET component that performs functions like spell checking or file uploading. Components that perform spell checking or file uploading are so general that they could be utilized by, and therefore should be shared globally with, all applications that need access to them.

If you want to share an assembly locally with a certain set of assemblies, you have to put a copy of the shared assembly's DLL either in each of the folders of the dependent assemblies or in the private search paths of the dependent assemblies. On the other hand, if you want to share an assembly globally with assemblies in any application or if the assembly will be used in COM+ components, you have to put the shared assembly's DLL in the global assembly cache (GAC).

Let's use the Account component as an example. The component has the following classes: Tx, TxLog, Account, CDAccount, CheckingAccount, SavingsAccount, AccountController, and AccountFacade. Each of them is in its own C# source file. Our naming convention for the C# source files is the class name followed by the file extension (.cs) for C# source files. For example, the definition of Account is in Account.cs. Grouping all the classes into one component means compiling all the source files into one assembly. To compile the source files into one assembly, we first compile each of the source files into a module. Then we generate the assembly from the modules.

The command below compiles Account.cs into a module. The result module contains the MSIL code and metadata for the Account class. The module filename is Account.netmodule.

```
csc /t:module Account.cs
```

The following four commands compile CDAccount, CheckingAccount, SavingsAccount, and AccountController into their own modules respectively. Because the four classes reference the Account class in Account.netmodule, we have to indicate that reference in the commands using /addmodule.

```
csc /t:module /addmodule:Account.netmodule CDAccount.cs
csc /t:module /addmodule:Account.netmodule CheckingAccount.cs
csc /t:module /addmodule:Account.netmodule SavingsAccount.cs
csc /t:module /addmodule:Account.netmodule AccountController.cs
```

The command below compiles TxLog.cs into a module. The module filename is TxLog.netmodule.

```
csc /t:module TxLog.cs
```

The command below compiles `Tx.cs` into a module. Because the class `Tx` references the `Account` class in `Account.netmodule`, we have to indicate that reference in the command using `/addmodule`.

```
csc /t:module /addmodule:TxLog.netmodule /addmodule:Account.netmodule Tx.cs
```

The following command compiles `AccountFacade.cs` and all the previously created modules into a DLL named `AccountFacade.dll`.

```
csc /t:library /addmodule:Account.netmodule /addmodule:Tx.netmodule
/addmodule:CDAccount.netmodule /addmodule:CheckingAccount.netmodule
/addmodule:SavingsAccount.netmodule /addmodule:AccountController.netmodule
/addmodule:TxLog.netmodule -out:AccountFacade.dll AccountFacade.cs
```

The `AccountFacade.dll` and all module files together are our `Account` component. In other words, the `Account` component in our `Bank` application is a multi-file assembly that consists of `AccountFacade.dll` and the module files. The DLL file contains not only the MSIL code and metadata for the `AccountFacade` class but also the assembly's manifest.

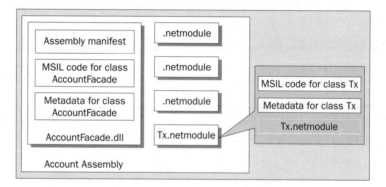

This figure above illustrates the relationships among modules, assemblies, manifest, and metadata. It is important to note that the purpose of this section is to show you how to technically package classes into an assembly in the .NET platform so that you have a more solid feeling of the correlation between conceptual design and physical implementation. However, just because you know how things are done physically doesn't mean that you should put everything you know in a design document. UML is platform independent and not tied to the build process of a specific platform. How the components of your application are built is irrelevant to UML. Therefore, don't model the build information in an UML component diagram.

Map Components to Physical Deployment Nodes

The Component diagram shows the various modules of our application but it does not tell you which module will go on which hardware platform. The job of a Deployment diagram is to fulfill that need and provide designers with a standard way of documenting system deployment.

Thanks to Visio and its UML Model Diagram Template, creating a deployment diagram is a breeze once you have the component diagram ready. If you know how to leverage the help Visio provides, you'll find that the time and hard work you invested in drawing a component diagram is rewarding when you are trying to prepare the deployment diagram. Let's open up the component diagram we made previously. If you don't see the Model Explorer window, then open the UML menu, point to View and click on Model Explorer to bring up the Model Explorer window. In that window, you should see the Implementation model we created previously in the tree hierarchy.

We'll now add a Deployment diagram to the model under the Top Package subfolder of the Implementation Model folder and name it BankDeployment. In the drawing space of the newly created BankDeployment diagram, we can now drag and drop elements from the UML Deployment stencil as well as elements in the Top Package. This saves us a lot of headache because in BankDeployment, we can reuse elements that we added to the model when preparing the BankComponent diagram.

During the requirements analysis phase, we knew from interviews with our client that they have two database servers, one for storing account records and the other for storing customer records. For performance reasons, we decide to deploy the Account component on a machine close to the database server that stores account records. Similarly, we'll deploy the Customer component on a machine close to the database server that stores customer records.

So we'll have four nodes in our deployment diagram, one for the Account component hosted on one app server, one for the Customer component hosted on another app server, and two nodes for the two database servers. This is shown in the diagram opposite. Notice that we made the decision of deploying the Staff component on the same machine as the Customer component. Besides the four nodes, we also see some others. The Staff component accesses an LDAP server shared by our Bank application, client's HR system, and a central management console. Here in the deployment diagram, we only show the LDAP server because our Staff component connects to it directly. The HR system and central management console are not relevant to our system deployment and they shouldn't be modeled in the diagram.

In the diagram below, a node runs the web server hosting web pages for B2C electronic banking. On the side of B2B electronic banking, we have an app server for hosting the three B2B components.

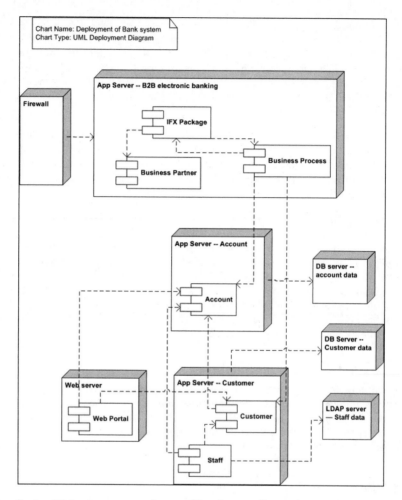

The beauty of using Visio to prepare a diagram like the one shown above is that you only need to drag node shapes from the UML Deployment stencil and component elements from the Top Package, place them where you would like them to be in the drawing area, and name them properly. The dependencies among components are automatically carried over from the BankComponent diagram. We'll now walk through the steps of creating the above diagram in Visio.

1. Add a Deployment diagram

First, we'll add a Deployment diagram to the Implementation Model under the Top Package and name it BankDeployment. Right-click on the Top Package subfolder of the Implementation Model folder and select New | Deployment Diagram in the pop-up menu. Rename the newly created diagram to BankDeployment by right-clicking on the node representing the diagram in the Model Explorer, selecting Rename in the pop-up menu, and then typing in BankDeployment as the new name for the diagram.

2. Add Node shapes

In the BankDeployment diagram, we'll add Node shapes for each of the eight nodes shown in the above diagram. To add a Node shape to the drawing space of a diagram, locate the Node shape in the UML Deployment stencil, drag it, and drop it on the drawing area. To add the Web server node to the BankDeployment diagram, drag and drop the Node shape to the drawing area and rename it to Web Server.

Notice that as you add the Web Server Node shape in the drawing area, an element appears in the Model Explorer under the Top Package folder. This is the same as what we've seen in previous sections where we added Component shapes or Interface shapes to a Component diagram. Repeat the steps for adding the Web Server node and add the other Node shapes to the BankDeployment diagram.

3. Add Component shapes

After the Node shapes are in place, the next thing we'll do is model the information of what component of the Bank system resides on which node. We do so by dragging and dropping the Component elements in the Top Package folder. This reuse of Component elements we created in an earlier Component diagram is a time-saving feature of Visio. It also reduces the chance of having inconsistencies between Component diagrams and Deployment diagrams. As you place the Component elements in the drawing area of the BankDeployment diagram, you'll notice that the dependencies among components are carried over from the BankComponent diagram.

4. Add additional Dependency shapes

The Dependency shapes that are carried over from the BankComponent diagram are dependencies among components. Besides those dependencies, we might need some others for denoting the dependencies between two nodes or between a node and a component. To model those extra dependencies in the BankDeployment diagram, we'll drag the Dependency shapes in the UML Deployment stencil and drop them in the drawing area. In the BankDeployment diagram, we have a dependency between the Staff component and the LDAP Server node, a dependency between the App Server – Customer node and the DB Server – Customer Data node. We also have a dependency between the App Server – Account node and the DB Server – Account Data node, and a dependency between the Firewall node and the App Server – B2B Electronic Banking node.

After completing the above steps for preparing the BankDeployment diagram, the Model Explorer should look like the one shown opposite. We can see that under the Top Package, we have a few new elements. They are the various nodes in the BankDeployment diagram.

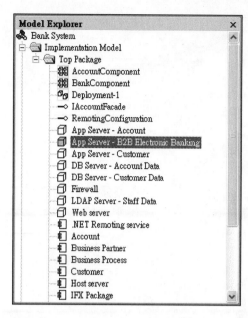

We would like to make a point before ending this section. Showing how components are distributed is the purpose of a deployment diagram. When we say how components are distributed, we don't mean the physical means you use to install programs on production machines. What we mean is the logical topological placement of components. The physical means that you use to distribute components of your application is irrelevant to UML design. One can choose to package assemblies into .cab or .msi files and let users install the application by using tools such as InstallShield or Microsoft Installer. So, don't model this information in an UML deployment diagram.

Summary

We have looked at the various aspects of distributed system design and the .NET infrastructure for distributed programming. We examined the specific problems that challenge designers of distributed systems and then went through the design process of distributed systems by going through an example application. We created a custom stereotype for modeling .NET Remoting objects and their activation modes. The custom stereotype we created is just the tip of the iceberg. We hope you have fun in creating your own!

In the next chapter we look at the crucially important area of database modeling using Visio, which includes an in-depth look at Object Role Modeling (ORM), reverse engineering a database, and much more besides!

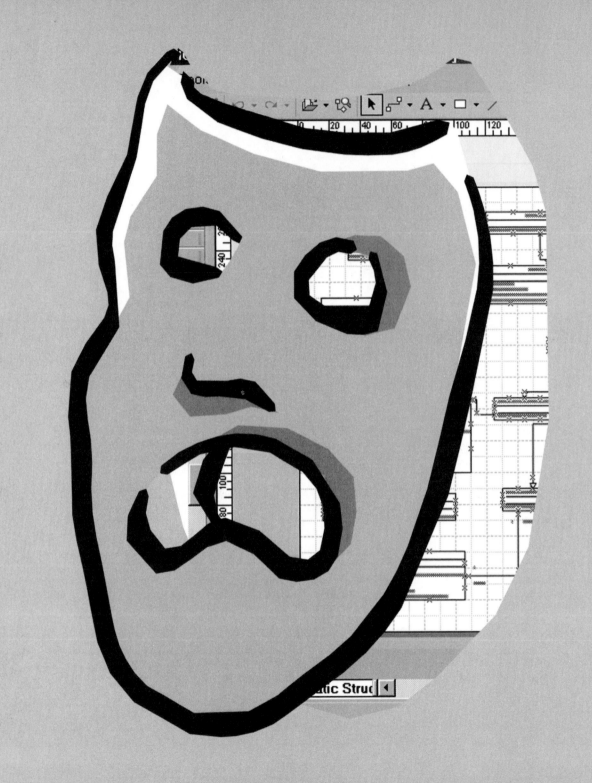

Database Modeling with Visio for Enterprise Architects

The preceding chapters of this book have shown how to use Visual Studio .NET and UML to help architect an object-oriented solution that fulfills business needs. In order to accomplish this, Requirements were gathered and analyzed, conceptual designs were constructed, logical and functional diagrams were created, and a framework for the implementation was generated. All of this was accomplished from a truly object-oriented, code perspective. This chapter intends to illustrate how to do much the same thing but rather from a data-centric view. We will show how the new tools available to us can be used to achieve more speed, reliability, pertinence, and efficiency throughout the development process.

Specifically, these tools include:

- ❑ Database modeling
- ❑ Object Role Modeling (ORM)
- ❑ Visio Data Projects
- ❑ ORM Source Diagrams
- ❑ Entity Relationship Source Diagrams
- ❑ Reverse Engineering the database
- ❑ Generating/Updating the database

Design Process Overview

We begin by looking at where the details of the rest of the chapter fit into the development of a business solution. When we first set out to build a project, we have an idea of what the solution will entail and how it will be built. It's getting there by extracting the details of our idea that is the aim of the design process. In order to prevent us from getting lost in these details, however, our aim in the next section is to provide a bigger picture, so that you can have an idea of how and why VS.NET's data-modeling capabilities can help you develop better solutions.

Database Modeling

When a problem is presented to us, we first need to understand the nature of it. The only ones who can do this are the ones who have the problem in the first place. In order to help them, we need them to communicate it to us. The main concern at this point is this communication. But how can we communicate effectively when the parties come from different backgrounds? Finding a common ground that is simple and intuitive between the technical domain and the problem domain is what a modeling solution hopes to accomplish. Neither party has to know the details of what the other side is doing when they can both agree that the model is correct. In this way, a model is like a contract (interface in object-oriented (OO) parlance) between the two groups. This will become clearer later on in the chapter when we see, as an example, that as long as they can both agree on the logical ER diagram, the programmer can develop their part of the solution independent of the physical database and the DBA can perform their optimization and administration however they please. Now replace DBA and Programmer with Programmer and Domain expert and you'll have an idea of where ORM fits in.

A concise description of the problem creates documentation. This is another benefit of modeling: documentation as an artifact is a by-product of the modeling process. Documentation should also serve as a defined deliverable, which can be used to measure progress of the project and minimize ambiguity and assumptions made on the part of both sides. The less assumptions made by both sides, the less risk is involved.

Visual Studio .NET for Enterprise Architects will greatly speed the iteration of the design steps and insulate the architect from the risk involved in changing scope or design decisions later on in the development cycle. One way this is accomplished is through the automation of mapping from one design phase to the other. While the improvements brought forth in this new tool are many, the database modeling aspects represent a tremendous leap in the development of effective databases. Most of us have used tools that can create DBMS systems based on logical diagrams and models. Many different tools exist that accomplish only this. In fact, most DBMS systems come with a suite of tools that will allow the architect to map out the database using the most popular of these models, the Entity Relationship diagram (ERD). These diagrams have become the de facto standard today and represent one layer of abstraction above the physical database. They can be used in a number of ways to directly manipulate or create scripts that can update the system to reflect changes made in the source model. This process has been greatly refined in the latest version of Visio for Enterprise Architects.

Although this is the way it has been done for some time and it is still part of the process of creating the system, Entity Relationship Diagrams were only developed to ease one aspect of the development cycle, namely the logical design phase. In order to address the other steps, VS.NET now tightly integrates **Object Role Modeling (ORM)**.

ORM has been around since the mid 1970's and is at a level of maturity where a formal specification has been adopted for some time. It was developed alongside UML as a data-centric modeling language and like UML, helps nearly all phases of the development process. It uses natural language to help gather and analyze requirements with subject matter experts, provides a modeling language to perform conceptual design, and maps well to Entity Relationship Diagrams to provide the logistics of the implementation of the solution. Like UML, it is flexible and broad enough to cover any situation, and yet finely detailed enough to be useful and convey most of its information to the next step of the design process.

Object Role Modeling (ORM)

ORM grew out of a combination of Binary Relationship Modeling, which studied the different types of relationships that could exist between two objects, and Natural Language Information Analysis Method (NIAM), which sought to dissect language to define objects involved and the relationships between them. The goal was to create a modeling language that was based on natural language, was intuitive, and mapped easily to existing database systems. In its current incarnation, developed by Dr. Terry Halprin it is supported by the latest version of Visio available with Visual Studio EA (see www.microsoft.com/office/visio for more details) as FORML (Formal Object Role Modeling Language). The result is a comprehensive modeling language that provides easy-to-understand language coupled with intuitive, easy-to-understand diagrams that map quite well to the logical design structures.

The benefits of its use are numerous. It greatly speeds up the requirements-gathering process by describing objects and the roles they play instead of trying to jump directly to creating tables with attributes to store the information. It provides stability and reliability by accommodating underlying changes easily and allowing the model to be populated with sample data to check the accuracy of the model. It is complete, in that almost any business requirement may be notated using the many constructs of the language. Finally, it helps comprehension so that the ideas conveyed by the model may be easily expressed to non-technical business stakeholders. The combination of all of these benefits makes ORM a very useful tool in most if not all of the steps of the design process.

Because ORM is closely tied to UML from an object-oriented perspective, it offers some of the same benefits and can actually help better refine a UML model.

It can be used to model many different levels of abstraction. For example, the entire system can be mapped on a single page showing only the major subsystems and how they interact with each other. Then it can be used to build the subsystems with a fine degree of detail and control over most of the implementation aspects. Even at this level, it still holds true to its name by representing conceptual objects as they are, not fitted into an implementation-specific modeling solution such as static structure or ER diagrams. Even at this level, its object-oriented nature shields users from implementation and technical terms such as tables and columns.

What is ORM?

ORM is a fact-based approach to modeling a solution. What does this mean? It means that we define the system or domain by defining the facts about what makes up the system. Instead of talking about objects and attributes or tables and columns, we talk about the roles an object plays in the system or what it *does* with another object. This allows a high-level discussion of the system, but don't think everything needs to be kept at a high level. ORM provides a level of detail specific enough to clearly define the rules and constraints that make up the system.

By expressing the parts that make up the system in simple sentences like these, we're able to begin the process of formalizing our design.

Elementary Facts

At its base level, ORM is composed of elementary facts. These are simple declarative statements about objects, and the roles they play. They shouldn't contain any extraneous information at this point, simply a subject and a predicate. Some examples from a system we're going to look at are:

- Flight *departs from* Gate
- Terminal *has a* Gate
- Airline *owns a* Terminal

Sometimes it is useful to express the inverse of the facts so that the statement is even clearer:

- Gate *is departed from by* Flight
- Gate *is of* Terminal
- Terminal *is owned by* Airline

The shorthand way to represent this is with a slash between the two forms of the predicate. We read these left to right, and then right to left so that none of the information above is lost:

- Flight *departs from/is departed from by* Gate (read as: Flight departs from Gate; Gate is departed from by Flight)
- Terminal *has a/is of* Gate
- Airline *owns/is owned by* Terminal

Here, the objects are the nouns in each of the facts and are capitalized so that they can be easily distinguished. Since there are two nouns in each of these facts, they are called binary facts. The number of objects participating in a predicate is the arity of the predicate. The default arity is binary, but we can also have unary facts that describe the state of an object (for example, Gate is occupied), ternary facts that we'll see later, and even quaternary facts (with an arity of 1, 3, and 4, respectively). The predicate of the sentence defines the roles (arrives, has, and owns) that the objects fulfill in the fact.

This is the verbal aspect of ORM and is a great way to express information about the system. Another method is used in concert with this verbalization. This is the graphical depiction of these elementary facts using ORM notation.

ORM Notation

To visually represent the facts above, we use ORM notation.

Objects and Roles

Objects are depicted as ovals, while the roles are depicted as boxes as shown:

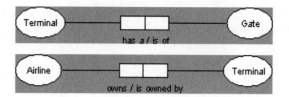

We can see that each object fulfills one role above represented by a box. These boxes together represent the predicate of the fact. The entire diagram together depicts the fact type.

Constraints

Constraints are the bread and butter of the ORM. They are how we define the rules of the system and further refine the relationships between objects represented by their roles. For example, we could say that an airline must own at least one terminal in order to be considered an airline. This is known as a Mandatory Constraint and it asserts that in order to exist, the object must participate in this role. Mandatory Constraints are depicted in ORM notation by a dot on the line connecting the object to its role. Coming from the other side of the predicate, we could assert that every terminal is owned by at most one airline. This is a uniqueness constraint stating that the Terminal object can only play the role once or not at all. This is represented by an arrow over the role played by the Terminal object. You can see this in the diagram below:

These are simple constraints that we've entered to demonstrate some of the notation. We'll show some more complex constraints in a bit, but first let's take a look at a procedure that has been designed to help us come up with the objects, roles, and constraints. This is the Conceptual Schema Design Procedure (CSDP).

The Conceptual Schema Design Procedure

This procedure was created specifically for ORM modeling to help create ORM diagrams. The steps of the procedure are as follows:

- ❑ Transform familiar information examples into elementary facts, and apply quality checks
- ❑ Draw the fact types, and apply a population check
- ❑ Check for entity types that should be combined and note any arithmetic derivations
- ❑ Add uniqueness constraints and check fact types
- ❑ Add mandatory role constraints and check for logical derivations
- ❑ Add value, set comparison, and subtyping constraints
- ❑ Add other constraints and perform final checks

We'll go through each of these steps with a straightforward example. Suppose we need to create a system that manages a number of the day-to-day operations of an airline. This would be quite a large system, so we'll break it down into more manageable parts. We've been told that the part they're having the most problems with is how to get the right meals to the right flights. This will be the domain or Universe of Discourse we'll begin with.

Step one of the procedure accepts as its input requirements and examples from the users of the system. When we say examples, we mean just that. One of the benefits of ORM and this procedure is that it accepts example data from the users and can even use it to generate parts of the model. One of the best ways to obtain this type of data is with a report or input screen that the users expect the system to fill with data. This offers an extremely intuitive way for the users to specify requirements. People are familiar with reports and they'll usually know what kind of information they will need from the system and what kind of information they will need to enter.

We meet with the people currently responsible for the part of the system we're beginning with and they provide us with an auditing report that the system would produce. We quickly scan through and removed some of the monotony and repetition of the report to give a clearer picture of the types of information needed:

Flight Number	Departure Time	Terminal	Gate	Seat	Meal Type
5468	8:30 AM	A	A34	B12	Kosher
5468	8:30 AM	A	A34	B13	Regular
5572	9:00 AM	C	C28	E23	Vegetarian
5695	9:30 AM	C	C15	F11	Regular
5433	10:30 AM	C	C12	D15	Regular
5211	11:15 AM	C	C12	F11	Regular

So applying the method described in the first step of the CSDP we derive the following fact types:

- Flight *has* Flight Number
- Flight *has* Departure Time
- Flight *departs* Gate
- Gate *has* GateCode
- Terminal *has* Gate
- Terminal *has* TerminalLetter
- Flight *has* Seat
- Seat *has* SeatCode
- Meal Type *is delivered to* Seat

This takes us all of five minutes after we've got the report above. We quickly write them down and show them to the client for some quick verification that these really do capture most of the objects in the system. This is another great feature of ORM. Because it uses natural language, we don't need our clients to learn anything at all just yet. We simply make some statements about the system and see if they nod their heads.

Objects Types: Entity and Value Types

At this point, let's discuss the different types of objects that will play a role in our facts above: object types and value types.

Objects are anything that can take part in a fact. They are what the system will be composed of and can be real-world physical objects (Terminals, Gates) or more abstract (Takeoff Times). A value object represents an object that will not be broken down further and usually represents a numeric or string constant. Think of value objects as the primitive data types in a system. They are usually restricted to participating in one role with an entity type object.

An entity object on the other hand represents a more complicated real-world object that can play many different roles with both values and other entity types. Entity objects are represented by solid ovals while value objects are dotted ovals.

Entity objects must have a reference scheme that identifies the objects within their roles.

> *The reference scheme is used so that you can get a clearer picture of which object* instance *is playing in the role* instance.

The experts of the system will help with defining the reference scheme for your entity object types. For example, we find that:

- ❑ Flight is referenced by its `FlightNumber`
- ❑ Gate can be referenced by its `GateCode`
- ❑ Terminal is referenced by its `TerminalLetter`
- ❑ Seat is referenced by its `SeatCode`

The reference scheme is depicted in the diagram in parentheses below the Entity object name, as shown for our `Terminal` object:

Value types that do not serve as reference schemes for entity types are constants. They have an implicit reference scheme that is omitted from the diagram. For example, an instance of the `TerminalLetter` object could be `'B'`.

After coming up with our reference schemes for our entity objects, we have the following fact types:

- ❑ Flight (`FlightNumber`) *has* Departure Time
- ❑ Flight (`FlightNumber`) *departs* Gate (`GateCode`)
- ❑ Terminal (`TerminalLetter`) *has* Gate (`GateCode`)
- ❑ Flight (`FlightNumber`) *has* Seat (`SeatCode`)
- ❑ Meal Type *is delivered to* Seat (`SeatCode`)

The next step in the CSDP is to draw the fact types. Since we're going to use Visio to do this, it will help to understand some things about how Visio structures and organizes our source models.

Visio Data Projects

When Visio is launched, it assumes you would like to begin a new modeling project or diagram and presents you with a number of modeling solutions. Selecting the **Databases** category presents you with the choices shown below (depending on which models you chose to install in the Visio setup application). The diagrams that we are concerned with throughout this chapter are the Database Model Diagram, the ER Source Model, and the ORM Source Model. The cornerstone of the Visio Data Project will be the Database Model Diagram (DMD).

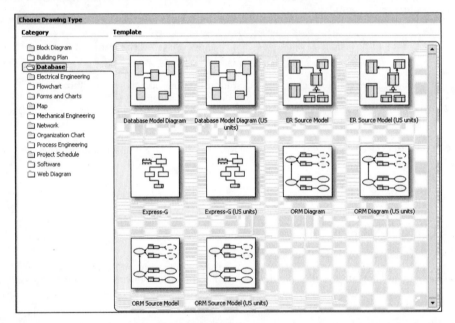

The DMD is mainly an **Entity Relationship** (ER) diagram with project management capabilities. The drawing surface itself is a standard ER diagram with standard ER shapes that are used to map out your logical design. However, unlike the standard ER Source Model, it has a number of features that make up the structure of a data project. Most of this functionality is accessed through the database menu. Opposite, we show a standard ER source model's database (right) menu compared with that of the Database Model Diagram on the left.

The DMD is the only diagram from which a database can be generated or updated. Think of the DMD as a staging area for the project. As we'll go into detail later, while ORM is a great tool for gathering/analyzing requirements and creating a conceptual design, it wouldn't be a good idea to directly create a physical database from it. There has to be an intermediate step depicting some of the logical design details. As we'll see, at interim steps in the conceptual design, the project can be built to produce the logical design as encapsulated by the DMD. Here it can be given final implementation details before the generation or update of the database takes place. We'll go into each of the differences in detail in a while, but for completeness, we'll briefly explain what each represents.

The Show Related Tables menu choice is merely a UI change; it will add to the drawing surface all the tables in the model that are directly related to the currently selected table. The model menu includes the Model Error Check function and a new function called Refresh that will refresh the model with any changes in the underlying database. The Project sub-menu is the most important change from ER diagram to data project. It provides the functionality to add existing models to the data project and maintain the synchronization between the source models and the DMD.

Creating the Data Project

We noted earlier that a data project's functionality is based around the Database Model Diagram. This is best explained in terms of the Project submenu of the Database menu pictured above. As you can see, the Project menu contains functionality to build the project, manage the project documents, and maintain the source models. The first step is usually to add a source model to the project. Since this is a completely new system that we intend to design, we will begin by adding a new ORM source model so that we can get back to our example. Clicking this option prompts you to name and save your new source model. After it is finished saving, you should see the project window partially covering your drawing. Your new file should appear in the project window; double-clicking it will open your new ORM diagram alongside your DMD.

You now have all of the files you need to create your solution in Visio. The ORM source model will facilitate requirements gathering, analysis, and creation of the conceptual design. The DMD encompasses an ER diagram that will accommodate all of the logical design requirements and allow the detail needed to generate or update the physical database you plan to use.

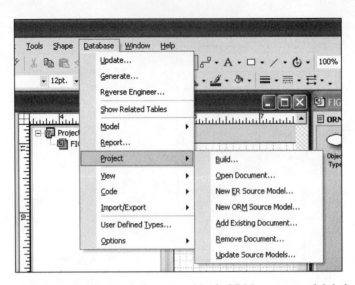

Now that we have a data project that includes a new blank ORM source model, let's get back to our example.

Step 2 – Drawing the Fact Types

There are many ways we can draw fact types in Visio. We're going to show how all of them work so you can decide which one you like best. The first thing most people notice when they create a diagram in Visio is the stencil shapes. Looking in the stencil, we notice that there are only three shapes. This is very misleading because the ORM notation provides many shapes we can use to display information about the system.

As we'll see later on, most of the shapes will be displayed on the diagram depending on properties and information we set using dialogs Visio provides. To get an idea of most, if not ALL of the shapes used to represent relationships in ORM, take a look at the stencil of an ORM diagram instead of an ORM source model. ORM diagrams are used to merely draw the diagram using the shapes. They cannot be used to generate the logical model as source diagrams can.

It turns out that dragging shapes from the stencil is one of the most tedious ways to define objects and fact types. A much better way is the Business Rules Window

The Business Rules Window

The Business Rules window is usually located as a tab at the bottom of the screen. This area can be occupied by windows and editors that can all be selected from the View submenu of the Database menu pictured below:

The Business Rules window is composed of two panes: the **Object Types** pane where we can create and define some of the properties of our objects, and the **Fact Types** pane where we do the same thing with our facts.

Taking our first example fact: Flight *departs* Gate, let's begin by adding the two objects in the fact: **Flight** and **Gate**. Double-click the first row to create a new entry. Name the object type **Flight** in the object types column, then double-click to add a new object type and name it **Gate**. Don't worry about the other columns just yet.

So now we have two objects, let's define the relationship (or fact) type between them. Bring the **Fact Types** tab forward and double-click the row to add a new fact type. The fact type editor is displayed:

The Fact Editor

The Fact Editor consists of five tabs. The first of these, the **Fact** tab, describes the basic elements of the fact including the objects and the relationships they take part in. You can choose to enter the fact in Freeform or Guided input styles. **Guided** is the default (you can change this in the properties; we'll show you how later) and allows you to select from your list of objects on each side and add the verbiage or wording of the roles each object plays. Notice that when the **Guided** input style is being used, the arity of the fact can be selected from the drop-down next to the **Guided** radio button. This lets Visio know how many boxes to put on the form for your object names and relationships. You can also enter the inverse of the relationship in the text box provided. Let's do this with our example so that the Fact Editor resembles the one overleaf:

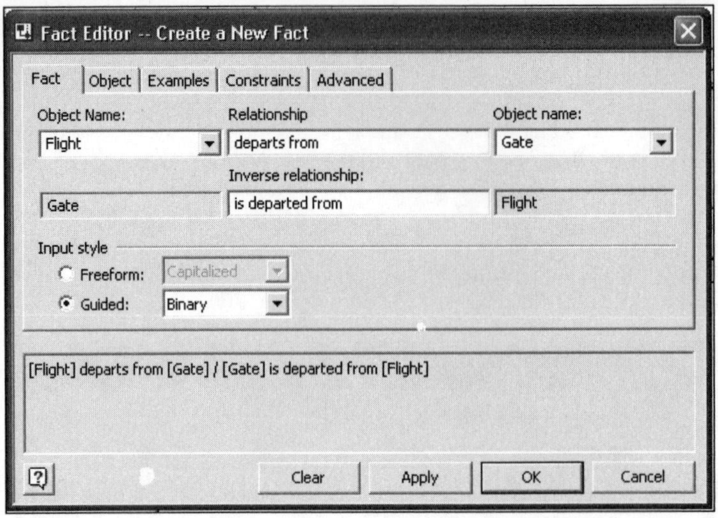

Freeform input allows you to simply type a fact into the editor. You can use either **Capitalized** or **Brackets** to distinguish your objects from the rest of fact by choosing from the drop-down next to the Freeform radio button. The freeform editor really is the best way because it is faster, easier, and allows you to enter your facts in the most intuitive way, as a sentence. In freeform input, the inverse is entered into the predicate by delimiting it with a slash.

We'll enter the first fact using guided input and then use freeform input to enter another fact. To enter our first fact select the **Flight** object from the first **Object Name** drop-down and type **departs from** in the **Relationship** text box. Next, select **Gate** from the second **Object Name** drop-down so that we have a completed fact. Fill in the inverse: **is departed from** in the **Inverse Relationship** textbox. Press the **Apply** button and the Fact Editor saves your new fact to the model and clears itself so that you can enter a new fact.

Now we'll enter the second fact type represented by the statement Flight *has* Seat using the **Freeform** input style. Select **FreeForm** and go ahead and leave the dropdown with **Capitalized** selected. Enter **Flight has a/is in Seat** exactly as shown next:

On your screen you will see that the objects are highlighted in red and the predicate is blue.

Moving onto the **Object** tab of the Fact Editor we see one way we can define the reference scheme for the objects in our fact.

The Fact Editor **Object** tab shows a box that has the objects that take part in this fact. Choosing an object in this box displays its attributes in the rest of the form so that you can modify them.

You can change the object kind or type using the **Object kind** drop-down box. The three available choices are: Entity, Value, and External. We've already gone over **Entity** and **Value** types. **External** simply means that the object is defined in another diagram somewhere else. This is extremely useful when you have a larger system where different teams are working on different parts of the system. If an object has been better defined elsewhere, then we can refer to it in our diagram as external and need only be concerned with the roles it fulfills in our system.

The Entity attributes box is where we define our reference scheme. As can be seen here, we have defined the FlightNumber to be the reference scheme for our Flight Entity object. The Ref Type dropdown allows you to better specify *how* the reference scheme identifies the entity object. The most common Ref Type is Identification, but you can also choose Measurement and Formatting.

Click OK to close the Fact Editor. Looking in the Object Types Pane of the Business Rules window, we see that the editor has created our Seat object for us with the reference scheme we specified.

Let's quickly add the rest of the fact types so that we can move on to the next step of the CSDP. Choosing Freeform input style, enter the rest of our elementary facts, pressing Apply after each one in the fact editor:

- ❑ Flight (FlightNumber) *has/describes* DepartureTime
- ❑ Terminal (TerminalLetter) *has/is in* Gate (GateCode)
- ❑ Meal Type (MealType) *is delivered to/receives* Seat (SeatCode)

After entering these facts, you should have the following facts and objects just like the Business Rules window below:

The object types should also match what you see here:

At this point it is really a good idea to save our drawing. Click Save from the File menu and save your file.

Now let's look at yet another tool Visio provides that helps us complete the steps of the CSDP. Remember, we still have to do a population check to make sure we have represented all the data in the report. To facilitate this, Visio provides automated reporting of our model so far.

Visio Reporting

To help with the steps of the CSDP and to better communicate our progress and ideas to the client access the different reports by clicking Report... from the Database menu.

The New Report Wizard will present you with a list of the different report types it provides. Even though we've only touched the surface of ORM so far, this is a good time to bring up this feature because it will help at this and the next stage of the CSDP.

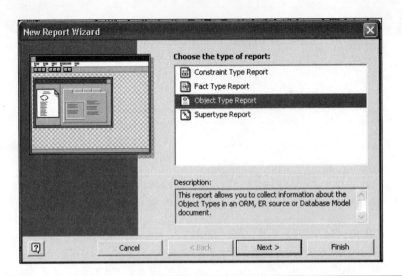

Report	Description
Constraint Type Report	Summarizes the different types of constraints in your model. You can select which constraint types you wish to include and what attributes you would like to report on. You can also describe how you would like what attributes you would like to sort, and group. As we'll see later, most of this information is pulled from the Add Constraint Editor.
Fact Type Report	Summarizes the information that is pulled from the Fact Type Editor form. It gives a report on the 'arity' of the facts you have entered so far, some of the simple constraints you have entered for the facts, and the example data you have entered.
Object Type Report	Summarizes all of the object types you have entered so far. Great resource to use when doing population checks and combining entities that are the same in different parts of the system.
Supertype Report	Provides a number of reporting options and figures to help understand the Subtype relationships and subset constraints of your model. Includes a hierarchical tree.

It's just a few simple steps to generate these reports but they provide a powerful way of checking your model and looking for discrepancies at this stage of the project. In fact, I would advise the reader to go ahead and bring up each of the reports and just click Finish (this will accept the defaults) in the first step. It only takes a minute and can give you a good idea of the type of information these reports provide.

Step 3 of the CSDP

Step 3 is the combination of entities and any objects that can be derived arithmetically.

Keep in mind that our example so far has been of one part of a fairly simple system. We may have two or more teams working on other parts of the system and probably a large portion of them will come up with, for example a flight object. Other parts of the system will want to describe other facts that include a flight, such as *Pilot flies Plane*. We don't want to duplicate efforts at this point. If another part of the system is defining the object with more detail than we need, we can simply mark it as external and define our own roles for it. This is definitely where the reports described in the last section can really come in handy.

Arithmetic derivations are just that. Any objects that can be derived arithmetically from a combination of others should probably not be objects in their own right. For example, suppose we created an object representing the total number of passengers aboard our plane, but we already knew the number of First Class Passengers and the number of Coach Passengers. The object representing the total number of passengers would be unnecessary, since we would simply add First Class and Coach Passengers to come up with the total.

Thus we perform this step on our model so far and are satisfied that our Flight, Gate, and Seat objects don't need to be combined and that there are no arithmetic derivations in our model. The next step in the CSDP is the addition of some constraints to our model.

Constraints

Constraints are the most important part of an ORM model. They help to further specify the business rules of your data model. We'll begin our discussion of constraints by looking at some of the other tabs of the Fact Editor.

The **Examples** tab is for adding example data to the model. This is one of the key benefits of ORM diagrams. Example data and test populations can, and should, be loaded directly into the model for every fact type. The integrity of the model can then be checked for validity against the example data. Constraints can even be derived from the example data.

Let's try this by starting with the following fact: **Flight (FlightNumber) departs Gate (GateCode)**. With this fact selected, right-click the fact in the Business Rules Editor and select **Edit Fact...**. Then, click the **Examples** tab. These rows are where you will add your sample data that represents instances that will eventually be stored in the database. Add the sample data as shown below:

Highlighting row 1 and looking in the bottom window, we see Flight 5468 departs from Gate A34. We mentioned earlier in the chapter that verbalization of facts is very important in ORM. Here is a prime example. We can use this to verify that our data and our facts really do meet the situation. We should make sure that we enter information that really represents the system we want to model. Notice that each Flight is unique and that each Gate is unique or that one Flight will depart from one gate and that one Gate is departed from by one Flight. It's important to remember that this doesn't mean that a Gate can only be used once. That's a *Primary* uniqueness constraint, and is explained below. Let's add these constraints to the fact using the Constraints tab of the Fact Editor:

Here you can add the following constraints:

Constraint	Description
Uniqueness Constraint	Specify that an instance of one or more of the objects in the role will be unique within the role. For example, *One* Flight leaves *One* Gate.
Mandatory Constraint	Specify that the object *must* play that role in order for the role to exist. In other words, a Flight *must* depart from a Gate if it is to exist as a flight.
Frequency Constraint	Specify the number of times, if any, an object must fulfill the role. Here it is just one, but in other situations it could be more. For example, Four Flight attendants are required to serve a Flight.

Enter these constraints using the Constraints tab so that they'll be reflected in our model. Visio provides questions to help us conceptualize the constraint. Clicking the Rephrase button will grammatically rephrase this question to further illustrate the constraints that relate to the fact.

The drop-downs above the Rephrase button present some of the ways we can answer the question that will allow Visio to set the constraints for us.

Constraint Question #1 relates to the role that Flight plays in the predicate while Constraint Question #2 will help us set constraints on the role that Gate plays. We will set Exactly One for both Constraint questions as we said above.

The Primary Uniqueness drop-down allows you to specify a primary uniqueness constraint over one of the roles in this fact. This means for example, that the object can only play in one of these roles ever. A Match (the one you use to light fires) object, or a Thirty-First Birthday object; these can only be used once. In other words, if there were a primary uniqueness constraint over the fact in the screenshot above, only one instance of Gate would ever exist for this role. A Flight could only depart from one gate once, then no other flights could depart from that same Gate – definitely not the situation we want here.

Now our Constraint tab should look like this:

> **Notice how Visio has verbalized our fact and its constraints. This is a great quality check to make sure that our constraints are correct.**

Another good way to verify our constraints is back in the Examples tab. Let's go back there and click the Analyze button:

This causes Visio to analyze the example data and make a suggestion about what constraints the data implies. If you have already entered constraints that do not match the data, an error will appear. I wanted to show how to add a constraint using the Constraints tab, but if we had done this first, we could have bypassed the Constraints tab and applied the constraints automatically after entering our example data by clicking Apply UC Constraints. This is another very good reason for adding example data to every fact.

Our fact now looks like this:

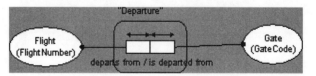

Notice the bars with arrows over the roles we have defined uniqueness constraints for, and the dots indicating mandatory roles.

The **Advanced** tab of the Fact Editor allows you to set some of the other properties of the role.

![Fact Editor -- Edit existing Fact dialog box showing tabs: Fact, Object, Examples, Constraints, Advanced. Advanced tab selected with Notes field, Objectify / Nest fact as field, Derivation of fact section with radio buttons None (selected), Derived, Derived and stored, a Derivation rule field, and External fact type checkbox. Bottom shows: [Flight] departs from [Gate] / [Gate] is departed from [Flight]. Buttons: Clear, Apply, OK, Cancel.]

Notes can be defined for pretty much anything in Visio. They can help document things that may need to be added later and are stored in the model.

The **Objectify / Nest Fact as:** textbox allows you to turn this fact into a full-fledged object that can then take part in its own roles. For example, let's say that we want to objectify the fact: *Flight departs Gate* as a Departure that can then take part in a role with a Runway object. We could type **Departure** into the textbox provided to accomplish this. ORM represents a nested fact as a soft rectangle around the predicate as shown:

![ORM diagram showing "Departure" nested fact as a soft rectangle around the predicate, with Flight (Flight Number) entity and Gate (GateCode) entity, connected by "departs from / is departed from" predicate.]

The **Departure** object is now an entity type with all of the properties of any other entity type.

The **Derivation** radio buttons and textbox allow you to add derivation rules for this fact type. A derivation rule is a way to enter more information than is formally allowed in the model about the way that the relationship is carried out. For example, let's suppose that there was a way to derive some other object in the system from the gate and flight. We could enter it here as a documented feature of the system that we'll enter later. The **Derived** radio button indicates that the derivation exists while the **Derived and stored** radio button indicates that the derivation exists and the value will be stored in the database.

External fact type allows you to specify your object as an external object type. Remember, this stipulates that the fact is defined in another part of the system and that we just want to show a relationship between it and our system without explicitly defining it.

Steps 4 to 7 of the CSDP

The rest of the CSDP presents a recommended order for creating the rest of the constraint types in the model. In this section, we'll define and give some examples of these constraints. To do this, we'll be taking a look at a better way to add constraints than the Fact Editor – the **Add Constraint** form. We're also going to end our above example here to look at a situation in which some of these more complex constraints occur.

Traveler, TicketPrice, and FrequentFlierMiles

We're going to look at the situation of how a traveler is charged for their flight. This will involve a Traveler entity object, a FrequentFlierMiles entity object and a TicketPrice entity object. We're also going to see a unary fact type that describes whether a Traveler is an employee of the carrier of the flight.

Our small part of the system is represented by three facts. Create these facts in the same manner as you did in previous examples:

❑ Traveler *pays* TicketPrice

❑ Traveler *uses* FrequentFlierMiles

❑ Traveler *is employee*

Let's not worry about the uniqueness constraints that we can create in the Fact Editor for these roles. The Fact Editor is limited to creating constraints for the particular fact that it is modifying. The **Add Constraint** form can create constraints *between* facts. Here are our facts so far in ORM notation:

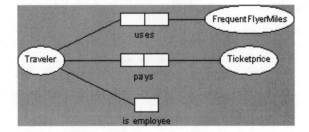

Here's the Fact Editor window showing the unary fact:

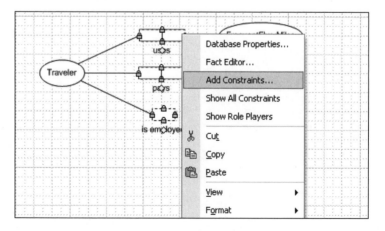

Here's an explanation of the constraint we'll add first: We know that a Traveler will not pay the TicketPrice if they are using FrequentFlierMiles or are employed by the carrier; this is an exclusion constraint. We also know that they must fall into one of the categories. They must be an employee, pay the TicketPrice, or use FrequentFlierMiles to take part in the system; this is a mandatory or inclusive constraint.

Add Constraint Form

The Add Constraint form allows an easier and better way for you to add constraints to your ORM diagram. To create our constraints, we'll select all three of the predicates of our diagram by dragging a box around them, or holding the *Shift* key (normally we would use *Ctrl* for this purpose in Windows!). Select Add Constraints... to bring up the Add Constraint editor.

The Add Constraint Editor

The Constraint type drop-down allows you to select the kind of constraint you would like to define for the roles you select. The Primary checkbox tells Visio that the constraint provides a primary reference for the role instance (much like we explained earlier with the Fact Editor). The roles we had selected are displayed in the first box so that we may select them to participate in this constraint. Finally, the box at the bottom will verbalize the constraint as we create it to help walk us through the process.

Select Exclusion as our constraint type and select the roles on the left-hand side, which represent those roles fulfilled by the Traveler object as shown:

Add Constraint

Constraint type:　　　Number of roles at each end:

Exclusion ▼ | 1 ⬍

Select the role box of each role in the constraint:

1	[Traveler] uses [FrequentFlyerMiles]
2	[Traveler] pays [Ticketprice]
3	[Traveler] is employee

For each Traveler t, at most one of the following holds:
　　　Traveler t uses some FrequentFlyerMiles;
　　　Traveler t pays some Ticketprice;
　　　Traveler t is employee.

Reset | Apply | OK | Cancel

Notice the verbalizer box at the bottom has grammatically stated our constraint. This is such a wonderful feature!

Also notice the **Number of Roles at each end** box that has appeared. This allows you to specify the number the roles that will be included over more than one instance of the constraint.

Click **OK** to add the constraint so that we now have the following diagram:

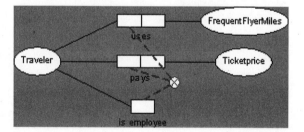

Notice that the circled **X** is used to indicate an exclusion constraint. Now we know that a Traveler instance cannot take part in more than one role, or said another way, they are disjunctive. Now let's add the other constraint. Select the predicates again and select **Add Constraint** to bring up the **Add Constraints** dialog. Select a **Mandatory** constraint type and choose the roles as shown:

Add Constraint

Constraint type:

Mandatory

Select the role box of each role in the constraint:

1	[Traveler] uses [FrequentFlyerMiles]
2	[Traveler] pays [Ticketprice]
3	[Traveler] is employee

Each Traveler uses some FrequentFlyerMiles or pays some Ticketprice or is employee.

Reset	Apply	OK	Cancel

Click **OK** to add the constraint so that the diagram now looks like this:

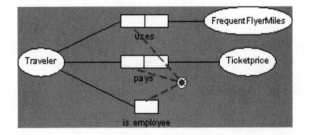

Remember that the notation for a mandatory role is a dot. Visio has drawn the dot on top of our exclusion constraint's **X**. You can right-click the constraint and select **Split X / OR** constraint to show them separately. The technical term for this type of constraint is an inclusive-OR constraint or a mandatory disjunction of the roles.

Here's a short explanation of the rest of the constraints (that we haven't looked at already) that you can add in the constraint type editor:

Constraint	Description
Subset	Much like a subtype relation that we'll look at later. It denotes that the population of one role must be a subset of the population fulfilling another role. In other words, a member of one role must also be a member in another role. For example, Travelers using FrequentFlierMiles must also play the role of Participating in the FrequentFlierProgram. The difference between this and an Equality constraint, is that Travelers participating in the FrequentFlierProgram don't necessarily have to use their FrequentFlierMiles.
Equality	Specifies that the populations of the roles must be equal.
Index	These constraints apply less to conceptual design and more to the performance advantages of an index defined in the physical database. They don't really specify any concepts but are included in ORM notation by a circled I.
Ring	There are many types of ring constraints; the Visio documentation actually has some good examples and definitions for all of them.

Although there is plenty of documentation in Visio on them, it's worth looking at an example of a Ring Constraint. Suppose we are to build a program for the review of pilots on the planes such that pilots review other pilots:

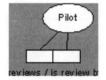

The constraint has to stipulate that a pilot cannot review themselves. Select the predicate and bring up the Add Constraints editor, select a Ring constraint type and then select both sides of the role to show the Ring Constraint Editor:

We'll select an Irreflexive constraint from the Ring Type: drop-down and click OK. Notice that the bottom of the Add Constraint Editor once again helps out by verbalizing the relationship: No Pilot *reviews* itself.

ORM notation depicts this with a circle to depict its cyclical nature and ir for irreflexive. The end result Oir is shown below:

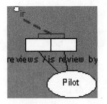

Creating the Conceptual, Logical, and Physical Database

We'll begin by creating an ORM source model. To create our new ORM source diagram, we select a new ORM Source Model diagram from the Database category of the main drawing menu. We now have a blank drawing surface with which to begin modeling. The simple example we are going to build is that of a part of an airport reservations system. We are only going to be concerned with a simple seating assignment data store. A report of some of our elementary facts is shown below:

❑   Fact1 – Airline *owns/is owned by* airplane

❑   Fact2 – Airplane *has a* seat

❑   Fact3 – Seat *has a* row number

❑   Fact4 – Seat *has a* location code (aisle, window, middle)

❑   Fact5 – Traveler *sits in* seat

❑   Fact6 – Traveler *rides in* airplane

Creating the Object Types

We're already familiar with the Business Rules editor, so let's just go ahead and create the objects below:

Object Name	Reference Mode	Kind	Data Type
Airline	Code	Entity	Char(10)
Airplane	Id	Entity	Char(10)
Traveler	Id	Entity	int
Seat	Code	Entity	char(5)
RowNumber	Number	Entity	int
LocationCode	Code	Entity	char(1)

Our business rules editor should now look like this:

Object Types	Physical Data Type	Kind	RefMode	
● Airline	char(10)	Entity	Code	
● Airplane	char(10)	Entity	Id	
● Traveler	int	Entity	Id	
● Seat	char(5)	Entity	Code	
● Row	int	Entity	Number	
● Location	char(1)	Entity	Code	
○ (Double-click here to add a new object t...				

All Folders
☐ 🗐 OrmExample.vsd
   🗁 Entire Contents

Contents of 'Entire Contents'

◄ ►|▲ Fact Types   **Object Types** ◄

× \ **Business Rules** \ Verbalizer \ Output \ Database Properties \

Creating the Predicate Types

Now that we have our objects, we will define the roles that they play in Fact 1. Remember, we can add facts by either creating them in the **Fact types** pane of the Business Rules editor, or by dragging a predicate object to the surface. Either way, the Fact Editor will help define the predicate as shown.

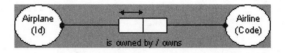

We will also want to define some simple constraints on this relationship. Here we need to think about how we are going to define what is and isn't allowed by the system. It is critically important, that we must not let our own assumptions guide us here. Once again, let's ask our point of contact for the system for advice about how the final product really should work. We don't want to define the constraints too strictly to allow for all combinations and relationships that will need to be depicted in the system. For this relationship, we decide that an airline can own more than one airplane at a time, an airplane must belong to one airline, and that an airline has to own at least one plane. This is depicted by the arrow over the **is owned by** side of the predicate and the black dot on the connector to our airplane and airline objects. Our Fact Editor will look as shown:

🗐 **Fact Editor -- Edit existing Fact**　　　　　　　　　　　 ☒

  Fact | Object | Examples | Constraints | Advanced |

Constraint Question #1

Each Airplane is owned by how many Airline?　　　　　Exactly One ▼

Rephrase

Constraint Question #2

Each Airline owns how many Airplane?　　　　　One or More ▼

Rephrase

1..3

Primary uniqueness: **None** ▼

[Airplane] is owned by [Airline] / [Airline] owns [Airplane]
   Each Airplane is owned by some Airline.
   Each Airline owns some Airplane.|
   Each Airplane is owned by at most one Airline.

[?]　　　　　　　　Clear　　　Apply　　　OK　　　Cancel

Remember that there is no primary uniqueness constraint because that doesn't apply here. Instances of the objects and their uniqueness are not defined by this role.

Fact2 states that Airplanes have Seats, Seats are in Airplanes. This is another simple constraint that we define as:

The Fact Editor's Constraints tab looks like this:

![Fact Editor -- Edit existing Fact dialog showing Constraints tab]

The Fact Editor dialog contains:

Tabs: Fact | Object | Examples | Constraints | Advanced

Constraint Question #1
Each Airplane has how many Seat?   One or More ▼   Rephrase

Constraint Question #2
Each Seat is in how many Airplane?   Exactly One ▼   Rephrase

Primary uniqueness: None ▼

[Airplane] has [Seat] / [Seat] is in [Airplane]
    Each Airplane has some Seat.
    Each Seat is in some Airplane.
    Each Seat is in at most one Airplane.

Buttons: Clear   Apply   OK   Cancel

Primary uniqueness constraint

The other fact types are pretty much the same except that one thing has been left out that I would like to mention. A seat has a Row and a Location. One might have just taken the same road as for all the other constraints and defined these predicates like this:

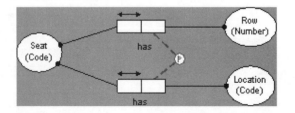

That's perfectly fine, and would probably result in a model that would work. Both of these are mandatory and their values actually define each seat. This is because the reference scheme for the Seat (SeatNumber) is a combination or composite of the reference schemes of the Location (LocationCode) and the Row (RowNumber). The point is that a seat doesn't necessarily have a need for its own unique identifier because this is provided by the roles it fulfills with the Location and Row objects. How do we go about adding this relationship (called a composite primary reference scheme) to the diagram? The best way to these types of constraints happens to be the **Add Constraint** form. Remember, to display it, choose both predicates either by dragging a box diagonally around them, or by holding down the *Shift* key and clicking both of them. Then either click on one of the shapes, right-click and select **Add Constraints...** or do the same from the **Database** menu.

Here is our old friend the Add Constraint dialog again. Click each of the sides of the predicates shown so that they look like the diagram below and check the **Primary** checkbox. Notice the verbalizer window reads the constraint for you as you click each role.

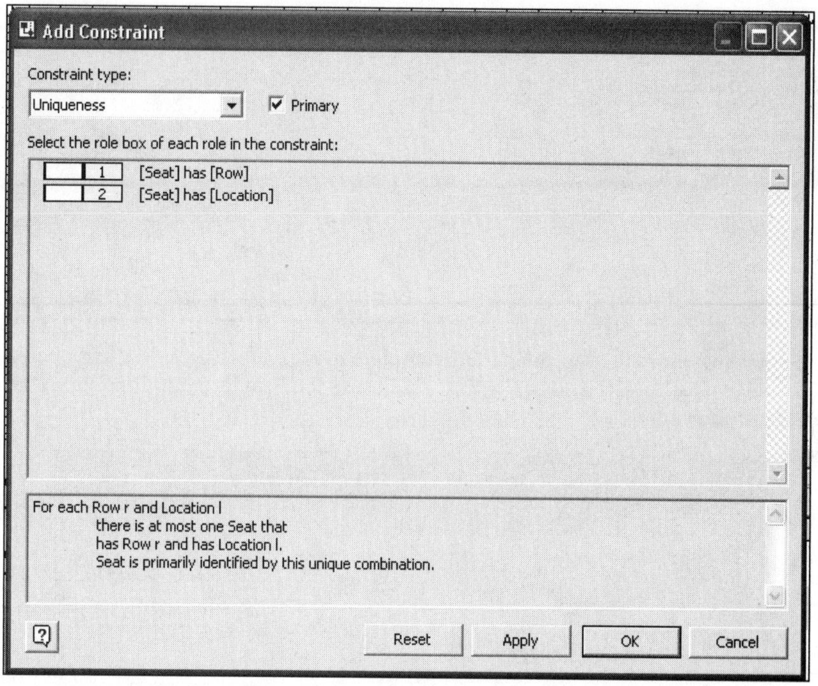

Now clear the reference mode of the seat object using the Business Rules editor.

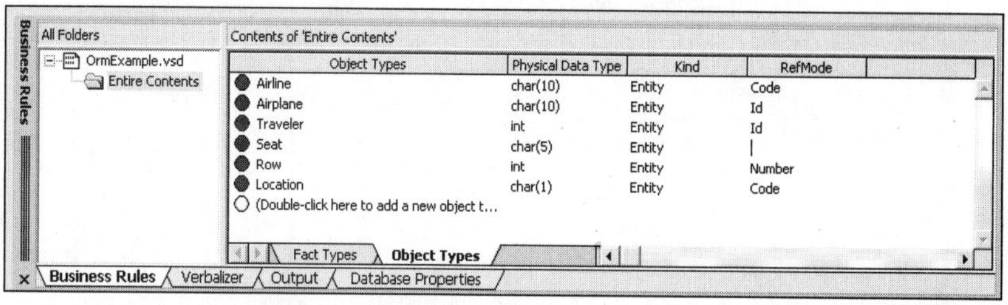

Your diagram should now look like this: the circled P represents the primary uniqueness constraint. This means that a seat is primarily defined by the unique relationships it plays with LocationCode and Rownumber.

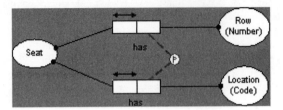

The Verbalizer grammatically states this:

```
Verbalizer

Seat has Location
        Each Seat has some Location.
        For each Location l, some Seat has Location l.
        Each Seat has at most one Location.
Seat has Row
        Each Seat has some Row.
        For each Row r, some Seat has Row r.
        Each Seat has at most one Row.
For each Row r and Location l
        there is at most one Seat that
        has Row r and has Location l.
        Seat is primarily identified by this unique combination.
```

Business Rules \ Verbalizer

We need to enter two more facts to define our complete model. Once again we just open the Fact Editor and type: Traveler rides in Airplane in the Fact tab (using the Freeform input method). We then define the constraints as shown below:

Fact Editor -- Create a New Fact

Fact | Object | Examples | Constraints | Advanced

Constraint Question #1
Each Traveler rides in how many Airplane?   Exactly One ▼
                                                    Rephrase

Constraint Question #2
How many Traveler rides in each Airplane?   Zero or More ▼
                                                    Rephrase

Primary uniqueness: None ▼

[Traveler] rides in [Airplane]
        Each Traveler rides in some Airplane.
        Each Traveler rides in at most one Airplane.

Clear   Apply   OK   Cancel

Next, we define the fact: Traveler sits in Seat. Type this into the Fact tab and define the constraints for this fact as shown below:

Fact Editor -- Edit existing Fact

Fact | Object | Examples | Constraints | Advanced

Constraint Question #1

Each Traveler sits in how many Seat?   Exactly One ▼   Rephrase

Constraint Question #2

How many Traveler sits in each Seat?   Exactly One ▼   Rephrase

Primary uniqueness: **None** ▼

[Traveler] sits in [Seat]
    Each Traveler sits in some Seat.
    For each Seat s, some Traveler sits in Seat s.
    For each Seat s, at most one Traveler sits in Seat s.
    Each Traveler sits in at most one Seat.

Clear   Apply   OK   Cancel

By now, your full diagram should look something like this (Remember, a great way to add the shapes is to right-click and select Show relationships):

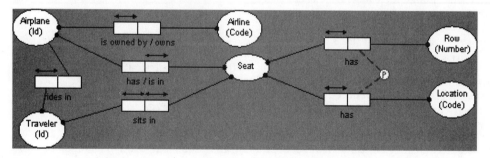

Before moving to the next section, it is a good idea to do a model error check. You can do this by selecting Model Error Check from the Database menu:

Database | Window | Help

Reverse Engineer...

Add Constraint

Model Error Check

Report...

View ▶

Import/Export ▶

User Defined Types...

Options ▶

301

This will perform a conceptual validation of your model. It will inform you of any problems with your model such as a lack of reference schemes or constraints that contradict the samples you've entered. All of this information will appear in the Output window. I've entered some faulty examples for one of the facts to demonstrate this. Otherwise, our model generates no errors and no warnings.

You can double-click the error/warning row and Visio will highlight the offending shape on the diagram. Since we have no errors or warnings in our current model (I'll correct the faulty examples I've entered before we continue!), we're ready to move one step closer to generating the database. That next step is:

Building the Logical Model

Now that we have a good diagram of the objects in our part of the system, it is time to see if our work has truly paid off. One of the best things about using an automated modeling tool like Visio is that you can regenerate the model at will in a few seconds. If you don't like the results, you can always go back and change things, then generate it again.

> At this point, I can't stress enough the need to get the Visio SR-1 from Microsoft. It fixes a number of really annoying and potentially destructive bugs in database diagramming and updating logic that can lead to, at the least, headaches, and at the most corrupted models! Do yourself a favor and get it from:
> http://msdn.microsoft.com/downloads/default.asp?URL=/downloads/sample.a sp?url=/MSDN-FILES/027/001/906/msdncompositedoc.xml

We begin by creating our Database Model Diagram and adding our ORM diagram to it by selecting Add Existing Document from the Database menu. The project window should come up at this point and we should see that our diagram is now part of our data project. Select Build from the Database menu and Visio begins to generate the logical model. The Output window will show the status as well as any errors and warnings that reflect mistakes or inconsistencies in your model. Remember, we can double-click the row to highlight the offending shape. After Visio is done generating your model, you'll see the tables it has generated in the Tables and Views Window. You can see in the Tables and Views window opposite, that it has generated three tables: Airplane, Seat, and Traveler.

This illustrates a point. When you first use Visio to generate a logical diagram from you ORM, you will sometimes wonder why it has chosen to do certain things. One of the aspects that seems counter-intuitive is that Visio didn't decide to put Airlines into their own table. They are an entity object aren't they? Why wouldn't Visio represent them with an entity in an ER diagram? The answer has to do with the algorithm Visio uses to map the objects. The simple fact is that it is optimized, while our perceptions (what we think should be generated) are not. We didn't define any value types or other roles extending our airline object. Visio therefore, has taken the simplest and best way of representing them, by showing them as a required column in our Airplane table.

Let's see how Visio defined the relationships between our objects. The easiest way to do this is to drag one of the tables to the drawing surface and select Show related tables, either from the context (right-click) menu or the Database menu. Visio adds the shapes to the drawing and lays them out for us as seen below:

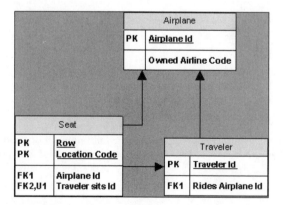

At first glance it doesn't look pretty. Even though many databases allow column names to have spaces, this still isn't necessarily a good practice. Why is Row by itself as a field name while Location has its reference scheme included (LocationCode)? Also, what's with the Rides Airplane Id of the Traveler table?

The answer to these kinds of problems lies back on our ORM diagram in the document properties. Although at first, they can seem confusing, changing these settings can save a lot of time and help generate truly usable ER diagrams. I will try to explain each of the properties and how each one can affect your ER diagram. Go back to the ORM model by double-clicking it in the Project window, or the Window menu if it's already open in Visio. Open the document properties by choosing Database | Options | Document.

The first tab of the ORM Document Options Window simply asks if you want to show constraints that only impact on the physical model. This pretty much means indexes that you define for the sole purpose of speeding performance.

The Abbreviation tab is where things start to get interesting. It displays some common default words and the abbreviations that Visio inserts in place of other words when the logical model is generated. Any of these words appearing anywhere in your model will be replaced by that abbreviation. This is how Visio maps your objects/predicates to fields and tables. If we don't do this, many of the sits in, rides, and such like, can make their way into the logical model. Notice that most of the words have no abbreviation at all. This is not by accident; the simple fact is that most of the time you don't want any of these "conceptual" words to even appear into your model. Let's add some of our own. Enter in the words: sits, rides, and owned into the bottom of the list so that your list now looks like this:

This also explains our Row, RowNumber problem – the field names Location Code and Row are derived from the ORM reference schemes LocationCode and RowNumber. If you look in the Abreviation tab we've just added to, number is there. Erasing this will solve our issue.

> This scenario illustrates a great way to find out the nuances of what's going on with the names Visio uses when you build your model. If when you are building your ER diagram you're not sure why Visio did chose a certain name, it usually relates to some of these document properties.

Just to show exactly what this fixed, let's rebuild the logical model. Press **OK** and open your DMD. Build the data project again and you should get what I have below.

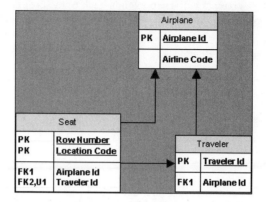

As you can see, the extraneous words were removed! The spaces still remain, but we'll show how to get rid of them below.

From the **Prefixes** tab, we can set prefixes that Visio will use in the naming of our columns and tables. For columns, we can choose to have no prefix, a prefix based on the first few letters of the table name, or a custom prefix on a per table basis. This can go a long way to creating uniformity in the names of objects in your database. We can also specify a custom prefix for our table names. Hopefully in a later version of Visio, there might be an option to have a column prefix based on the column datatype. Either way, this is an extremely useful feature that can go a long way in setting some consistency across your architected database solution without most of the work.

The **Suffix** tab allows you to define a custom suffix to append to the end of column and table names.

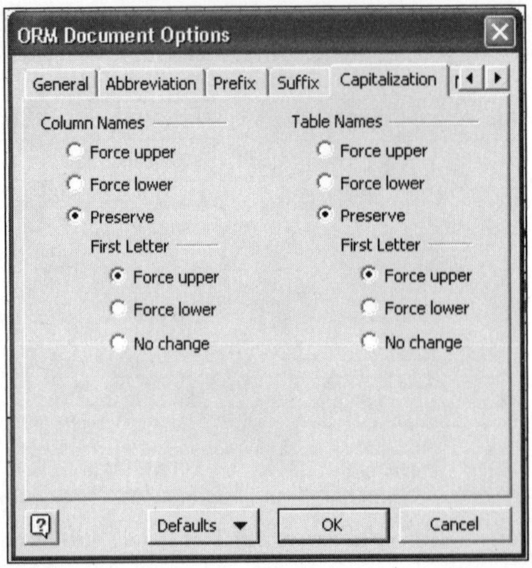

The **Capitalization** tab allows you to specify the rules to apply to the capitalization of both column and table names. You can choose to force all upper or lower case punctuation or have it determined by the first letter.

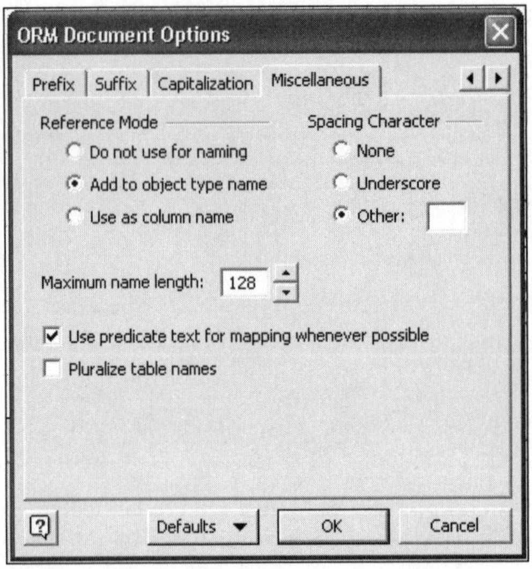

The **Miscellaneous** tab has a number of options that we can use to tailor our logical diagram. It is here that we find the reason behind the spaces in the column names of our ER diagram. Looking at the **Spacing Character** label in the above screenshot, we see that the **Other** radio button is selected by default. This is very misleading and I'm not sure why it's been designed this way, but inside the **Other** textbox, there is a [space] character – of course, you can't see it! Usually one would want to set it to something else. We'll choose **None** for the **Spacing Character**, although an underscore could do nicely too (This would make LocationCode become Location_Code); this is really a matter of personal preference.

The **Reference mode** options are useful but are also misleading in some cases. The option I have found to be the best is to use the reference mode as the column name. This sets whatever you put in the reference mode box to be the name of the column that represents the primary key in the table represented by your object, or the column name that represents your object (remember how the primary key of the Airline table was named?). The reason why this is misleading is because Visio seems to have done this. I usually set it to **Add to object type name**, and then make sure I name my columns with the name of the object type plus an **ID** or **Code**.

The **Maximum name length** can be used to restrict the maximum length of column names. The **Use predicate text...** checkbox tells Visio to use the predicate verbiage to help name relationships and columns.

Finally, the Pluralize table names checkbox is very useful and I usually set it. It will take your objects (which are singular in the conceptual view) and pluralize them so that your airplane object becomes an Airplanes table, for example. I usually set them to be the defaults for all documents I create. After setting these properties, and building the model again, the end result appears below.

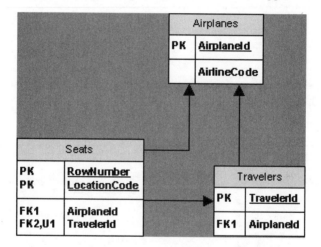

We now have a fairly complete logical design created from our conceptual design without having to define one table or column! The benefits that we have realized as developers are numerous. Not only have we collected requirements about the specification of the system we need to build and a conceptual design of our system, but we also have a very good start at logical design! The truly great part is that we can make changes to our conceptual design and rebuild the logical model with one click on a menu, thus insulating us from the risk of downstream changes.

Meanwhile, it is good to keep in mind that our data model is not dependent on any vendor-specific DBMS. We have used SQL server's driver here because that is the database that we will generate this model to, but we could just as easily have chosen another vendor's driver. We could do so right now as a matter of fact, by opening our ORM diagram and choosing **Driver...** from the **Database | Options** menu.

In fact, when we do, we see the screen overleaf and find that there are a number of properties we can define that specify how our model will map to any database we choose. Specifically, we can specify the way we want our data types to map and how we want DDL scripts to be generated.

Generating the Database

Now that we have our logical model defined, we can begin to generate our physical database. The process is exceedingly easy since Visio provides a wizard to walk us through the process. Select Generate... from the Database menu of the data project to begin. You are presented with the screen below:

The checkboxes provided allow you to decide exactly how you want the database to be generated. If you would like to generate a DDL script, you can select that checkbox and choose where you would like to save the text file. Clicking Generate new database will instruct Visio that you are indeed ready to create the actual database. The Store current database... checkbox is extremely useful as we'll see later. It instructs Visio to take a snapshot of the database so that it will be easier to update and replicate changes back to the model at a later date. Make the choices to suit your needs and click Next.

The next screen lets you configure your data source that points to the server or file that you want the database to be generated in. Remember the "data source" is really just a pointer to the database you want to generate, don't get confused by the wording. You can have Visio create the database or use one that already exists. In this example, using the SQL Server driver, you must specify a data source to a SQL Server you can connect to. Clicking new brings up the Create New Data Source wizard:

After you have configured your data source to point to your server, Give your database a name in the Database Name textbox and hit Next. The wizard now has a summary screen that shows you the tables you are about to create in your new database. Hit Next and Visio does a final physical validation of the database to make sure that the model is consistent and that there are no errors.

Clicking **Finish** on the wizard starts the generation process. If you have chosen to create a new database and you didn't create one in the data source creation wizard, Visio will ask you for a logical file name for the database and transaction log as well as the path and other physical characteristics. When the generation process is done, Visio asks if you would like to see the generated DDL script.

You now have a completely generated database that should exactly match your logical model. You can verify this by opening SQL Server's Enterprise Manager or Visual Studio .NET's Server Explorer and seeing for yourself – the database listed with all the others

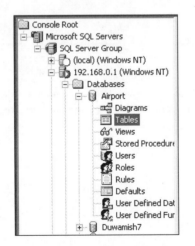

The first thing to do when you have verified that your database is set up the way you like, is go back to your data project and save it. You'll be presented with this message box:

This dialog can come up many times when you are working on a project and can be intimidating at first, mostly due to its wording. Here's what it means – the collective model is just another name for the data project or Database Model Diagram. In this instance, changes were made to it that you would like to keep, changes made by Visio when you generated the database. When it stores the database model, it marks all the shapes in your model as reverse engineered. This is some kind of internal trick to help Visio merge and synchronize your model with what's in the database. If you choose to build your project, your source models are used to build the logical design in the DMD, overwriting anything in the DMD. So, in this instance, we will choose Yes to update the source models so that the shapes in our ORM will also be marked as reverse engineered, but there will be many times when you're working back and forth between the two that you may choose not to.

Organization of the Data Projects

Another point to bring up is third sentence in the dialog. This is a true statement and can be a point of confusion and even aggravation.

Working with multiple source models in this version of Visio just isn't a good idea at this point. In fact there isn't really all that much need. Keep in mind that the DMD is just an ER diagram so you really don't need any of those. Visio won't update multiple source models with new objects, only change existing object names. A logical diagram (provided by the DMD) and an ORM diagram are all you need to model incredibly complex systems.

Also, when your diagrams get very large, there are many ways to spread them out and organize them. You can right-click on the tab at the bottom of the current drawing page in either diagram to create a new page representing a conceptual group of objects and relationships:

Also, another extremely useful feature for organizing your drawings is the folder system of the **Business Rules** window. You can right-click to create a new folder, and then drag fact types into that folder as shown below:

Refreshing the Model from the Database

The database is now in the hands of the DBA and in action in the real world. No matter how good the design, there always seems to be someone or something that wants to change it. Sometimes it's simply a data type or column name change, or the addition of an index you may not have thought of to increase performance. Sometimes the change can be downright huge such as combining tables to decrease joins. You can be sure that a well-normalized schema will be lost on some and it may be beyond your control to prevent it. Luckily, you can at least find out what's gone on and update your documentation to reflect the changes. The reporting feature mentioned later can also be of great help here. Also, a good idea is to make sure that you have backups of your existing model so that you can always revert to your pristine design idea.

Let's suppose that the "powers that be" have decided that Airlines are now going to own terminals in airports. This isn't that far-fetched after all – we had already broached the subject that Airlines should possibly have been in their own table. The problem comes that, instead of coming back to you to architect the solution, they just take it upon themselves to create the Airlines and Terminals tables themselves. Here is what they have done:

❑ Created an `Airlines` table with an `airlineCode` primary key

❑ Created a `Terminals` table with a `terminalID` primary key

❑ Added an `airlineCode` column to the `Terminals` table

Your first step is to open up your diagram and choose refresh from the model submenu of the **Database** menu:

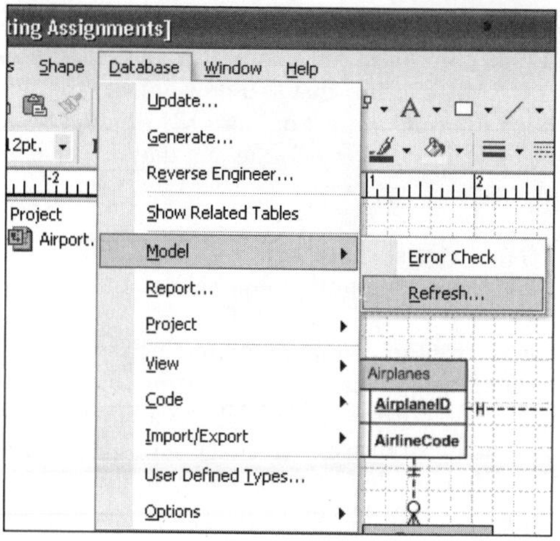

The wizard asks for a data source. You should already have one configured, but if not, create one as described in the *Generating the Database* section and click Next. Visio searches for conflicts between your model and the way it thinks the database is, and the way the physical database has changed. It should find two conflicts pictured below:

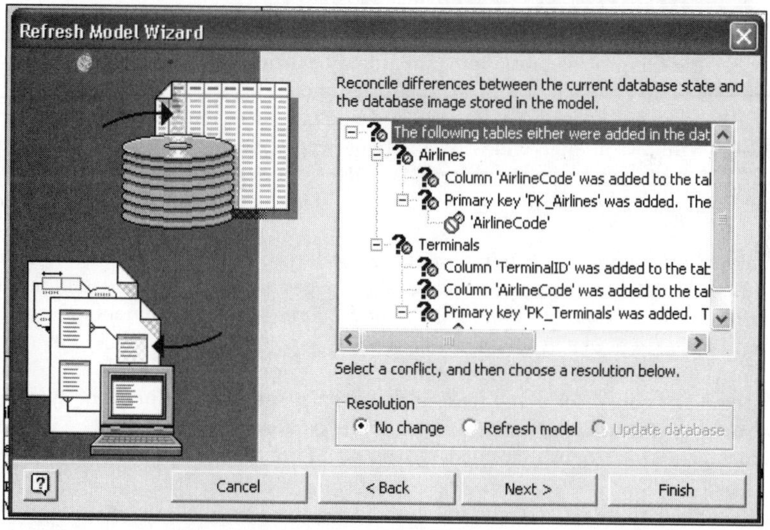

We will want to refresh our model with these changes, so make sure the top of the hierarchy is highlighted and click the Refresh model radio button. Visio generates the tables for us in our data project. We realize this by looking at the Tables and views window. We should be able to have Visio lay them out on the diagram by right-clicking the Airplanes table and selecting Show related tables. This doesn't work and, to our horror, we see why – no foreign key constraints were defined!

We save our model and the Update Source Models dialog comes up. Click Yes so that our ORM and ER diagram will be updated (you could also just choose Update Source models from the Database | Project menu). Opening our ORM we affirm that two new object types are there, but no new fact types. You can see that there has been minimal impact on our ORM model besides the two new objects. Some of the reference mode names have changed due to the fact that our changes to the document properties were not used for the new objects.

We also notice another problem. Because there were no constraints and the names didn't exactly match up, the airlineCode field that was added in the physical database is now a value type object.

This shows a problem with the current implementation of Visio's reverse engineering. Visio doesn't use the properties of our document or model that we've set during the reverse engineering process. This is a major flaw because it causes Visio to corrupt the model when you refresh it from the data source. I have no doubt that this will be fixed in later releases. However, let's bear in mind that ORM is a conceptual design procedure and wasn't really intended to map exactly to the underlying database model. It is better to use an ER diagram for the kind of maintenance duties that we must perform.

We mentioned reverse engineering the database in the previous paragraph – now it's time to have a deeper look at this process.

Reverse Engineering the Database

Reverse engineering is the process of mapping an already existing physical database and automatically developing a model so that it can be more easily understood – a viewable model is always more intuitive. There aren't many who would claim that a command-line interface is more intuitive and easier to understand than a Windows interface. Obviously, if you were to learn the command-line and get used to it, it can be a faster way to interact with the system. In order to understand what is really going on, nothing beats a viewable diagram or model. This is what documentation is for and why it is so important.

Unless it's combined with updating/generation of the database, which we'll look at later, the creation and maintenance of documentation is reverse engineering's biggest purpose. Many databases are designed from the outset with little or no regard to documentation. Even if solid documentation of the database exists, it is often so grossly outdated that it does not really represent the database in its current implementation. While the database is being constructed, design decisions may be made on the fly. This should be expected and occurs for many reasons that are beyond the control of the system designer. The design can prove to be unfeasible given the choice of the database system used. The implementation of the database can include optimizations that the designers could not foresee the need for.

The list of objects that can be reverse-engineered and depicted by Visio depends on two things:

❑   The model to which you choose to reverse engineer

❑   The features supported by the driver that Visio uses to communicate with the database

Visio uses an algorithm to pull metadata from the underlying database system. The different types of objects you can reverse engineer depend on what the driver you have installed supports.

Reverse Engineering an ER diagram

Reverse engineering a database in Visio is an extremely simple process. How it actually does it is much more complex. Let's start by going through the process with the SQL Server Northwind database and examining what comes out on the other side.

The Reverse Engineer Wizard

We begin by creating the diagram we want to reverse engineer to. We will start with an ER diagram. We can have either a Database Model Diagram or an ER Source Diagram. Either way will provide us with the capability to reverse engineer an ER diagram. Selecting Reverse Engineer from the Database menu brings up the Reverse Engineer Wizard. This wizard will guide us through the process.

We begin by selecting the database we are going to connect to and the driver we are going to use. Visio shows you a combination of the OLEDB drivers and ODBC data sources you have on your system. Selecting the SQL Server driver, which is the default, will filter the list of available data sources to only those that are configured to point to SQL server databases. Any of the drivers in the list may be used to reverse engineer the database; however, the features available will change because some of the drivers or the DBMS you are using don't support all of them.

Notice that there is also a Generic ODBC driver. This driver is the ODBC driver for OLEDB providers and allows you to select any database for which you have an OLEDB provider. If you already have a data source set up, you may select it, or you can create a new one to point to your database.

In the next step of the wizard you are asked to choose which object types you would like to reverse engineer. This depends upon the database system you are trying to reverse engineer as well as the driver you have selected to connect to that database. The object types supported are checked by default, while the unsupported ones are grayed out. You can choose to filter which objects are displayed in subsequent steps by unchecking unwanted types. The object types indented below the tables objects describe the different properties/attributes of a table that Visio can map to the model.

Clicking the **Next** button will cause Visio to connect to the source database and retrieve a list of the tables and views from the source database. You can then select which tables and views you would like mapped to your diagram by putting a check in the box next to the tables you want. Clicking **Next** will then provide you with a list of the stored procedures. You can again select which objects you want by putting a check mark in the box next to the desired selections.

The next step in the wizard asks you if you would like Visio to add the resulting shapes directly to the diagram. Clicking **Yes** will cause Visio to attempt to add the shapes to the current page of the diagram, while clicking **No** will simply add the generated shapes to the underlying model allowing you to add them later. At this point, you can choose to click **Finish** and have Visio begin the reverse engineering process, or clicking **Next** will allow you to view a summary of all the objects and catalog information that you have selected. Finishing the wizard will begin the reverse engineering process. As you can see, the **Output** window is brought into focus.

Once the reverse engineering process has begun, the **Output** window will come up. Visio begins by extracting the columns of all the tables, then it moves on to constraints beginning with checked constraints, primary key constraints, indexes, foreign keys, and triggers. For any stored procedures you have selected the code will be extracted and placed in the underlying model. Visio then performs an error check on the model to alert you to check consistency and integrity of the system. Finally, it provides a summary indicating how many objects were engineered and how long it took for each group. If you had chosen to have Visio automatically add the shapes to the drawing, they would now be laid out on the surface. Otherwise, you can view all of the objects in the **Tables and Views** window. Dragging a table or view object from the **Tables and Views** window to the drawing surface results in that shape being placed in the drawing.

If this window isn't visible, it can be accessed by Database | View, and clicking Tables and views. Any code that was reverse engineered will show up in the code tab of the tables and views window. These shapes may not be added to the drawing and are merely there to provide completeness in the model and allow you to make edits to the code if need be.

As soon as the reverse engineering process is complete, Visio stores the data in an underlying model using its own format. This underlying model stores everything that it reverse engineered, not only what appears on the drawing surface.

From its visual depiction on the drawing surface one can see a number of properties that Visio has reverse engineered for that object:

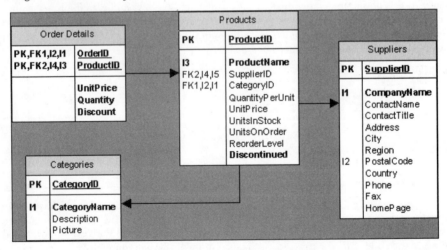

The table name is displayed in the gray section at the top of the object. As with standard entity relationship diagrams, the objects columns are displayed on the right-hand side while constraints and attributes are shown to the left of the column name. Primary keys are shown underlined and with a PK identifier on their left. Required columns are shown in bold. Indexes are marked on their left with an I. Uniqueness constraints are depicted with a U. Foreign key constraints are depicted with an FK next to the columns they are defined for.

This notation is not the only way objects can be depicted in Visio. On the **Database** menu under **Options,** you can select the document choice to bring up the database document options window.

Here you can decide the symbol set for graphically modeling the system. You can choose either relational, which is the default, or the IDEF1X symbol set. You can also choose whether to display conceptual names, physical names, or both. Conceptual names are only useful for reverse engineering if they have been defined in the underlying database or if you plan to define them later in the model; otherwise they will be the same as the physical name.

The **Table** tab allows you to choose the level of detail you would like to depict in your drawing. For example, you can choose not to display keys and indexes and you can choose to display both portable and physical data types for each column:

The **Relationship** tab provides options to display the attributes of the relationships defined in the underlying database in many different ways. For example, you can choose to display the physical name or the verb phrase of the underlying key relationship (not shown in the diagram below).

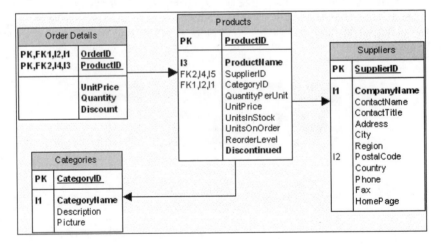

You can choose to display either cardinality notation or crow's feet, and you can use referential action to display the triggers involved in cascading additions and deletions. The verb phrase is defined by the conceptual predicate role defined for the object in the relationship.

The Database Properties Window for ER diagrams

Right-clicking on a shape and selecting Database Properties brings up the Database Properties window. This window usually appears as a tab at the bottom of the drawing.

This window is extremely useful for viewing all of the underlying properties of a database object, many of which cannot be depicted visually. On the left are the categories of properties that are defined for each object, the first of which, Definition, includes all of the properties that define that object including the physical name, owner, and source database. There is also a property here that lets you define a conceptual name for this object.

The Columns category depicts all of the columns and their attributes that are defined for this table and allows you to set mandatory constraints, primary key constraints, and the physical or portable data type for each column. Selecting a column and pressing the Edit button to the right brings up the Column Properties window.

Column Properties

The Definition tab allows you to specify a default value as well as a conceptual name. Conceptual names provide more documentation and can help to map back to the conceptual model. The Sync names when typing checkbox ensures that the names are the same in order to ease the creation of conceptual names. Creating a default value for a field in the database can be very useful to use as a boilerplate for new data to be entered into the table.

The **Data Type** tab gives greater freedom to select and control data types, both portable (a general data type that may be easily mapped to any physical database) and physical (a native data type based upon the default driver you have specified). The **Collection** tab allows you to specify a collection type, which is used if your database supports object-relational models. Let's move onto the **Check** tab:

The **Check** tab allows you to define check constraints placed upon this column. You can define values and/or ranges of values that the column can accept. The **Show check clause code** radio button allows you to customize code to meet more specific check clause needs. The **Extended** tab will allow you specify any extended properties defined by the driver of your database system. Finally, the **Notes** tab allows you to enter free-form annotations that you would like in order to more fully document this column.

Now let's return to the **Database Properties** window. The **Primary ID** category allows you to define the column or columns that will uniquely identify each row in your table. Add columns by selecting them from the available columns list box and clicking the **Add** button. They will then be depicted in the primary ID column list box. You can also choose how you would like the primary key to be enforced, the physical name of the constraint, and whether you want to create an index on that column or columns.

The Indexes category is used to identify the columns you would like to create indexes for. Click New to create a new index, select the index type from the drop-down menu then add columns to it from the available columns list box. The Options button allows you define any driver-specific options you would like. The trigger category allows you to define code triggers that will be executed based upon certain actions on your tables. Click Add to bring up the code editor window. The code editor window is used to type DDL scripts that will create or alter objects in your database.

Back on the Database Properties window, the Check category will allow you to add check clauses to your table in much the same way as you defined triggers. The Extended category will allow you to define extended attributes defined by your database driver. Once again the notes column allows you to annotate your table.

Remember, that at this point all the tables are in the underlying model. If your drawing surface gets too cluttered, you can select them and press the *Delete* key. Be sure not to remove the tables from the underlying model (unless of course this is really your intent). A useful tip for retrieving many of the shapes back onto the drawing surface is to select any object already on the surface and either right-click and select Show Related Tables, or select Show Related Tables from the Database menu. This will add any shapes to the drawing that are related directly to that table. This will also add to the drawing all the relational objects that define how all these table relate to other.

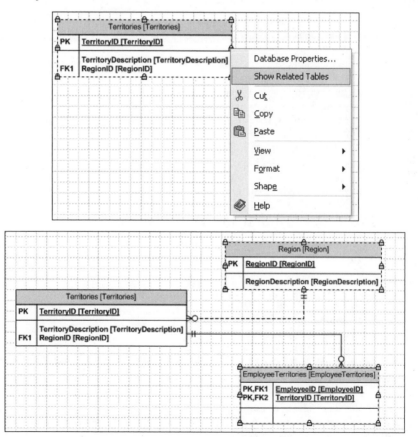

Reverse Engineering an ORM Diagram

The reverse engineering process for an ORM source model is almost exactly the same as that for an ER diagram. The same steps are involved. This makes sense because the way Visio internally stores all of the metadata that it pulls from the underlying physical database is the same for both diagrams. The only difference is the notation and the way that this information is graphically depicted for you. Once you have gone through the wizard, chosen the objects you wish to reverse engineer and completed the reverse engineering process you will be presented with all of the object types in the underlying database. All of the objects are listed alphabetically in the object types window. A better way (because the objects are easier to drag from it) is to view the results of the reverse engineering process by using the Business Rules window. Choosing the Object Types tab displays all of the object types, both entity and value, while the Fact Types tab displays all of the facts or predicates that define the roles the objects play. Objects can be dragged directly onto the drawing surface from either of these tabs. As with ER diagrams, an extremely useful way to add shapes to the drawing and have Visio lay them out for you is by right-clicking on any type on the drawing surface and selecting Show Relationships:

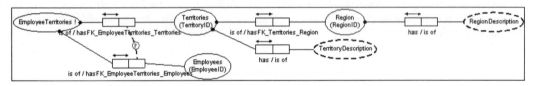

As can be seen from the diagram the Territories object plays three roles. The foreign key constraints in the underlying database have been mapped to a system of predicates, roles, and constraints. As can be seen from the Territories is of Region fact type, the physical name of the foreign key defined in the database (FK_Territory_Region) has been used to create the inverse text of the role. The uniqueness constraints are shown as the familiar arrow-tipped bars over the role they constrain. We can also see the primary uniqueness constraint (a circled P) that denotes that Territories and Employees provide a primary composite reference scheme for the EmployeeTerritories object. Although the ORM modeling notation is very good at graphically depicting many of the objects in a database in an intuitive manner, there are still many properties that are left out of the visual representation. Just as in ER diagrams, the Database Properties window can be extremely useful in viewing these properties.

The Database Properties Window for ORM Diagrams

The Database Properties window also outlines the properties of the currently selected object in categories listed on the left:

Selecting different objects results in a multitude of different properties being displayed that can be defined for each particular object type. We will go over the different types of properties that can be defined for both fact types and object types.

Selecting an object in the **Object Types** tab of the **Business Rules** window and then looking at its database properties, let's have a look at the first category of **Definition**.

We see that you can define the name of the object, and specify whether the object is an entity, value or external type. The **External** checkbox states whether this object is defined here or if the object is merely being used as a proxy for an external object defined elsewhere. We can specify the name space it belongs to if our project is large enough that we want to define namespaces so that name collision does not occur. The **Independent** checkbox allow us to determine whether we define this object as independent or not with regard to whether it has to play a role in a predicate to exist. Finally, we can give Visio's Verbalizer some help in the verbiage of our model by telling it whether we want it to use his/her instead of its when constructing fact types.

The **Ref Mode** category is used to define the identification scheme for your object. Value types may not have a reference mode since, as you'll remember, they represent strings and numeric values or primitive types. For entities, we can define the name of the reference and the type of reference it is. If a reference mode is specified, it can be identification, formatting, or measurement. Identification means that the reference is an unique identifier for each instance of your object. An example of formatting identification type would be a table of a certain screw type where the screw size uniquely identifies each screw. A measurement identification type would be a type whose value is measured by/as its primary identification scheme. The **Options** section will decide how you want the primary reference scheme to be used for naming. We'll keep **Use Document's setting** for now, and we'll take a look at the choices and how to change the default document's setting later.

The **Data Type** category allows the detailed definition of the data type of the object in order to achieve a more precise mapping to the physical database. We can choose any data type that is specified in the driver we are using for this model. If the **Show portable data type** radio button is checked, the portable data types that aren't specific to the particular DBMS in question are used. If the **Physical data type** is checked, then Visio will update and tailor the screen so that each of the options reflects the specific driver you have chosen for your model. For SQL server, you can define whether the column is an identity column by clicking the **Edit** button.

The **Composite Type** category allows you to define whether this type is a composite type and if so, what kind of composite type the object is.

```
Categories:
  Definition            Mapping Option
  Ref Mode                (•) Does not result in a composite type
  Data Type
⇨ Composite Type          ( ) Named row type
  Subtype
  Value                   ( ) Unnamed row type
  Nested Roles
  Notes                   ( ) Domain

                          ( ) Distinct type

  × │ Business Rules │ Output │ Database Properties │ Verbalizer │
```

The **Subtype** category is for use when the object is defined as a subtype of another type. The only selection that is not grayed out by default is the **Map to a separate table** option.

```
Categories:
  Definition            [ ] Map to separate table    Primary supertype: [        ▼]
  Ref Mode
  Data Type             [ ] Create table inheritance
  Composite Type
⇨ Subtype               Subtype definition:
  Value                 ┌──────────────────────────────┐
  Nested Roles          │                             ▲│
  Notes                 │                              │
                        │                              │
                        │                              │
                        │                             ▼│
                        └──────────────────────────────┘

  × │ Business Rules │ Database Properties │ Verbalizer │
```

Although this is very useful when the type is a subtype, it can also be useful if you want to make sure that your object is represented in the logical diagram as a separate entity or table. Adding a subtype relationship to the diagram and relating it to the object and its supertype will allow the other options to be entered. You can define the supertype, instruct Visio that you want to use table inheritance, and enter notes documenting the subtype/supertype relationship.

The **Value** category allows you to define and restrict the value that your object can take. This is tied up with the reference mode or identification scheme that you have defined for your object. Taking our example of the wood screw above, screw size can only be so big or small, so you would want to restrict its value here.

```
Categories:
  Definition            Range                        Defined values/ranges:
  Ref Mode              From: [        ]              ┌──────────────────────┐
  Data Type                                           │ <New Value/Range>    │
  Composite Type          (empty = no min or no max)  │                      │
  Subtype                                    [ Add ]  │                      │
⇨ Value                 To:   [        ]              │                      │
  Nested Roles                               [Remove] │                      │
  Notes                 Value                         │                      │
                        [        ]                    └──────────────────────┘

  × │ Business Rules │ Output │ Database Properties │ Verbalizer │
```

We've already explained what a nested role (objectified) predicate is. When the object you are looking at is a nested role, this category presents you with readings that you can change to help verbalize the relationship you have now created.

As you can see, the reverse engineering process is the simple part. It's the understanding of what's going on that can be difficult.

Summary

We've covered a lot of material in this chapter about a topic that will be fairly new for many people. I think we can derive from its support in Visio that Microsoft believes ORM to be a way of conceptually modeling systems that can help communication between the system designers and the solution stakeholders.

Keep in mind that ORM can even be used in many ways that aren't just related to database design such as Requirements Specifications for Requests for Proposals and can certainly help with UML for modeling the relationships between classes and objects without the complexity of attributes and methods.

We have also discussed a framework, the Conceptual Schema Design Procedure for modeling using the ORM. ORM notation has been discussed as well as the different object types, fact types, constraints and subtypes. We looked at how all of these are mapped (or not) to the underlying ER diagram when we are ready to move beyond conceptual design, to the logical design.

ER diagrams have been revisited and we have shown how to tweak the properties of our logical model, which allows a fine level of control over how the database is finally generated/updated in the underlying DBMS. Once this is accomplished, we've shown how we can use round-trip engineering so that our model and our DBMS will stay synchronized. With this synchronization comes the benefit that we get to use our design tool to design the database instead of having to rely on the tools included with our specific DBMS.

For more information on ORM I recommend the following web sites/articles:

1. www.orm.net – this site is managed by Terry Halpin, the father of ORM who now works for Microsoft. There is a tremendous amount of good reference material here.

2. *Object Role Modeling, an Overview* – This article, as well as it's more detailed parts, is one of the best papers out there for learning ORM. It is also written by Terry Halpin and includes many examples of using Visio to model the solution. It can be found at: http://msdn.microsoft.com/library/default.asp?url=/library/en-us/dv_vstechart/html/vstchvsea_ormoverview.asp?frame=true

3. Episode 25 of the .NET Show – Microsoft decided to devote an entire episode of the .NET show to the ORM. Terry Halpin is a guest and discusses some of the benefits and ways in which ORM has been used, not just in database-centric view. It can be found at: http://msdn.microsoft.com/theshow/Episode025/default.asp

Hopefully you now have an idea of why Microsoft and others have placed a lot of emphasis on the ORM. It really is an excellent way to model a solution conceptually and with the automated features that Visio provides, can help improve the quality and reliability of your next system.

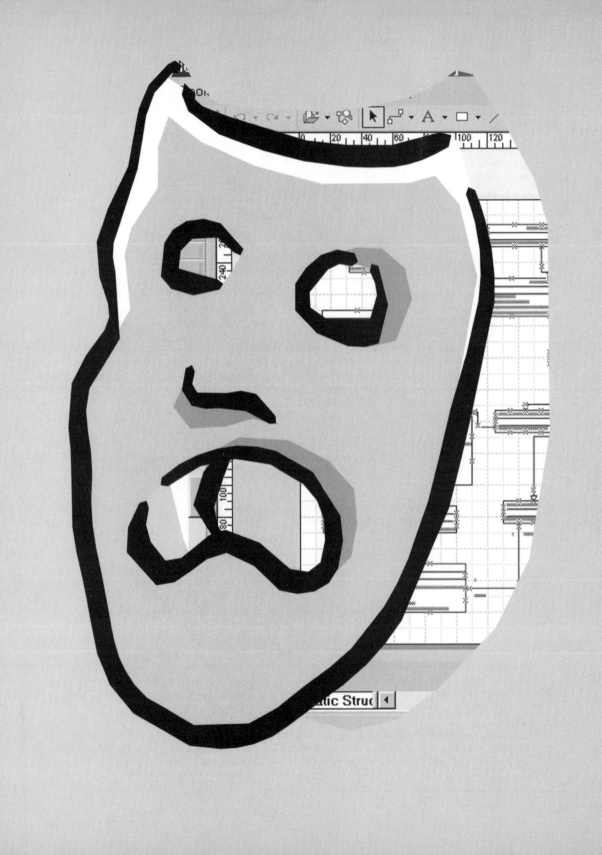

Index

A Guide to the Index

The index is arranged hierarchically, in alphabetical order, with symbols preceding the letter A. Most second-level entries and many third-level entries also occur as first-level entries. This is to ensure that users will find the information they require however they choose to search for it.

N

namespaces
creating namespace packages, 79
navigability information
detailed design documentation, 223
nested activation shape, 126
nested classes
Reverse engineering UML model structure, 184
nested role, Database Properties Window
ORM, 327
NET Framework
see .NET Framework.
New Report Wizard
drawing fact types in Visio, 283
options for reports, 284
no source code reverse engineering
see assembly based reverse engineering.
node
UML deployment diagram, 23, 264
Node shapes
deployment stencil, 266
UML deployment diagram, 266
non-compiled projects
Reverse engineering, 181
normalization
Database Model diagrams, 67
normalizing application logic with business objects, 77
notes, Database Properties Window
Entity Relationship diagrams, 323

O

object
creating object types, 296
entity types, 275
ORM notation, 272, 275
UML sequence diagram, 17
value types, 275
Object Constraint Language
see OCL.
object in state
UML activity diagram, 14
Object Lifeline shape
adding actor to sequence diagram, 111
adding business objects to sequence diagram, 118
retrieving checked out media, 122
representing user interface, 113
sequence stencil, 111, 118, 122
UML Shape Display Options Dialog, 112
Object Management Group
UML, 11
object modeling
Booch method, 11
compared to data modeling, 74
distributed systems, 240
Object Oriented Software Engineering, 11
OMT, 11
UML, 11
Object Modeling Technique
see OMT.
Object Oriented Software Engineering
object modeling, 11
object pooling
distributed systems, 242

Object Remote Procedure Call protocols
see ORPC protocols.
Object Role Modeling
see ORM.
Object Types pane
Business Rules Window, 279
Objectory
see Object Oriented Software Engineering.
OCL
UML, 12
OLE diagrams
see COM and OLE diagrams.
OMG
see Object Management Group.
OMT
object modeling, 11
Operation Properties Dialog
see UML Operation Properties Dialog.
operations
adding methods to class, 141
UML Operation Properties Dialog, 141
adding operations to data access base class, 82
marking operation as abstract, 89
specifying operation parameters, 86
UML Class Properties Dialog, 83
UML Operation Properties Dialog, 84, 91
adding overloaded operations to business object, 99
UML Class Properties Dialog, 99, 100
adding properties to class, 138
UML Operation Properties Dialog, 138
adding properties to interface, 145
UML Operation Properties Dialog, 145
Code-to-UML mapping, 189
compared to methods, 89
representing methods as operations, 189
method bodies, 191
representing properties as operations, 190
table of operation types, 139
viewing code generated from operations, 140
order entry application
code documentation, 225
detailed design documentation, 222
high level design documentation, 218
requirements development documentation, 212
software development lifecycle, 212
testing documentation, 226
UML documentation, 212
ORM, 276
adding to Database Model diagram, 277, 302
advantages of using, 271, 274
building logical model, 302
compared to Entity Relationship diagrams, 271
Conceptual Schema Design Procedure, 273
creating diagram, 296
creating object types, 296
defining roles, 297
model error check, 301
setting constraints, 297
data modeling, 271
database drivers option, 307
Database Properties Window, 324
composite type, 326
data type, 325
definition, 325
nested role, 327
ref mode, 325
subtype, 326
value, 326